Gichi Bitobig, Grand Marais

T0345937

Gichi Bitobig, Grand Marais

Early Accounts of the Anishinaabeg
and the North Shore Fur Trade

TIMOTHY COCHRANE

UNIVERSITY OF MINNESOTA PRESS

MINNEAPOLIS ♦ LONDON

Publisher's note: This book reprints the journals of Bela Chapman and George Johnston, as well as the records of the Fort William Hudson's Bay Company, exactly as they were written in the early nineteenth century. Some of the language and descriptions in the journals, including those of Native Americans and Native culture, are offensive, but the original text has been preserved to maintain the historical authenticity of these documents.

Maps drawn by Philip Schwartzberg, Meridian Mapping

Published by the University of Minnesota Press
111 Third Avenue South, Suite 290
Minneapolis, MN 55401–2520
http://www.upress.umn.edu

Printed in the United States of America on acid-free paper

The University of Minnesota is an equal-opportunity educator and employer.

24   10 9 8 7 6 5 4 3

Library of Congress Cataloging-in-Publication Data
Cochrane, Timothy, 1955– author.
Gichi Bitobig, Grand Marais : early accounts of the Anishinaabeg and the North
    Shore fur trade / Timothy Cochrane.
Minneapolis : University of Minnesota Press, [2018] | Includes bibliographical
    references and index. |
Identifiers: LCCN 2018016686 (print) | ISBN 978-1-5179-0593-4 (pb)
Subjects: LCSH: Fur trade—Minnesota—Grand Marais—History—19th century. |
    American Fur Company—History—18th century. | Ojibwa Indians—
    Minnesota—Grand Marais—History—18th century.
Classification: LCC HD9778.U63 C64 2018 (print) | DDC 381/.43970977675—dc23
LC record available at https://lccn.loc.gov/2018016686

This book is for Jean, who, like me, relishes our time on the North Shore.

Contents

Map of Lake Superior (Gichi Gami)   viii

Map of North Shore Anishinaabeg Territory   x

Introduction   1

1   In Grand Marais 25

2   American Fur Company and the Trade 47

3   Espagnol's Dilemma and the Anishinaabeg 95

4   "Fort Misery" 125

The Journals 141

The Log of Bela Chapman 151

The Journal of George Johnston 181

Excerpt from the Fort William Hudson's Bay
Company Records 201

Acknowledgments   205

Notes   209

Index   257

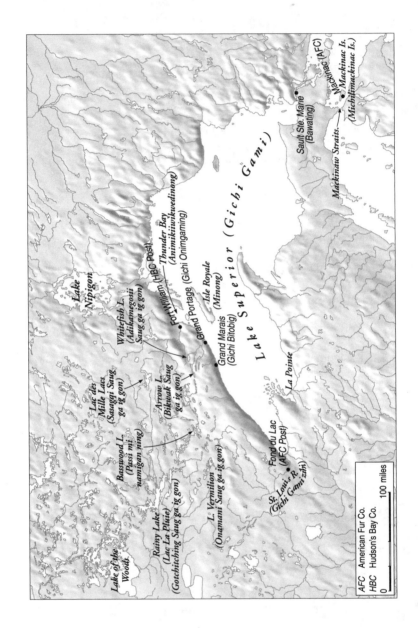

Lake Superior (Gichi Gami)

Sault Ste. Marie (Bawating)

Mackinac Is. (AFC)
Mackinac Is.
Mackinaw Straits
(Michilimackinac Is.)

Thunder Bay (Animikiwikwedinong)

Grand Portage (Gichi Oningaming)

Fort William (HBC Post)

Isle Royale (Minong)

Grand Marais (Gichi Bitobig)

La Pointe

Whitefish L. (Adikamegosii Saug ga ig gon)

Lake Nipigon

Arrow L. (Bikwak Saug ga ig gon)

Lac des Mille Lacs (Sasaggi Saug ga ig gon)

Basswood L. (Passi mi namigan ing)

Fond du Lac (AFC Post)

St. Louis R. (Gichi Gami zibi)

L. Vermilion (Onamani Saug ga ig gon)

Rainy Lake (Lac La Pluie) (Gotchitching Saug ga ig gon)

Lake of the Woods

AFC American Fur Co.
HBC Hudson's Bay Co.

0   100 miles

viii

Lake Superior

Place-Names

Lake Superior	Gichi Gami
La Pointe	
Fond du Lac, St. Louis River	Gichi Gami zibi
Vermilion Lake	Onamani Saug ga ig gon
Grand Marais	Gichi Bitobig
Grand Portage	Gichi Onimgaming
Isle Royale	Minong
Whitefish Lake	Adikamegosii Saug ga ig gon
Arrow Lake	Bikwak Saug ga ig gon
Lac des Mille Lacs	Sasagqi Saug ga ig gon
Basswood Lake	Passi mi namigan ning
Rainy Lake, Lac La Pluie	Gotchitching Saug ga ig gon
Lake of the Woods	
Thunder Bay	Animikiiwikwedinong
Lake Nipigon	
Mackinaw Straits, Mackinac Island	Michilimackinac Island
Sault Ste. Marie	Bawating
American Fur Company Post (Fond du Lac, eighteen miles upriver)	
Hudson's Bay Company Fort William Post (present day Fort William, on lake edge)	

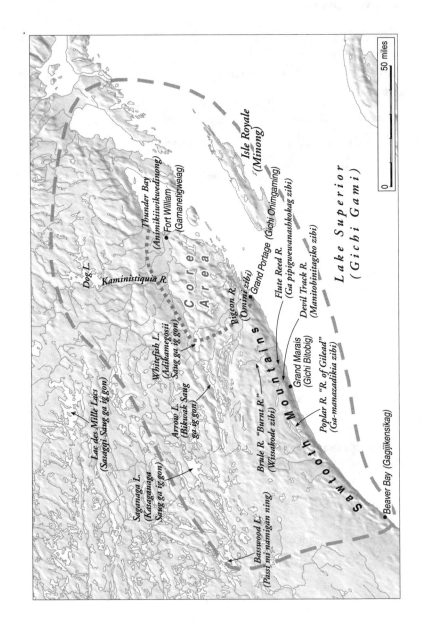

Lake Superior (Gichi Gami)

Isle Royale (Minong)

Grand Portage (Gichi Onigaming)

Flute Reed R. (Ga pipigwewanashkokag zibi)

Devil Track R. (Manitobinitagiko zibi)

Grand Marais (Gichi Bitobig)

Poplar R. "R. of Gilead" (Ga-manazadikia zibi)

Sawtooth Mountains

Beaver Bay (Gagijikensikag)

Pigeon R. (Omimi zibi)

Brule R. "Burnt R." (Wissakode zibi)

Basswood L. (Passi mi namigan ning)

Saganaga L. (Kasaganaga Saug ga ig gon)

Arrow L. (Bikwak Saug ga ig gon)

Lac des Mille Lacs (Sasaggi Saug ga ig gon)

Whitefish L. (Adikamegosii Saug gu ig gon)

Kaministiquia R.

Dog L.

Thunder Bay (Animikiiwikwedinong)

Fort William (Gamanetigweiag)

Corell Area

50 miles

0

North Shore Anishinaabeg Territory, 1825

Place-Names

Lake Superior	Gichi Gami
Beaver Bay	Gagijikensikag
Sawtooth Mountains	
Poplar River ("River of Gilead")	Ga-manazadika zibi
Grand Marais	Gichi Bitobig
Brule River ("Burnt River")	Wissakode zibi
Devil Track River	Manitobinitagiko zibi
Grand Portage	Gichi Onimgaming
Pigeon River	Omini zibi
Whitefish Lake	Adikamegosii Saug ga ig gon
Arrow Lake	Bikwak Saug ga ig gon
Lac des Mille Lacs	Sasagqi Saug ga ig gon
Saganaga Lake	Kasaganaga Saug ga ig gon
Basswood Lake	Passi mi namigan ning
Flute Reed River	Ga pipigwewanashkokag zibi
Fort William	Gamanetigweiag
Kaministiquia River	

Introduction

Grand Marais, 1823

Bela Chapman was frustrated, windbound again, short of his destination. His foot was aching, and he wasn't sure how far he had to travel. Not far from the mouth of the Poplar River, on the North Shore of Lake Superior, he heard the roar of surf pounding the rocky shoreline. Large dead swells kept him and his men on shore, despite the wind having lain down. The next day the wind freshened again in earnest from the south, and the waves prevented him from reaching Grand Marais. His concern stemmed from a late start and an extended, ten-day journey. He of course could not know this at the time, but his successor the next year, George Johnston, would start almost four weeks earlier, and it would take Johnston and men only six days to reach Grand Marais from Fond du Lac.[1]

Traveling up the North Shore, camping along the way where it was safe to get off the lake, Chapman and the other American Fur Company (AFC) men had not seen anyone. So perhaps they were not disappointed when they finally paddled into Gichi Bitobig and no one greeted or heralded them ashore. Compared with the headlands and rugged shoreline, the tidy protected harbor was a welcome relief.

There was little to suggest traders had overwintered there before. Once they were onshore, it was obvious no one lived there year-round but that it was a traditional camping ground. There was evidence of the comings and goings of Anishinaabeg and voyageurs.[2] Chapman and his men hauled gear into an opening of matted-down grasses and flowering asters, skirted by hazel, thimbleberries, and raspberries. A slight fragrance of sweetgrass greeted the men. Camps were placed on the edge of the wood to find shelter from the incessant, cold lake winds. Higher up on a bench of level ground there were remains of a number of old fires ringed with stones. A tripod of three stout sticks marked the most recently used fire pit. Littered on the ground were torn birch bark, remains from edges of old cedar mats, and a partial frame of a domed lodge made of saplings lashed together.[3] Underfoot in between the red stones were fragments of white clay pipes. Above the first bench, in loose stone, were a series of collapsed pits a few feet deep. These empty pits were Anishinaabeg food caches, once lined with birch bark and dried grass to keep smoked lake trout dry. Smaller trails led off from the back of the opening, but only the one leading to the sugar maples, or "sugar bush," was well trod. The harbor was now solitary but strewn with hints of a prior Anishinaabeg presence.

Before the day was over, the Anishinaabeg "found" Chapman and his men hastily setting up camp. The principal leader, Espagnol; an Anishinaabeg family head, Grand Coquin; and their families paddled into the harbor. They readily displayed the goods recently received from the Hudson's Bay Company clerk at Fort William, more than eighty miles northeast along the lake, and they tested Chapman's knowledge of customary greetings and gift giving among traders and Anishinaabeg. Chapman was preoccupied: there were trees to be found for building nearby, a post to be built, fish to be caught for their main winter food supply, gill nets to be "knit," and his wife, Mary Chaurette, was due to give birth. Still, even with the blur of activities during the first days, he needed to create a trading partnership, a connection, with Espagnol and other area Anishinaabeg.

Roughly a year later, Johnston and men and his small family arrived at Grand Marais to find the buildings they hoped to quickly occupy had been burned to the ground. Fortunately, they thought, they had brought a grindstone, and they sharpened their axes and immediately began to rebuild. Like Chapman, but more pessimistic, Johnston aspired to make something of his time at Gichi Bitobig and to prove his value to his AFC employers. Both clerks struggled at the newly founded post of Grand Marais.

Grand Marais and the Fur Trade

Only a few historians have known about the fur trade journals penned by Bela Chapman and George Johnston in the cold weather months in Grand Marais between 1823 and 1825. Few have had a chance to consider what it was like for the beleaguered AFC men on the North Shore, or have followed the canny leadership of the Anishinaabeg ogimaa, Espagnol. Instead, there has existed an inadvertent gap in the historical record: the time after the fierce North West Company (NWC) moved to Thunder Bay in 1803 and before the 1854 treaty and the tide of Scandinavian immigrants that swept into the Minnesota Arrowhead. I certainly did not know about this historical gap when I moved to the North Shore. Slowly, from obscure sources, I learned there was history to discover and plenty of surprises as well. I believe many residents living along the shore assume that "the fur trade stuff" only happened at Grand Portage (summer headquarters of the NWC—the Walmart of its day), Fort William, and sporadically at Duluth but had little impact on Grand Marais. Or as historian Bill Raff expressed it, there were only a "few white people on the North Shore except the leftovers of fur trade at Fond du Lac and Grand Portage."[4] If there was any mention of an earlier beginning of Grand Marais than the post–1854 treaty settlement, it was with regard to confusion about which fur trade company was located on the horseshoe-shaped harbor. The accepted local narrative was that the town was established after the 1854 treaty by Scandinavian immigrants, who made a living by fishing, subsistence farming, and making do in the rocky and forested land. Little was known about the pre-treaty use of the stony harbor now known as

Grand Marais perhaps because the sources of information to piece together that story are to be found so far away.

With some historical digging I learned that voyageurs and fur trade clerks had paddled by the harbor on voyages between the NWC's depot in Fort William, now Thunder Bay, and Fond du Lac (up the St. Louis River from modern-day Duluth). But was there more to this story than just tracing fur trade "leftovers"? And there was that pesky question, much debated locally, what does *Grand Marais* mean? The simmering debate about the meaning and origin of the French Canadian–derived name Grand Marais encapsulates the lack of knowledge about its early days. Could a more dedicated look at the early fur trade documents shed some light on the name and, more importantly, any substantive use of the nearby environs?

After reading this book and the journals of Chapman and Johnston, residents of and visitors to Grand Marais can theorize about the location of its fur trade post, its historical wellspring (the only real clue being it must have been high enough off the water that a small cellar was dug).[5] We are reminded again that before Scandinavian immigrants, the first visitors on its shore were African Anishinaabeg Americans, Yankees, and Métis fur traders. Johnston, with Caribou clan roots (from his great-grandfather) on the North Shore, scorned Grand Marais. Ambrose Davenport Jr., who returned to the North Shore to trade again in 1832, seven years after his initial posting at Gichi Bitobig, was the son of a Virginia soldier who defied the British Redcoats during the War of 1812 at Michilimackinac (roughly at the junction of Lake Huron and Lake Michigan and not far from Lake Superior) and was nearly hung for it. Many of these first traders were from Michigan and returned home. Chapman became a delegate to the first territorial congress for Michigan. But as it is today, Grand Marais was linked to the regional hub of Fond du Lac. Its corporate beginnings belie the fierce individuality of today's residents.

More interesting to me was discovering what we can about Anishinaabeg living in Grand Marais and nearby during this historic period when some of the first Yankees made their way here. Unfortunately, though, this story appears to be about events and people beyond the reach of Grand Portage elders' oral history. Thus, we are dependent upon these new-to-us but brittle records to attempt to answer such questions as the following: Was Grand Marais an important Anishinaabeg settlement? Did their mobility in the area—as yet unconstrained by significant acculturative forces such as English teachers or missionaries or government Indian agents—include much use of Grand Marais? And can early records help us understand the first relationships between area Anishinaabeg and a powerful American business concern—the American Fur Company? It appears that, in fact, the "founding" of Grand Marais may very well be a story about a powerful corporation allied with many American interests seeking to yield a profit in the old Northwest.

These journals, above all, remind us that Grand Marais, or Gichi Bitobig, the harbor proper, was an Anishinaabeg place long before what later settlers would think of as the Anishinaabeg residences on the eastern edge of town called Chippewa City. It was a home place for Espagnol and family. His family made maple sugar above town, following in the footsteps of his mother's relatives, who had maple sugared there. Their maple sugar gear was snugly cached above town, it being taboo to take and use some other families' mukuks, kettle, cake sugar molds, wooden spoons, and such. Gichi Bitobig was a place Espagnol knew intimately. He was a well-regarded North Shore Anishinaabeg leader, who died just prior to the treaty years. Because of his responsibilities to his band, he, too, was a traveler, ranging far from Gichi Bitobig. He was knowledgeable about the region's geography and its limitations and advantages. Thus, he would frequent Gichi Bitobig during particular times of the year when he could catch trout or make maple sugar. He would regularly canoe and snowshoe to Gichi Bitobig, fish from in and out of its double bays, and live along its shoreline. Like their gichi ogimaa, North Shore Anishinaabeg resided seasonally at Gichi Bitobig long before whites would try to eke out a livelihood on its beautiful, but not always bountiful, terrain and waters.

Through time, three giant fur trade companies reached into Lake Superior country. The oldest, and sometimes mistakenly thought to be the only company there, was the Hudson's Bay Company, or HBC. Some observers would profanely declare that "HBC" stood for "here before Christ." Given a British royal charter in 1670, for decades the HBC timidly traded from posts on the shores of Hudson Bay. But by the 1820s it was led by the ambitious Governor George Simpson, and the "Honorable Company" held a powerful monopoly in British Canada centered on Hudson Bay and extending westward to the Rocky Mountains. The company would claim "Rupert's Land," or the exclusive commercial domain of one third of Canada lands, its southern boundary abutting the border route and Grand Portage.

The NWC, with its summer depot once in Grand Portage, was run from Montreal and heavily dependent on extended canoe routes and thousands of voyageurs. It used a Native American technological invention—canoes—to perfection. Operated on a share basis among its partners, the NWC once had more than 120 posts in the interior of British Canada and in the northern tier of the United States. But in 1821, a once unthinkable event occurred, and the two cutthroat competitors merged. The North West Company name was given up to the HBC, but North West men dominated the ranks of the refashioned HBC. A trade monopoly was only briefly regained, however, as the upstart Yankees finally made their way into the fur trade and into Lake Superior country. Owned by a German immigrant, John Jacob Astor, the AFC on the Great Lakes was run by a Scot, Ramsay Crooks. Astor's and Crooks's trading acumen and adept political maneuvering positioned the AFC to obtain a fur trade monopoly on the American Great Lakes beginning in the late 1810s. Profits from the fur trade—and then from real estate—made John Jacob Astor the richest man in America and one of the country's most influential men. In a competitive tit for tat, the HBC maneuvered to close AFC posts on British soil in Georgian Bay in Lake Huron, which stimulated Astor and Crooks to look for ways to counter. Less than a year later, the AFC had a handful of small posts in what became northern Minnesota, challenging the HBC on the border trade.

Fortunately, two fur trade journals exist that document the first steps of the AFC enterprise in Grand Marais during the 1820s. Until now, they have never been fully transcribed nor published. These journals were written by two AFC clerks—Bela Chapman and George Johnston—who were working to establish a new trading post at the harbor. Readers may have read bits and pieces of Chapman's journal, as it was synopsized in the primary work on Grand Portage National Monument, Carolyn Gilman's *The Grand Portage Story*.[6] The journals of Chapman and Johnston provide a doorway to local history and its links with national economic and political affairs. The story remains very local, dependent on local conditions and actors, but it is also directly connected to the continental aims of Astor, the actions of his main lieutenants, and their competition with the Hudson's Bay Company. And because of Astor's power and influence, government policy was involved in this story of the "fur trade history."

There is almost a two-year run of historical entries. Chapman began writing in the fall of 1823 and ceased in May 1824. George Johnston resumed writing the successive fall of 1824 until he unceremoniously lapsed in March 1825. These entries provide a local record of the playing out of competition among corporate giants and of the conditions local Anishinaabeg faced in trading and of the strategies they used in their dealings. This record throws light upon a very different and early Grand Marais. A third "journal," or really multiple documents, also exists from the Hudson Bay Company's Fort William post that provides a comparative—and a competitor's—perspective on trade in the area.

◇◇◇

Some may be surprised to learn that Grand Marais—what some with tongue in cheek have called "the Norwegian American Riviera" on Lake Superior—began with corporate struggles, fought by tycoons living in distant cities and involving political elites in America and England. But the story also begins on the most intimate scale, that is, with the struggles of mostly young men in a rugged, new environment trying to make a living and a profit—though mostly for their bosses and Astor. And we also, to the degree possible, try to understand those few years from the perspective of area Anishinaabeg, particularly from the perspectives of Espagnol, an influential leader, and Grand Coquin, the primary male Anishinaabe who traded at the little AFC post at Grand Marais.

Unfortunately, the journals rarely mention Anishinaabeg women, and thus our knowledge of what they were doing can only be inferred. Obviously Anishinaabeg women were living there, both as tribal members and also as spouses to traders, often traveling miles from their home places and families. While only a "shadow" of their presence is identifiable in some journal entries, we know they brought necessary skills to make daily subsistence and the small trading post possible.

What can we surmise about the Anishinaabeg perspective on the AFC coming to Grand Marais? With the merging of British fur trade companies, Anishinaabeg had fewer trading options. Posts were fewer in number and more distant—sometimes weeks' worth of travel away. Anishinaabeg had witnessed the downsizing of Fort William after the NWC and HBC merger in 1821. There were noticeably fewer "servants" at the HBC post. Further, the HBC was less interested in having them work as guides or help harvest potatoes or put up hay and had less interest in trade for canoe bark, gum, and local produce. As one scholar summed up, "The feudal state of Fort William is at an end, its council chamber is silent and desolate, its banquet-hall no longer echoes the auld-world ditty."[7] So, on one hand, the appearance of the Yanks brought back competition more favorable to Anishinaabeg traders. Perhaps this was why the Anishinaabe leader Espagnol promptly advised Chapman that there was relatively good fall fishing at Grand Marais.[8] Having the Americans close provided more trading leverage and maneuvering for the Anishinaabeg. But it was also a foreshadowing of more Americans creeping into the country, into Lower Michigan and the Ohio Valley. As allies of the British in the War of 1812, North Shore Anishinaabeg must have viewed the coming of the Americans to Grand Marais as a mixed blessing.

The old fur trade journals also occasionally reveal surprising connections with today. One notable example is the fur trade custom at Grand Portage persisting from the NWC period to the 1960s of conducting New Year's festivities. The fur trade companies provided a day off and special food and drink on New Year's, and Anishinaabeg and "free men" visited their posts and made courtesy calls on post clerks. In Grand Portage residents went from house to house to enjoy food, sweets, and conversation with each other. An older description of the custom is provided by Henry Schoolcraft on January 1, 1825: "New Year's day here as among the Metiss . . . is a day of friendly visiting from house to house, and cordial congratulations, with refreshments, spread on the board for all."[9] These journals, then, while old, can directly link to the present.

Determining what is the most appropriate name to use for the Native Americans who lived on the northwestern shores of Lake Superior during the 1820s is challenging. Readers are probably familiar with older names, such as Chippewa, Ojibway, and even Saulteaux, used commonly in Canada, and the more modern Ojibwe. These names refer to the same group, variously named through time. Today, however, Grand Portage people prefer the name Anishinaabeg (in its plural form) and use the term in their school and on the entrance sign to the reservation. As Anishinaabeg is their own name for themselves, it is the most fitting to use here. "Indian" is also informally used in Grand Portage today, so I have used it sparingly as an alternative to Anishinaabeg.

Traders did not worry about using the "right" name, preferring the simple and yet misunderstood term "Indian." But even employing more specific names—Grand Portage Anishinaabeg or Grand Portage Band, as commonly used today—is not quite right, as the historic group we are talking about included Anishinaabeg who now reside in Fort William, part of Thunder Bay. Anishinaabeg is an overarching name for a widespread Algonquian-speaking people. Thus, there are many bands of Anishinaabeg. Most commonly each group is designated by a vital geographical feature they inhabit, such as the Anishinaabeg of Rainy Lake, Fond du Lac, or Nipigon.

But there is not a consistent name for those people residing along the northwestern shore of Lake Superior that was used prior to the division of the Grand Portage and Fort William Anishinaabeg in the 1840s and 1850s.[10] At the time of this story, this group had not yet been separated by the border or religious factions. So they were commonly called the Grand Portage Ojibwe when the NWC was in operation at Grand Portage. Only a few years later, when the post moved north, writers talked of the Saulteaux or Ojibway of Fort William. Since these people residing on the northwestern shores of Lake Superior were truly a maritime people, Ojibway historian William Warren suggested that they might be known as Ke-che-gum-me-win-in-e-wug, or Men of the Great Water.[11] But there are many Anishinaabeg bands that live along Lake Superior, and this general term does not distinguish one from another. Further, it appears that Anishinaabeg at this time did not have their own specific name for this group either—at least not one that has been recorded and includes Native people on both sides of the border.

These Anishinaabeg depended on two primary geographical features: Lake Superior and the canoe and portage routes westward. There were two routes westward: one along the present-day international border, and the other following the Kaministiquia River westward until the northern route connects with the international border. But Lake Superior was the dominant presence in this traditional use area. And by today's naming conventions, this area is called the North Shore, despite really being the northwestern shore of the Gichi Gami. Hence, I propose the tentative name of North Shore Anishinaabeg. I remind readers, however, that North Shore Anishinaabeg is not a historical name but one that describes the group at the time.

A goal of this book is to open a window into the past with as humane a record as I can assemble. All the actors were under varying levels of stress, sometimes including hunger, and a tremendous measure of uncertainty. On the AFC side was a world made up largely of young men, although both clerks brought their wives along. The North Shore was new to Chapman and Johnston, while Chapman's men, the Bonga brothers, and their father before them had coasted the shore in the past. On the Anishinaabeg side was a corner of their homeland that was not comparatively heavily used. And many changes were afoot, often coming from afar. Anishinaabeg were ever devising strategies for their families to prosper in a tough country. They were continually pressed to figure out what of their past would be useful in the future. They were also adopting new practices and some objects when they concluded it was in their best interest to do so. The story here, then, is of two very different groups purposefully colliding, sometimes cooperating, and in the midst of this oftentimes misunderstanding one another. To tell this story of the North Shore fully, we must begin by introducing the two clerks: Bela Chapman and George Johnston.

Bela Chapman

Bela Chapman was the sixth child of a large rural New England family, born on July 19, 1793. His father was one of the first doctors in

Cornish, New Hampshire, a town located a couple miles from the Connecticut River, which is the border with Vermont. When Bela was seventeen, his father died, and not long after this Bela left home to find work.[12] Eventually he found himself in the frontier fur trade town of Michilimackinac. At the age of twenty-seven, he married Mary Chaurette, of mixed-blood descent. Mary was the daughter of Simon Chaurette, a fur trader, and Kinistenokwe, an Anishinaabe woman. Father-in-law Chaurette had clerked at posts in northern Wisconsin, such as Lac du Flambeau, and worked for the XY and NW Companies, and eventually for the AFC at Lac du Flambeau.[13] Mary Chapman's grandfather was the Anishinaabe ogimaa, or leader, Kishkemun of Folle Avoine in what is now Wisconsin.[14] Bela and Mary Chapman had eleven children, most of whom were born at Mackinac Island. However, their second-born, Reuben Chapman, was born in Grand Marais in 1824.[15] Bela Chapman was a devout Presbyterian and likely the only Presbyterian at the post. His men, such as Boucher and the Bongas, were likely Catholics with many traditional Anishinaabeg beliefs.[16]

The last available clerk at Fond du Lac, Chapman must have wondered where he would be sent. Older for a clerk—thirty years old—he was new to the country. Eventually, he learned that he would be sent up the North Shore to start an AFC operation at Grand Marais, with trips to Grand Portage. He must have felt some pride in being chosen to establish a new AFC post. But it would be a small post, and Grand Marais was a new location for the AFC, so questions surrounded the fledgling operation. From the men's perspective it compared poorly with the settlement at Fond du Lac and the civility of the town of Michilimackinac. The task before Chapman was daunting: establish a working post, be a thorn in the side of the HBC at Fort William, create trading relationships with local Anishinaabeg, maybe make some profits, and keep his men under control. Further, as the clerk in charge, he needed to lead his men to work in concert and trade productively.

Barely a year later, after leaving Grand Marais, he was connected enough to government officials that he was a witness to the 1825 Prairie du Chien treaty seeking peace among the warring Sioux, Chippewa, Sacs, Fox, and others. A year later Mary, his wife, "daughter of Equameeg," was allotted a one-section land grant from the U.S. government as part of the "half-breed" settlement in the 1826 treaty at Fond du Lac.[17]

Despite his short and frustrating stint at Grand Marais, Chapman continued to work for the AFC, in the early 1830s at the St. Mary's Outfit at Sault Ste.

Bela Chapman was the first American Fur Company clerk at Grand Marais. He directed his men to build the first post along the harbor shoreline in the fall of 1823.

Marie. Working on "shares" for the AFC, he tried a number of ventures, including leasing a sawmill and running the AFC store. Only a matter of days after learning his terms with the AFC for running the store, he was informed the AFC was closing it. In June 1835, the AFC repurchased the goods and let Chapman go. Looking for work, he went to Milwaukee, then returned to Michilimackinac.[18] In 1836, Chapman was falsely listed as a "half breed" in the 1836 treaty register. He was not provided treaty payment, but Mary, his wife, and his children were, for a total of $5,460.34. Following the custom of the day, all treaty money was provided to the male head of household, or Bela Chapman. For a period of time, Chapman sought to work with the AFC. As late as 1840 he inquired of AFC officials if they might consider him restarting trade at Mackinac.[19]

After his stint in the fur trade, Chapman led a distinguished life as a resident of Michilimackinac. In the 1830s he was deeply involved in territorial affairs, signing petitions to Congress for better roads, courts closer to home, trade licenses, and new county boundaries. In 1835 as a Whig candidate, he was elected a delegate to the constitutional convention of Michigan Territory, beating out James Schoolcraft by two votes.[20] He returned to Michigan state government for one term in 1867. He twice became "President" of Mackinac Village and repeatedly served in county government. Later, he became a probate court judge for Mackinac County for four different stints.[21] Eventually he homesteaded land in Cheboygan County, Michigan, and became equally prominent there. In fact, the first Cheboygan County jail was located on the second floor of the Chapman house.[22] Bela Chapman died in 1873 and was buried in his adopted home of Michilimackinac.[23]

George Johnston

George Johnston descended from distinguished lineages on both his father's and mother's sides. His father, John Johnston, was a "stocky, red-headed young Irishman, with . . . bright blue eyes." Shortly after arriving in North America he determined to be a fur trader. He was renowned for his civilized upbringing and devotion to his Anishinaabe wife, Susan O Shau-gus-co-day-way-qua. While raised as a nobleman, he was financially strapped during most of his adult life. His wife, known by Susan, was the daughter of Waubojeeg, or White Fisher, one of the most celebrated Anishinaabeg civil and war chiefs of the region, living in La Pointe, an old village and fur trade town in the Apostle Islands. She was a "strong character" and a person "who wonderfully adapted herself to her strange position . . . [and] was loved by her family."[24] She taught her children Anishinaabemowin and traditional manners, beliefs, and oral literature. While she hosted dozens of English-speaking guests and dignitaries through the years, she declined to speak publicly in English.

George's grandfather Waubojeeg led numerous war parties to fight the Fox and the Sioux, including a decisive battle that led to the Anishinaabeg possession of the St. Croix River valley.[25] His hunting grounds reportedly "extended along the southern shores of Lake Superior from the Montreal River, to the inlet of the Misacoda, or Burntwood [Brule] River." He was a tall man, being six feet six inches, and slender. He died in 1793, about forty-five years of age, of consumption.[26] George's great-grandfather Ma-Mongositea, or Big Foot, was of the Caribou clan, and his father before him was from Grand Portage.[27] Ma-Mongositea, an ally of the French, "was the ruling chief during the war of conquest of the Canadas by the British crown."[28]

Johnston family members were proud of their heritage as descendants of important Anishinaabeg ogimaag. For example, George Johnston's younger brother wrote the following about their great-great-grandfather Noka: "The grandfather of the chief White Fisher killed in one day's hunt starting from the mouth of the Crow Wing River, sixteen elk, 4 buffalo, five deer, three bear, one lynx and one porcupine."[29] Through his mother's distinguished lineage, George was related to members of the Caribou clan (sometimes called Reindeer clan by whites) living on the North Shore.

John Johnston came to Sault Ste. Marie, or Bawating in Anishinaabemowin, in 1793. He resided and spent most of his trading career at the Soo, working most commonly as an independent trader.[30] His strong bearing and self-determination made him a man of influence. He largely maintained his independence from the giant fur trade companies until he joined Astor and the South West Fur Company in 1816. He remained a British subject and participated in the War of 1812 as an officer. His British services in the war led to troubles in getting paid back for American lands and trade merchandise confiscated during the war.[31] His sons Lewis and George also served on the British side. George served in the army and was in the engagement at Mackinac Island on August 4, 1814.[32]

John and Susan Johnston had eight children. George Kal-

Mestayaho Johnston was the second born, in 1796, three years after his older brother, Lewis. Both Lewis and George were sent away to Montreal for school. He was remembered as a "great reader," following his father's penchant of reading to his young family on long winter nights.[33] The Johnston's third child was Jane, born in 1800, who would eventually marry Indian agent and aspiring ethnologist and author Henry Schoolcraft. She wrote poetry, although little of it was published in her lifetime. Jane was surrounded by three younger sisters and two younger brothers; the last, John McDougal, was born in 1816. In 1837, another brother, William Miengun Johnston, married Susan Davenport, sister of Ambrose Davenport Jr., who was one of Chapman's men in Grand Marais.

George began his adult life working for his father. George "was a very well educated man, conventional and very ceremonious in manner, uniting in himself very noticeably, the studied manners of his 'rank' in both nations, the Irish and the Indian."[34] He shared his father's cultivated taste in classic literature, clothes, and manners. His tastes for refined things never diminished; for example, even as a trader he purchased a cashmere-trimmed vest when a more practical one might do. The result was he was frequently in debt and quite often to the AFC, for which he worked off and on.[35] "George grew to be relatively tall and fluent in French, English, and Ojibway."[36] He saw himself as elite and was self-important; for example, he read and copied favorite poetry in his notebooks. He purposefully made stylish allusions in his journal entries to demonstrate his classical education.[37] Further, his father gave George and his siblings a vigorous sense of religion. Thus, George wrote the following verse in his journal:

Though I walk in the midst of troubles,
My god will not forsake me, if I put
My whole trust in god my Savior,
He will receive me: he shall stretch

Forth his hand against my enemies,
And his right hand shall save me.[38]

He was particularly proud to be his father's aide and confi-
dante and later defender. Prior to his stint in Grand Marais, young
George's most shining moment came when he was taking care of his
father's fur trade business while he was away. Territorial Governor
Lewis Cass and twenty soldiers approached Sault Ste. Marie in the
summer of 1820 to treat with local Anishinaabeg. He wrote:

> Their party landed opposite the present site where Fort Brady is
> now situated and formed their camp on the green near the shore
> of the St. Marie River, and within gunshot of the Indian village sit-
> uated on an elevated bank, and at this season of the year was well
> populated by the Indians who had arrived from different regions
> of the country from their winter hunting excursion; and beside
> the local population, many little fleets of canoes having arrived
> from the north and southern shore of Lake Superior on their way
> down to visit their English father at Drummond Island, and to
> receive their annual presents from the British government....
>
> My father, John Johnston, Esq., being absent from home, I
> called on his excellency, the governor, and invited him and his
> party to partake of the hospitalities of our home, and on the fol-
> lowing morning I received a message from the governor desiring
> me to attend the contemplated council he was to hold with the
> Indians.... soon the chiefs and head men seated themselves, the
> interpreter was ordered to bring in some tobacco for the chiefs to
> smoke, and the interpreter, agreeably to his instructions, brought
> in an armful of plug tobacco and which he threw upon the ground
> and within the Indian circle. At this time I observed standing near
> the marquee [tent] door a young chief, Sessaba, dressed in full
> British uniform and appeared too important a character to take
> a seat on the ground with the elder chiefs. At this time one of the

head men observed and casting his eye on the pile of tobacco before him, I presume, said he, that this tobacco is designed for our
smoking, and, drawing one of the plugs of tobacco towards him
with his belt and commenced cutting the tobacco, and at this instant, Sessaba, stepping inside the marquee, shoved the tobacco
lying on the ground with his foot, and addressing himself to the
head man who was cutting the tobacco, and with a frown, said
to him "How dare you accept of tobacco thrown on the ground
as bones to dogs," and instantly wheeling around, he walked off
towards the village and hoisted the British colors, and while the
chiefs and all were amazed at Sessaba's course it was reported to
Gen Cass that the British flag was hoisted and waving in the Indian village and so soon did the general spring to his feet, calling his
interpreter to accompany him, they marched toward the village,
and Lieut. Pierce and his men sprung to their arms. This broke up
the council and the chiefs dispersed.... [Indian women and children flee in canoes in confusion.] In the meantime the British flag
was hauled down by the general. At this time I walked home and
I met my mother opposite my office and she, appearing much
agitated, accosted me saying: "For God's sake, George, send instantly for the elder chiefs, for that foolish young chief, Sessaba,
will bring ruin to the tribe, and get them assembled here." I immediately dispatched messengers for the chiefs and elders. And
the chiefs, soon obeying the summons, were assembled in my
office and I addressed with the following words: "My friends and
relatives, I am young and possess very little wisdom to give you
advice at this present time; it is from you I should receive it, but
on this occasion allow me to give you a few words of warning;
and I do not design to be lengthy; a few words will suffice. You
are all of you aware that hostilities between Great Britain and the
United States have ceased. Peace now exists. The two nations are
now living on friendly terms; one of your young men has misbe-
haved himself and has given a gross insult to the government of

Michigan, a representative of the president of the United States, by hoisting the British flag on his acknowledged territory. You can not expect that the British government will sustain him in such an act. I understand that he has gone to arm himself and raise warriors; now be wise and quick and put a stop to this wild scheme and suppress the rising of your young men. The firing of one gun will bring ruin to your tribe and to the Chippewas, so that a dog will not be left to howl in your villages."

My mother at this time came in and with authority commanded the assembled chiefs to be quick, and suppress the follies of Sessaba, the chief. Shingwackhouse, the orator of the tribe, and who had been a partisan during the past war, was selected with other braves, and they had orders from the chiefs to stop Sessaba's proceedings, and they forthwith started upon the portage road, and they met Sessaba, who, having divested himself of his regimentals, and now appearing painted and in war accouterments, leading a party of warriors, prepared and determined for a desperate encounter with Gen Cass. Shingwackhouse, on meeting Sessaba, and addressing the party with him, said to them: "My friends and relatives, I am authorized by our chiefs and elders to stop your proceedings." Sessaba, instantly replying to, said to Shingwackhouse, "You was a war leader when my brother fell in battle; he was killed by the Americans, and how dare you come to put a stop to my proceedings?" and raising his war-club, struck at Shingwackhouse and grazed his left shoulder and Shingwackhouse, undismayed, still kept up his oration and with his eloquence and the power vested him by the chiefs, he prevailed on the party to return quietly to their respective lodges. [Johnston suggested the chiefs apologize to Gen Cass; they do, and a few days later their treaty negotiations conclude.][39]

While this account is written in a self-serving fashion, others, too, credit Johnston and his mother with preventing bloodshed.[40]

One of the more predictable results was that Cass, who would later become a presidential candidate, thought highly of Johnston. Both Cass and Henry Schoolcraft, Johnston's brother-in-law, would employ him periodically as an interpreter or Indian agent. For example, in 1822 Cass appointed Johnston as captain of the Militia of the Territory of Michigan, only a couple of years after he became a U.S. citizen. Two years later, Cass appointed Johnston as sheriff of Brown County, Michigan Territory.[41] Their relationship also meant that Johnston fielded odd requests from Cass, such as when Cass, then in Washington, requested Johnston send him "a few beaver tails" as objects of interest for polite society.[42] In 1826, Cass agreed to Schoolcraft's request that Johnston be named his subagent at La Pointe. Or as the letter of appointment reads, "Mr. Johnston has been temporarily appointed sub agent for your agency and has been directed to report to you for instructions. . . . Duties: These will relate principally to the conduct of the Indians, and of Traders, and to be the dissemination of foreign counsels and influence. The Indians must be conciliated by firm and prudent conduct."[43] Johnston was paid a then-handsome sum of $500 per year.

Schoolcraft was appointed Indian agent at Sault Ste. Marie in 1822, by Secretary of War John Calhoun at the urging of Governor Cass.[44] Before long, Schoolcraft and Jane Johnston began a courtship. And a year later, George Johnston became Schoolcraft's brother-in-law, when Schoolcraft married Jane in October 1823. For some observers, this meant there were three social climbers in the family: Henry, Jane, and George.[45] Particularly during his early years of marriage to Jane, Schoolcraft would do what he could to employ George or assist him in finding gainful employment. For example, Schoolcraft advocated for George to accompany him and others on two major expeditions, in 1831 and 1832, to find the source of the upper Mississippi.[46]

For a number of years rumors swirled of Schoolcraft's nepotism toward Johnston. Johnston's position in the desirable job as an

George Johnston was the second American Fur Company clerk at Grand Marais. He was a brother-in-law of Henry Schoolcraft. Courtesy of the Bentley Historical Library, University of Michigan.

Indian agent and his sometimes erratic and petty behavior set fertile ground for rumors. Schoolcraft's (and Johnston's) close association with Governor Cass contributed to a sense of connections that rankled some. This issue came to head in 1841 when Johnston was dismissed by Schoolcraft's successor as Michigan Superintendent of Indian Affairs. A different political party, and thus agent, was in charge, and Johnston's irregularities were more visible. He was dismissed.[47]

Johnston was an accomplished interpreter who served in three treaties. By chance, he translated for General Cass when he arrived at the Sault and negotiated for a small tract of land. Johnston was the official interpreter at the 1826 Fond du Lac Treaty, in which North Shore Anishinaabeg observed but were not signatories. And ironically, he served as the official interpreter for the British during the Robinson-Superior Treaty held at the Canadian Soo in 1850. The Robinson-Superior Treaty ceded much of the Canadian North Shore of Lake Superior (to the height of land), including from the Pigeon River to Sault Ste. Marie.[48]

Working to foster his relationship with his brother-in-law, Johnston could be overtly earnest, such as signing off a letter "Your sincere Friend & Kinsmen."[49] But this would not last, as eventually Johnston and Schoolcraft had a falling out. To be away from his influential brother-in-law, Johnston spent a great deal of time in the British Sault (across the St. Marys River) in the 1830s.[50] For a short period of time he became a fish dealer and entrepreneur and established a fishery in Batchawana Bay, up the east coast of Lake Superior.[51] Their mutual good friend Cass intervened and counseled Johnston to get over any hard feelings between them, saying his brother-in-law was concerned for his well-being.[52]

Johnston married twice. In October 1822 he married Louisa Raymond, or Wassidjeewunoqua, and their first child, Henry William Johnston, was born a year later. They eventually would have three children, two sons and one daughter. Their second child was born August 19, 1825, meaning Louisa must have been in Grand

Marais with Johnston despite the customary lack of mention of family members in journals.[53] Further, they had their first child, barely over a year old, with them in Grand Marais. Wassidjeewunoqua and Louisa Maria and Henry William, the oldest children and thus alive at the time of the 1826 treaty, were to receive one section of land.[54] Louisa died in December 1832.[55] Johnston then married strongly religious Mary Rice, and they had four children together, three sons and one daughter. Mary died in September 1858, leaving Johnston with seven children ranging from twelve to thirty-five years old.[56]

In many ways, Johnston lived a tragic life. He outlived two wives, and he witnessed his father never regain his inheritance and economic position. After his father's death, Johnston tried to assist his mother, who was forced to live on in modest means. For every step forward, such as good paying and responsible employment as an Indian agent (at La Pointe, Mackinac, Traverse Bay, and the Soo), he would commonly take a step back, returning to more hardscrabble circumstances, often going back to the frontier as a fur trader. Like his father, he would entreat the U.S. government to redress wrongs he believed were done to him through the loss of wages. And like his father, he met with little success. And his mixed-blood heritage, being a member of a family once seen as one of the most capable and even noble, would not be much help in his later years. In the eyes of the U.S. government, Johnston's children, and indeed Johnston, were classified as Indians. In the 1840s, he became a business partner with Schoolcraft's brother, James, to profit from the copper rush in the Upper Peninsula of Michigan. Johnston thought his contacts with area Anishinaabeg, who knew where copper ore was located and would willingly provide that information to Johnston, gave him a business advantage over others. But that enterprise came to a tragic end when his partner, James Schoolcraft, was murdered by an unknown assailant in 1846.[57]

Although only sixty-five when he died in 1861, Johnston must have been an old man, broken in spirit and feeling that his life had been a failure. He disappeared from his home one January blizzard day and was found frozen to death near the St. Marys Rapids. Many believed this was peculiar, as Johnston knew his way around the Soo better than most, and he knew how to take care of himself in wintertime.[58] Perhaps the most charitable part of his death was that he did not live to see his three sons die shortly after him in the Civil War.

In Grand Marais

Neither Chapman nor Johnston knew what to expect at Grand Marais. Apparently, neither did their bosses. Johnston's first impression of Grand Marais was detailed, quick to judge, and harsh:

> I arrived here this morning a lonely and dismal place it is, by the very first appearance. The Bay is semicircular, and by observing it from the lake, resembles very much a horse shoe, the beach is gravelly, the main shore is perpendicular rocks. It would be a good harbor for two or three vessels at a time on utmost emergencies, and the only one between Fond du Lac & Grand Portage, distance from the former place by computation forty five leagues & from the latter fifteen, about three miles from this passes a high range of mountains, which I am told go beyond Fort William. It is in some places perpendicular and at others sloping from top to the margin of the lake. The growth of Timber is vis Spruce a few stunted pines, poplar, white birch, cedars, and at some distance into the interior, here and there, a cluster of maple. The appearance of the country in general, is sterile in fact I cannot but lament my situation considering that I have nearly ten months to remain in this I may safely say Siberian exile, no one to converse with but Ignorant Canadians, and the Natives, the latter are chiefly, murderers, Robbers & thieves.[1]

Johnston's view was incensed by one unhappy discovery. The post Chapman's men had built, and they were to inhabit, was burned to the ground.

> I shall attempt to give you a cursory view of our proceedings in this post during our exile in it, intending to reserve something to discuss upon, should the Almighty enable us to meet again. We arrived here on the sixth after leaving Fon du Lac, without unloading or any accident happening [to] our boat. We found all the houses burnt which makes this place look dismal enough.[2]

Compounding his dismay was that Johnston knew that he had been sent to and had arrived at a fur trade backwater. While Chapman arrived exhausted, he was somewhat optimistic about Grand Marais and businesslike in his first impressions. There was much to be done and little time for writing.

Getting to Grand Marais was a culmination of days crossing much of Lake Superior. Johnston and likely Chapman had left Michilimackinac on Lake Michigan, and their boatmen rowed, sailed, and paddled into Lake Superior and westward to Fond du Lac. After a week or two at Fond du Lac on the St. Louis River, they started anew in canoes and a bateau (boat) to reach Grand Marais.[3] It was not likely that either clerk paddled or rowed. However, their young wives and any kinfolk along (but remaining unnamed) likely did in separate canoes.

It was the young clerks' responsibility, however, to insure the trade goods were secure and dry and arrived at their destination. Chapman's trip did not start well. The first night out he discovered that a whiskey barrel was empty, a container of lard broken and half gone, and a bag of pork empty. He never was able to determine who had plundered his supplies.[4] Keeping the goods dry, especially when seas were rough and landing precarious, was particularly tricky. If the goods got wet, the crew would be obliged to stop and dry them so they would not spoil. Or if the waves were too threatening, the crew would be windbound and lose precious days to be productive. Chapman rued that he was windbound six days on this trip from Fond du Lac to Grand Marais.

While traveling along the south shore of Lake Superior, the men encountered Anishinaabeg and other traders. Near the Ontonagon River, Johnston learned of the murder of four Americans traders by an Anishinaabeg war party. His Indian informants were anxious to make clear it was a "mistake" and the war party had intended to attack Dakota.[5] Nevertheless, their receiving this news and other information along the way illustrates that news flew quickly and the men lived largely in an oral society, or really societies. They were particularly vulnerable to rumor when they did not receive written news and letters from one trader to another.

State of the Country

Lake Superior dominated Chapman's, Johnston's, and their men's time at Grand Marais. It was their primary avenue to trade with Anishinaabeg and ultimately their escape route back to Fond du Lac. Fish from the lake provided much of their food. Indian traders would often come or leave by way of the lake, even late into the season, as the big lake remained free of ice for many winter months. When the men tried to fish, paddle, or sail, winds commonly whipped off the lake, numbing them or pinning them onshore. And the sound of the waves crashing, or slapping, or lapping the shore was ever present. Henry Schoolcraft would romantically recall a sweeping view of the eastern shore of Lake Superior that would have equally described the AFC men's experience:

> The water in which the men struck their paddles was pure as crystal. The air was perfectly exhilarating from its purity . . . the broad view of the entrance into the lake burst upon us. It is magnificent.

... Beyond it is what the Chippewas call Bub-eesh-ko-be, meaning the far off, indistinct prospect of a water scene, till the reality,
in the feeble power of human vision, loses itself in the clouds and
sky.... We clambered up and over ... till we ... stood on the highest pinnacle, and gazed on the "blue profound" of Superior, the
great water or Gitchigomee of the Indians.[6]

One year prior to the arrival of AFC men at Gichi Bitobig, David Thompson paddled by it. The head of the British survey team
sent to locate the international border, Thompson described the
place while coasting the lakeshore from the south:

Held on along low Lands and mostly very fine Beaches of red
Pebbles with swampy like ground directly behind. . . . Passed a
fine ship Harbor . . . many Midges and a few Musketoes. 2 Indians came to us from their lodges in the Bay. They and their looks
pleaded Hunger.[7]

A few years later, in June 1843, a prospector named George Cannon described entering Grand Marais harbor much like it must have
been for Chapman and Johnston and their men:

Toward night we put into a small Bay, named by the voyageurs
Grand Marais, or Good Boat Harbor. . . . June 5—The sun rose
clear and pleasant, and the night had been extremely cold, so as
to freeze the gravel along the water's edge sufficiently hard as to
bear up a person....

We had noticed at a short distance from our previous encampment that the Rock had changed character from a porous
Trap to a compact Greenstone, and here is assumed a Basaltic, or
columnar appearance, with the columns well defined, and varying
in height from one to twenty feet, being four, five, and six-sided.
There were inclined at every angle, from that of a perpendicular,

to a nearly horizontal position, and in many places the columns were broken off and fallen into the bed of the Lake. In many places, where the rock assumed a more compact form, were noticed spar veins having a direction nearly at right angles to the general bearing of the rock, which was east and west. This rock formed two sides of the Little Bay, which was nearly excluded from the Lake, forming a safe and convenient harbor for small boats.[8]

Cannon further observed this was a country of rock and thick, heavy moss. It was a place of "immense swarms of black flies, thicker than the leaves of the forest." Landing first at the "Burnt Wood River"—the Brule River today—he wrote that "the Timber along the river is principally the White Birch, which forms the majority, and a few scattering Norway Pines, with Fir, Cedar, a few Tamerack and Mountain Ash." He was struck by the sublime beauty, but after twenty days of prospecting, he saw no sign of big game—moose, caribou, or deer.[9]

Exploring the highlands above Poplar River (near where Lutsen is today), Cannon and fellow prospectors passed through sugar maple groves that had been harvested by Indians, as evident from the maple sugar implements cached at the foot of trees.[10] The area was heavily wooded, with no sign of forest fire. There was little sign of cutting beyond the edge of their camp on the harbor. Cannon met a few Anishinaabeg, living in small family groups. From the water, they first saw the smoke from the campfires. He befriended a generous family, and then he noted an Anishinaabe grave and old camping ground. For him, it was a wild but occupied country.

James Ferguson, an American surveyor seeking to put to rest any question about the exact location of the international border, noted "that nearly the whole of the northern shore of Lake Superior consists of these sheer rocky escarpments, from six hundred to nine hundred feet high."[11] In a different report he noted "the poverty of the country and its inhabitants."[12] In 1822 he stated, "The Whole interior is in a state of starvation, at Rat River [Kenora], a dozen frogs were sold for four dollars."[13] Others called it a barren country. While in this area in the summer of 1822, David Thompson said, "nothing of Pigeons, Partridges, etc. can be seen . . . [and on August he met] . . . 8 to 10 canoes of the [Anishi]nabe Indians, they had only Berries to eat."[14]

The most detailed comment about the area at the time was made by the Hudson's Bay Company factor at Fort William, John Haldane:

> The Indians about Fort William are not so numerous as they were some years ago—some having going to Nipigon—others to Fond du Lac, and a small portion to St. Marys.—The number still frequenting this establishment, generally, may amount to 28 men & lads.—There is one principal Chief to whom the others in a great measure look up—the only name he goes by, even with the Indians is "Espagnol." This band are beyond the old Grand Portage, yet last year he gave us almost all his years hunt amounting to 60 Beaver Skins besides a good many Otters and Martens. . . .
>
> All this part of the Country, in former times produced a good many Beaver & Otters—the Indians now complain of a scarcity in those Animals—there are still many Martens & Cats, but Foxes, Fishers, & Bears are not numerous & the Musquash not so much so as in other parts of the Country, near the Lake.— Formerly there were Moose Deer—at this time not one is to be seen, being literally extinct—Carribou was also at a former period, and not a great many years since very numerous—few now are seen. The scarcity of those Animals is greatly felt by the Indians. In Winter their sole dependence for subsistence, is on Rabbits (A species betwixt the English Hare & Rabbit—& which does not burrow) & Partridges of various kinds.—In the Summer & fall the Indians are furnished with Nets & in the fall they are supplied with a good stock of ammunition. Notwithstanding

these supplies they are often necessitated to have recourse to the establishment when we give them fish, potatoes & Indian Corn. Humanity & interest compel us to be kind to them, & they are generally grateful to us.

The face of the Country from the lines and then taking a range inwards of 100 Miles from the margin of the Lake, is mountainous, the flat parts being composed of innumerable small Lakes & Rivers—those Lakes & Rivers producing fish of various kinds as—Pike, Pickeral, Trout, Carp, White Fish, Loche (Mithy by the Indians) [burbot in English] & Sturgeon in some of the rivers only.

In Winter few fish are taken anywhere—this the poor Indians feel severely—almost everything then becomes an article of food—that is capable of being eaten—and they are at the same time pinched with cold from their scanty covering. Indeed were it not for the supply of European woolens, which they receive from us in the fall, they would literally require to lie dormant the whole winter. In other parts of the Country the natives can clothe themselves in Skins, but in these parts they must depend on the Company even for Leather & Parchment to make themselves Mockassins & Snow Shoes. Such is the case with all the Indians in the Lake Superior District.[15]

A year later, Haldane's counterpart described the "vegetable production" of the Rainy Lake region, highlighting wild rice and Jerusalem artichokes. Artichokes grew in sunny, sandy grounds far from the wild rice beds. Artichokes had one drawback: if relied upon too heavily, they resulted in "Flatulency & cholic."[16]

Most of the observers who came through this area did not mention Grand Marais or take great pains to explore the area nearby. The U.S. border surveyors—Ferguson, George W. Whistler, and Joseph Delafield—did not extend their maps as far south as Grand Marais. Thompson and the British-Canadian survey team, which proposed that the border run along the St. Louis River, did not name Grand Marais. Their Royal Navy counterparts, led by Lieutenant Henry W. Bayfield, affixed the "improperly named . . . Grand Marais" on their chart, but for years the chart was difficult to obtain. For most explorers and fur traders prior to the AFC efforts, Grand Marais remained a backwater, an infrequently used yet welcome refuge from Lake Superior's fury.

The Post

Was Grand Marais the best place for the post? Or was Chapman given vague instructions to build at Grand Marais? Why not locate it at Grand Portage, which is closer to the border, had a significant tradition as a trading post, and was an Anishinaabeg gathering place? It is clear that the AFC was not very familiar with the North Shore. If the AFC were to establish a post at Grand Portage, it would be hurtling into head-to-head competition with the Hudson's Bay Company at Fort William.[17] At this time, the exact location of the international border was not clear, although most thought Grand Portage was in American territory. But there still was a lingering sense at the time that Grand Portage was British territory, to the point that Henry Schoolcraft wrote that the United States should "take possession of, and raising our flag at, Old Grand Portage, (L[ake] S[uperior]) long the seat of the commercial and political power wielded over the north by the Northwest and the X.Y. Companies."[18] And on the other side of the border, as late as 1831, the HBC clerk at Fort William observed that "the Old Grand Portage would be a more convenient and advantageous situation for the Outpost [than Arrow Lake]."[19] Building a rival post at Grand Marais, then, was inching toward the border and the HBC but clearly keeping to American soil. The AFC men thought it was suitably located to intercept Indians coming to or from the wild rice beds at White Fish Lake and South and North Fowl Lakes and those canoeing by on Lake Superior.

Anishinaabeg would frequently travel along the lake, making Grand Marais an advantageous location for trade.[20] And it had a minor reputation among voyageurs traveling along the North Shore as a good fishing place.[21]

The AFC men hoped it was an opportune time to challenge the newly reorganized HBC. The North West Company and XY Company had merged in 1805, and the combined enterprise moved from Grand Portage northward to the Kaministiquia River and Thunder Bay. The subsequent bitter competition between the North Westers and the HBC depressed profits, and traders and innocents were killed, as they fought for supremacy for much of the northern half of North America. After the rancorous 1821 merger of the two titans, a final border clash resumed between the reorganized HBC and the upstart Americans. Companies eschewed competition; direct competition between fur trade companies diminished profits as each company had to become more liberal with gifts to Indians and agree to higher values for pelts.

The few AFC men had their hands full—particularly initially—with the many tasks involved in establishing the Grand Marais outpost. The post needed to be built, and simultaneously Chapman and Johnston hoped to begin trading. Food had to be secured, particularly fish from Lake Superior. Trade goods were given on credit to the Anishinaabeg with the hope they would promptly move to their trapping grounds—called hunting grounds in the journals. Men would have to fashion snowshoes and travel to Indian camps to bring goods so Anishinaabeg could trap in the cold winter months. Going to Anishinaabeg camps further insured they did not trade with a competitor. Fully provisioned Indians could trap harder and thus pay off their debts.[22]

The exact dimensions, number of buildings, and even location of the Grand Marais post are unknown. But the first steps in building a hypothetical post are described by fur trade scholar Grace Lee Nute:

The first duty of the voyageurs on reaching their wintering ground was to erect a fort under the direction of their clerk....A consultation was frequently held with the chief Indians as to the best site. [Anishinaabeg told at least one prior trader that Grand Marais had good fishing.[23]] When this was determined, a clearing was made, trees were cut and hewed into proper lengths and a storehouse and "shop" was erected. Next came the clerk's house, then a house for the men....

Chimneys of mud and sticks were put up at the ends of the dwellings and roofs were thatched with boughs held down by poles or sticks. As nails were expensive and heavy to take into the interior, the logs were held in place in a unique way. Grooves were cut in upright logs set at each corner of the foundation. Down these grooves were slipped the ends of the logs, which were cut into fit exactly between the uprights. Thus one log lay in place above another, held in position by vertical logs. A certain kind of white clay served admirably in place of plaster and whitewash and gave a neat appearance to the interiors. Puncheon floors were laid in the living quarters, bunks were constructed against the wall, rough tables and stools were made, and windows—one or two to a cabin—were covered with oiled deerskin in lieu of glass.[24]

The dressed skin or parchment windows had another advantage: if the men were starving, they could "live upon your parchment window" by consuming it.[25] Overlapping cedar bark often served as roofs for temporary buildings. If constructed with care, they were watertight.[26] And like at other AFC posts, a flagpole was likely erected, and it was customary to raise the American flag on the Sabbath.[27]

Chapman and Johnston give us a few details about the structures at Grand Marais. Chapman and men built a storehouse first, then Chapman's house. While it is not mentioned, they likely built a "men's house" as well. These "houses" may have been connected, more like apartments sharing a wall and perhaps even internal doors.[28] The living quarters must have had chimneys, but not necessarily the storehouse since a colder building cut short the time spent trading with Indians as few wanted to linger in the chill. Since iron was expensive and heavy to transport, and nails were still made by hand, the men likely had few or no nails to hold the logs together. Their building method was different than what was used for the notched or dovetailed log buildings built by later immigrants. Building a French Canadian–style structure with logs anchored in place with mortise and wooden pegs takes specialized skills and special tools to do well. The walls of this style of structure are more prone to falling until the whole structure is in place, and if the corner posts are not placed deep enough in the ground or mortises are improperly set. Chapman's men were apparently inexperienced builders with few or no nails to hold the structure together, resulting in the partially built house falling down. Eventually, the main problem for Chapman was that the roofs leaked badly in a heavy rain. Arriving late in the year, the men would have had difficulty peeling birch bark for roofing material, so they may have had to make do with cedar bark or poles with dirt on top.[29]

Warned about the leaky roofs of his predecessor, Johnston directed his men to put more effort into making water-repellent roofs. They paddled to the abandoned fields at Grand Portage to harvest over a hundred bundles of grass for thatch and then paddled back to Grand Marais. To hold the thatching in place, they applied four inches of dirt on top of the thatch, under a layer of poles. Johnston's house was the only one for which we have the dimensions: twenty feet by sixteen feet. His men were able to both put in a floor and dig a cellar in his house.[30] Neither Chapman nor Johnston were fond of their quarters, and both left or planned to leave them for tents at Grand Portage in the spring months.

What was life like at the post? It was particularly frantic when they first arrived. There were buildings to construct, cords of firewood to be cut, tables and chairs to be fashioned out of round timbers, and rudimentary beds to be made. Trade goods had to be guarded. Information was sought about the HBC fur rates and how much credit they might offer. Each clerk endeavored to identify an initial competitive method to counter the HBC. At the same time, food needed to be gathered, caught, or shot. Fish, some game, and basic staples such as flour and wild rice were the main sustenance for traders elsewhere.[31] Unlike at other posts west of Grand Marais, there is no evidence the AFC men collected or traded for wild rice with area Anishinaabeg. But they might have brought a limited amount with them from Fond du Lac (not far from productive wild rice beds).

Fishing for trout with gill nets was the most important food production at the post. But fishing also led to chores such as repairing boats and canoes, sewing up holes in gill nets, and sometimes "knitting" new nets. When Chapman first arrived at Grand Marais, he first knit more than six gill nets. At Fort William fish was put in a salt brine in barrels and stored for the lean winter months. Dozens of barrels of salted fish were put up each fall. Chapman made no mention of salting, but Johnston did.[32] This meant he brought both salt and barrels—at least a few—with him to Grand Marais. Chapman likely had his fish smoked or simply frozen. They were the primary foodstuff as indicated by their having been put "under key," likely in the storehouse.[33] And as their frozen, smoked, or even salted trout ran low, so too did other food stocks.

Chapman and Johnston men's diet was plain and repetitive. They likely brought cornmeal, flour, crackers and biscuits, tea, lard, and butter as staples. Johnston mentions that Fond du Lac produced wheat, Indian corn, squashes, and potatoes, so perhaps they were able to bring these staples. Potatoes were a mainstay at Fond du Lac.[34] Cornmeal mushes and bannock (because of little or no leavening) were likely common fare. If they were fortunate, perhaps they had limited amounts of luxury goods such as cheese, pepper, chocolate, "loaf sugar," "Spanish wine," and even coffee. Perhaps they had some barley or oats and a cask or two of dried peas from the Fond du Lac gardens. But these would have been in limited quantity.[35] Watching each one of these foods run low, or worse, run out was a gloomy prospect for the men. Chapman may have had one or two of his hogs butchered especially when cold weather came. But he held out and kept some until the spring. This meant, however, his men had to be careful to keep the hogs away from any frozen fish cached outside.

It is difficult to say what foods were locally harvested, as no mention is made of this, nor of the women, who more often than not would have provided that food. For example, rabbit snaring was typically women's work. Some of the meat from trapped furbearers was also eaten. Gathering the first greens in late spring would have made a welcome change to their diet, if not overdone. Late April meant the return of "Bustard," or wild goose, which was much sought after as a relief from hunger and a monotonous diet as well as a symbol of the return of spring.

As fall swung into winter, more and more effort turned toward cold-weather preparations, particularly getting the buildings chinked and firewood cut, hauled, and stored nearby. In heavy snow years, pathways had to be dug out. When not traveling *en derouine*— going to Anishinaabe winter camps to trade—the men had more time. Occasionally, boredom led to contests, such as documented a few years later at another post:

> Yesterday morning one of Mr. Davenport's men, laid a wager with another that he would eat at once a pan of [Maple] Sugar— (nearly 4 Qts—I should think). If he Succeeded he was to have the Sugar free—if not—he stake a *Shirt worth in this country* $4. The fellow soon gave up the attempt.[36]

With open hearths, cords of firewood were cut and burned. The Fort William journals regularly name who was cutting and hauling firewood, but not the AFC journals. If relatively dry firewood was a distance from the post, this would only aggravate this necessary chore, especially in deep snow. Birch-wood sledges may have been built to haul cordwood, as was done at other posts. It must have seemed like an endless task, as the chimneys would suck up much of the heat from the fires, leaving the "houses" cold, drafty, and dim with few windows.

The AFC men faced trying conditions. The day after Chapman "had the first addition to his family," his men finished the "body of our store house."[37] Mary Chaurette more likely gave birth in a tent or waakaa'igan than a house. Three weeks later, Chapman began plastering his house, and it promptly snowed. His men were likely sleeping in the storehouse at this time or perhaps even yet in tents. Cold weather set in early, and the Kaministiquia River froze fast on November 11.[38] Chapman's men and their families faced a very cold December in 1823, having a thirteen-day arctic spell in which temperatures rarely got above zero.[39] They shivered through a minus 37 degrees Fahrenheit low temperature in both January and February 1824. And yet there was one thaw, too, in January.[40] In the village of Sault Ste. Marie, Indian agent Schoolcraft described the winter: "A pinching cold winter wears away slowly. The whole village seems to me like so many prescient beavers, in a vast snow-bank, who cut away the snow and make paths, every morning, from one lodge to another."[41] A day after a cold snap, mild weather led to ice breakup on the Kaministiquia River on May 4, 1824.[42] A week later the ice went out of Thunder Bay.[43] With snowmelt and ice-out, travelers changed from snowshoes and dog teams to canoes, and their routes changed as well as winter forest trails gave way to moving across water and portages.

The snowmelt in the early summer of 1824 and thirty-eight days of rain resulted in relatively high water, leading to more dangerous canoe travel in fast water.[44] Rapids became dangerous as the force and speed of rivers rose. By the late summer months a different weather pattern had set in. If Chapmen and men had remained in Grand Marais, they would have smelled smoke. The forests west of Grand Marais had dried considerably, and two large forest fires broke out—a total of 131 square miles at Bald Eagle–Isabella Lakes and Long Island, Rush, and Loon Lakes.[45] Late in the summer of 1824 an early and heavy frost hurt the berry crop, leaving very few available.[46] In the first days of September, cold hit Anishinaabeg at wild ricing camps, including a hoar frost.[47] Johnston bemoaned the bleak November 1824 weather, with more days of snow and rain than any other month that year. The last three months of 1824, the snow fell a total of eighteen days, and the year went out with a coldest temperature recording of minus 24 Fahrenheit.[48] As was typical, it was a year of extremes with streaks of precipitation, dry spells, and cold weather.

Johnston and men enjoyed a comparatively mild late winter and spring of 1825, though he probably did not picture it as such. There were at least two winter thaws, and the coldest weather was not as numbing as years before. Ice breakup at Sault Ste. Marie was "ten days earlier than the oldest resident remembered." Southward at Fort Snelling, spring 1825 was one of the two warmest seasons in the 1800s, resulting in early ice-out on the Mississippi River.[49] Inland at Lac La Pluie (Rainy Lake), a trader wrote on April 23, "This is a most extraordinary circumstance. There is not within the memory of the oldest people in the country, such another instance of an early breaking up of the ice."[50] Even with the warmer spring weather, Johnston and his men were desperate, hungry, and fed up with their posting.

The AFC men knew little about the geography and resources of the North Shore. Aside from Grand Marais and several other places, few locations were identified by name. Chapman does call out known stopover spots, like the Isle of Encampment and Baptism River. Most of the shore remained unnamed, or locations had names not recognizable today. "River of Gilead" was likely the Poplar River. Later, Chapman sent his men "to Burnt River," likely the Brule River. Johnston, unimpressed with the geography, does not mention any site between Fond du Lac and Grand Marais, leaving the impression they arrived at Gichi Bitobig without any travail. However, someone of Chapman's men knew the country well enough to make a judgment about where to land each day, considering the options beyond where they were. It was unlikely that the designated guide, Boucher, made this call as later Chapman makes clear he was of little help. More likely, George Bonga was the person with some geographic knowledge, as we know he had traveled along the North Shore before, and Chapman later credits him with navigating inland trips.

Johnston wrote of a "high range of mountains" essentially walling off Grand Marais from the interior in his first journal entry at Grand Marais. These "mountains" are the Sawtooth Mountains, which parallel Lake Superior and indeed rise abruptly in a number of places. What little reconnaissance he had of the area may have come from his employers, William Aitken and William Morrison, or from his father. His father's published account said only this of the North Shore: "From Fond-du-Lac to Grand Portage, the distance is about sixty leagues; the mountains here high, one of them near the Portage is called 'The Thunder,' and is the Tenerife of Lake Superior."[51]

The AFC men's lack of knowledge about the area was evident in Chapman's assumption that it would be like the south shore and whitefish would be a commonly caught fish.[52] More critically, this lack of knowledge confined the AFC post to Grand Marais, where conditions for wintertime fishing were not favorable. Fall lake trout fishing was very productive, but once the deep cold set in, with shifting ice, harvesting fish by hook and line or spearing became very difficult and dangerous. Or as Johnston remarked, "Still cold I was in hopes that the Ice would have held, but it is constantly moving to & fro. We however ventured on the Bay but were not successful in catching trout." He then ruefully noted that "two months ago the Ice was firmly frozen at Pigeon River, where we might in our present situation get daily subsistence."[53] And then a week later the ice was solid in Grand Marais. In a word, the ice was unpredictable, and thus they could not reliably catch fresh fish in the depth of winter.

Chapman curiously predicted and then experienced three earthquakes while at Grand Marais. He wrote, "we have had two earthquakes since winter commenced and we shall shortly have a third or some other phenomena will make its appearance." A little more than three weeks later, he wrote, "We have had the earthquake as I prognosticated."[54] While it was possible that he and his men indeed experienced earthquakes, no one else in the region reported such phenomena. Chapman's report of earthquakes is more evidence of his lack of knowledge about the area than it is an accurate report on natural phenomena.

Chapman apparently brought hogs to Grand Marais, assuming good fodder for them would be present there. He also makes baffling comments about his hogs. Confusingly, he also uses the same term to disparage Indian trading partners that hung around the post longer than he would have liked. Nevertheless, Chapman kept hogs through much of the winter, naively hoping to find a market for them. This makes some sense, as fur trade employees often expected or demanded "grease" as part of their food rations. Perhaps the men assumed that their competitors at Fort William were regularly provided grease and sometimes pork for their diet. In some instances the HBC clerk would give grease to Espagnol and band.[55] In a diet low on fat, grease would have been a welcome addition to simple fare. It was so welcome a supplement to the "servants" diet that it was sometimes given out as a reward or treat at a regale. Chapman's troublesome hogs—often getting free—were a good idea largely before its time. The problem he never solved was the lack of a market.[56]

The Place-Name: Grand Marais

North Shore Anishinaabeg called Grand Marais Gichi Bitobig, or great double harbor.[57] Before the AFC men, voyageurs had been paddling by it for decades. Sometimes multiple brigades paddled by, looking longingly at its quiet, sheltered waters. In 1805, "fourteen large canoes ... [coasted by] necessary to carry over four hundred pieces of goods, of ninety pounds each, from Fort William to Fort St. Louis [Fond du Lac]."[58] Or rushing to beat a storm, they might pull out in the East Bay and haul their gear out of the reach of the crashing surf. To voyageurs, it was one of the best—and few—refuges from squalls on the North Shore. They paddled from the NWC's post at Grand Portage, and later its successor Fort William, to Fond du Lac and back. While paddling, they might tell the new clerk or bourgeois in the canoe its name or, more rarely, about pausing there. The French trader Perrault paddled by with his voyageurs in 1793. And the teenage British clerk George Nelson paddled by, perhaps calling it "Vieu Déser," French for old garden.[59] Any map that Nelson or Perrault might have consulted at the time would have left Grand Marais unnamed. It was undocumented except in the oral traditions of voyageurs. What the Americans were working with was trifling knowledge of the region and a handful of place-names passed down by word of mouth.

There was no doubt Chapman's crew were bound for a place already known as Grand Marais, though a single English spelling would not coalesce for a few decades. Its name preceded Chapman's and Johnston's arrivals by at least two decades. In 1804, trader Michel Curot paddled by it twice on his way to the NWC post in Thunder Bay, and he wrote it as Grand Marrais once, and then on his return he spelled it in its present form: Grand Marais.[60] Since most early traders who paddled the North Shore—like Curot—were French or French speaking, it was not surprising that it received a French name. If the pioneering North Shore travelers were accompanied by any Anishinaabeg or Anishinaabemowin-speaking men, such as Espagnol or even George Bonga, it would have been called Gichi Bitobig. Roughly translated, this means "grand twin bays" or "sheltered double bays."[61] Twin or double bays makes empirical sense as the two bays eventually became known in English as the "East and West Bays." More fittingly, Anishinaabeg gave it a name after its geographical uniqueness—two bays that are shielded from the open lake and are welcoming shelter from the surrounding, unforgiving rocky headlands.

Many North Shore place-names descended directly from Anishinaabemowin into English. For example, Mokomani-zibi was literally translated into Knife River. And it appears Two Island River was an English simplification of Minissan-nijogondeg, or two islands floating in the lake.[62] The Bongas and others knew the French place-names of some North Shore streams. Those who were bilingual would have known that many of these French place-names were derived from the Anishinaabeg language, or at least they shared the same meaning. A few have crossed over from Anishinaabemowin into French and finally into English. Moose Lake along the border route was first known as Mozo-sagaiigan, then Lac de l'Orignal [French for moose], and finally Moose Lake. Grand Marais and Brule River, or Wissakode zibi, appear to be Anishinaabemowin place-names that were translated into French but for some unknown reason did not convert into English.[63]

For the AFC men and other early travelers, knowledge of good harborage was paramount in uncharted and dangerous waters. For paddlers, the most important and desirable geographic feature is a safe and handy area to unload and load their canoes when buffeted by various winds and seas, especially compared with an otherwise unforgiving coastline. Few good harbors were available on the rocky headlands of the North Shore, so the east and west bays of Grand Marais were very welcome to paddlers and early sailors alike. For the eminent geographer and surveyor David Thompson, it was foremost a "fine Ship Harbor."[64]

Voyageurs speaking in a Canadian French or Quebecois French—a relatively archaic version of French—likely intended a different meaning for this safe harbor than assumed today. The similar pronunciation of Grand Marais and Grand Marée—only a French speaker who understands both formal and vernacular Quebecois

French can tell the difference—holds a clue to this mishearing and subsequent misunderstanding. In Canadian French *marée* means "pond" or "calm pool of water," which mirrors the Anishinaabe-mowin place-name.[65] Grand Marais—or great swamp—does not. Could the Grand Marée of the voyageurs have morphed into Grand Marais, especially when the writers were formally taught in classic French? A French linguist believes a mishearing of voyageurs' Que-becois French led to a "bad" transcription, which could account for this change. The vernacular Grand Marée became Grand Marais of the educated elites, including the map makers of the day. Thus, the meaning of the voyageurs' place-name was reinterpreted as "great swamp." The twin sheltered bays of the Anishinaabeg and voyageurs are rendered by later observers as Grand Marais, or great swamp.[66]

Royal Navy surveyors such as Bayfield and others knew only classical Parisian French, and those map makers and printers work-ing far distantly would have had no reason to dispute the spelling of a place-name or to be suspicious of the rendering of a frontier name. Nor did Bayfield have voyageurs in his survey crew who might have corrected him in his pronunciation of the name or explained its meaning in Quebecois French.[67] But when in the harbor measuring its depth and outline, Lieutenant Bayfield grew puzzled by its name. Assuming Grand Marais meant "Great Swamp," he wrote on his no-tably accurate (but unavailable) chart of Lake Superior "it is most inappropriately named."[68] The name made little sense to Bayfield as it did not accurately characterize the harbor, and no small marsh be-hind the cobblestone beach would have been of any interest to him. Clearly puzzled by this name, Bayfield chose to label it "Boat Har-b[or]" rather than Grand Marais in his concise and publicly available 1832 chart of Lake Superior derived from his admiralty charts.[69]

Figuring out the naming of Grand Marais is tricky, but deter-mining the exact location of the AFC post in Gichi Bitobig is even more problematic. The journals do not give us many clues about the location of the solitary post. Chapman started building before he

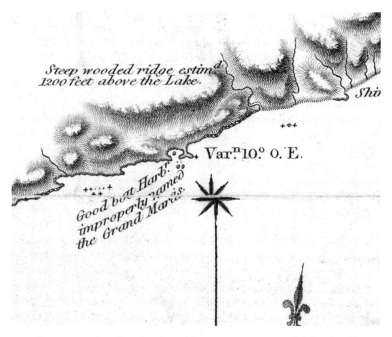

Grand Marais Harbor detail, enlarged from Lieutenants Bayfield and Collin's 1828 chart. A larger portion of this chart appears on the cover of this book. Bayfield also accurately depicted features such as the Devil Track River entering Lake Superior northeast of Grand Marais. Lieutenant Henry W. Bayfield assisted by Philip E. Collins, Admiralty Chart, British Royal Navy, "Survey of Lake Superior," Sheet 1, June 1828. Courtesy of the Library and Archives of Canada.

knew much about where the trade would take him, but presumably mostly to Grand Portage and inland. And in fact, Chapman's and Johnston's men did travel north (White Fish Lake and border lakes) and northeast (old Grand Portage) more than any other direction. Did this focus to the north and northeast mean the post was situated on the East Bay? And could the "little lake" sometimes mentioned be the more enclosed West Bay, within now what is even more protected by the breakwater built by the U.S. Army Corps of Engineers? If knowledgeable about situating a post, Chapman would have looked for a site near sheltered water and close to fishing grounds, and one protected from winds yet located so they could see Indians and any lake travelers approaching. They would have also sought gradually sloping topography into the lake (above and below the water) for ease of taking canoes in and out of the water, as the men would leap into the water to keep the canoes from hitting rocks. Also important would have been a beach or beaches with rounded pebbles or sand, which would not tear up or gouge the bark canoe bottoms.

It would also have been advantageous to be relatively close to both bays, as then they could launch or lift out canoes or bateau on the lee side depending on wind direction and thus be sheltered. This would have restricted the amount of portaging of goods and boats from shore to camp. Mostly, however, it would have been critical to have a sheltered place to lift canoes off the lake where wave surges would not threaten to swamp the canoes or wet the trade goods. And ideally the site would have been not too distant from good-sized trees to build with and to cut as firewood. Attractive locations would have included at the base of where the Coast Guard Point, or tombolo, meets the main shore and the edge of the present town. Alternately, it would be appropriate, if serendipitous, if the present-day "Trading Post" were located on the former location of the AFC post, but there is no direct connection through time to suggest this. Unhappily the exact location may be gone or greatly altered. In the late 1920s and early 1930s, six and half acres of land were removed for gravel for road building in Duluth.[70] The same gravelly shoreline attractive to AFC men was also attractive to those dredging and removing gravel bound for barges and construction sites in Duluth. And some of the original shoreline and nearby lowlands have been filled in, making locating any remains of the post particularly challenging.

2

American Fur Company and the Trade

In 1788, John Jacob Astor, an ambitious twenty-four-year-old, sat in a thirty-six-foot-long "Montreal" canoe amid four tons of packaged trade goods and a dozen French Canadian voyageurs paddling along Lake Superior's North Shore. Only four years in America, he was now a guest of Alexander Henry, one of the NWC partners, traveling to Grand Portage to witness the company's operations and broaden his grasp of the Indian trade. He had only recently given up selling musical instruments and plunged headlong into the fur trade. He left his young family in New York and traveled northward through Lake Champlain and then to the St. Lawrence and Montreal. A few days later, he was in a canoe bound westward to the great fur emporium of Grand Portage. There he would study the NWC, learn how to ramp up his profits, and, ironically, experience the country that the company he would found, the American Fur Company, would later come to contest. This was as far west as he traveled, though on this trip he purchased furs from the Red River country and returned home with a handsome profit. Travel weary, he reached home in October.[1]

Thirty-five years later, this German immigrant was one of the wealthiest men in America. In the 1820s, he spent more time in Europe than minding the daily affairs of the AFC. As a wealthy elite in a class-conscious business, he was aloof from the men making up the muscle of the AFC. Instead, he charged his senior managers to communicate with them—or, more commonly, to direct them unequivocally. His workforce was heterogeneous: Scots, French Canadians, Yanks, Métis, a few Indians, and others. His Grand Marais men would also include African-Anishinaabeg men. Collectively the AFC men traded at posts all along the northern American border from the Great Lakes to the Great Plains, Rocky Mountains, and the Columbia River basin to the Pacific Ocean. In one way, the make-up of the men of the Grand Marais "experiment" was a microcosm of the nation as a whole. However, Chapman's and Johnston's men were isolated from Astor, their superiors, and what Johnston would call civilization. Their task was not for the timid; the small band was sent out to challenge the colossal HBC and by their success ensure only American commerce—especially their own—within the Arrowhead region, an embryonic part of the United States of America. Incidentally, their anticipated success would also have the useful outcome of affirming the international boundary.

The Men

George Bonga appears to be the only man who was posted at Grand Marais both years; otherwise the makeup of the men changed. However, Johnston names him only as "George," so it is possible, but not likely, that a different George accompanied him. Johnston did not fully name his men as did Chapman, so it is unclear exactly who they were. In both years, the men were the last to leave from Fond du Lac and thus might not even have been AFC "servants" but rather "freemen" that William Morrison and William Aitken added to complete the Grand Marais workforce. Assuming "George" was George Bonga, he played a prominent role in both clerks' journals. During Chapman's time in Grand Marais, it appears that Bonga's two brothers were also initially along. Stephen, George, and Jack Bonga were African American and Anishinaabeg canoe men, fur traders, and interpreters. Their family had been in the upper Great Lakes region for three generations. When they worked at "Fort Misery," they were young men: Stephen, roughly twenty-three or twenty-four years of age; George, perhaps eighteen; and Jack, maybe seven.[2] We never learn why Jack accompanied his older brothers to Grand Marais. During their adult lives they more often worked apart, particularly Stephen from his younger brothers. They worked at fur trade posts in Michigan, northern Wisconsin, Minnesota, and even in North Dakota and Canada. Despite being half Anishinaabeg, George was "the blackest man I ever saw, so black that his skin fairly glistened, but was, excepting his brother Jack, the only black person in the country." George, who was a gifted storyteller, used to "paralyze his hearers when reminiscing by saying 'Gentlemen, I assure you that John Banfil and myself were the first two white men that ever came into this country.'"[3] While fur trade historians have long known about the Bongas, few have been aware that they were the dominant workforce at the first AFC operation at Grand Marais, then technically a part of Michigan Territory.

Stephen, George, and Jack were sons of Pierre Bonga, a black voyageur and canoe man, and an Anishinaabe woman, Ogibwayquay.[4] Pierre became a valued employee for a succession of fur trade companies: the NWC, South West Company, and the AFC. After living at Michilimackinac, he moved and lived for many years in Fond du Lac. He might accompany a trader for a year or two to a distant post but would return to his wife and growing family in Fond du Lac.

Pierre led a remarkable fur trade life. He accompanied noted fur trader Alexander Henry on a trip to the Red River in 1799. While at the Pembina River post, Pierre served as Henry's interpreter, and when Henry was absent, Pierre served as the man in charge. When a man threatened the order of the post and to kill Pierre, he instead "did not escape without a sound beating."[5] At least one child was born at Pembina in what is now North Dakota.[6] Pierre remained in the Red River district until 1806, when he returned to what would soon be called Fort William on the Kaministiquia River mouth. He then worked for the NWC in its heyday. There Jack Bonga was born in 1815. In the spring of 1816, Pierre arrested Lord Selkirk's agent during the overt hostilities between the two companies and their allies. No doubt as retribution, when Lord Selkirk seized Fort William six months later, Pierre was hauled from his hut and along with trader Daniel McKenzie was held in custody in the "gaol" for eight days.[7] In 1819, Pierre led a canoe brigade for the NWC, "substituting" for a bourgeois.[8] In 1820 Pierre was "an old negro in the employ of the company who has a squaw for a wife, and a family of four children residing in Fond du Lac."[9] Pierre would eventually become a clerk for the AFC at Lake Winnibigoshish and died there circa 1834.[10]

Through time, the Bonga family lived on both sides of the St. Louis River, not far from the fur trade establishment. Maragatt, their first child, was born in 1797. The oldest boy, Stephen, was told by his mother that he was born in the moon of ripening strawberries, or in June 1798 or 1799. Two sisters were born between Stephen and George. George was born in 1803.[11] The NWC post at Superior was relatively new, having been established in 1793. When his father was employed at Fort William, in Thunder Bay, a young George was sent to Montreal for an education. In his own words, he stated, "I did not get as good an education, as I might have had," because the impending strife between the NWC and the Lord Selkirk–led HBC interrupted his schooling in Montreal.

Exactly when Stephen, George, and Jack were considered old enough to join the fur trade is unknown. But by 1820, George was in the fur trade, and in the same year he acted as an Anishinaabemowin interpreter for Governor Lewis Cass at Fond du Lac. The Bongas may have been chosen to accompany Chapman because they had some experience on the Lake Superior North Shore, primarily at Fort William.

The Bongas were big, strong men. George was said to be six feet tall and weighed over two hundred pounds. He was legendary for his strength, and Alfred Brunson, a missionary and onetime Indian agent, witnessed one of his feats:

George Bungo, became first a clerk and then a trader. He was one of the strongest men I ever saw. He loaded himself, at the foot of the Porcupine Mountain, at the mouth of the Montreal River, with a pack of goods, and then bags of bullets, till the whole load amounted to eight hundred and twenty pounds, and carried them one thousand paces, up the side of the mountain, and won a bet.[12]

By 1834, George was a highly valued clerk at AFC's Fond du Lac post, earning a yearly salary much higher than his brother Jack and most men at the post. George was a skilled woodsman, and in 1837 for six days and nights he tracked down an Anishinaabe man wanted for murder.[13] It appears that George and Jack worked alongside each other at Fond du Lac until at least 1841, George as a "clerk," and Jack as a "laborer." George was high enough in the fur trade hierarchy that he was a claimant in the 1842 Treaty of La Pointe, in which he and "François St. Jean" [Bonga?] were seeking $366.84 in annuities for goods not paid for by his Anishinaabeg trading partners. Years later, George would become relatively well off as a trader, with posts from Otter Tail to Leech Lakes. He lived a mobile life, appearing in both St. Anthony Falls and Crow Wing, Minnesota, in the 1849 territorial census, and in Leech Lake and Pembina in the 1860 federal census.[14]

In the 1830s, Stephen Bonga worked as a steersman, or governail, of a large canoe, and as a fur trader at Folle Avoine on the Yellow and St. Croix Rivers, and at Fond du Lac. As a steersman he was routinely expected to know the lake, its geography, and hazards. At one point, Stephen became a trusted protégé of the trader at Fond du Lac in care of valuable goods.[15] Stephen would survive the 1850 Sandy Lake death march in which many Anishinaabeg perished. The march, the epitome of broken promises, removed a number of Anishinaabeg bands westward to Sandy Lake in the winter months, where they waited for food and annuities that never arrived. Congress did not appropriate monies for them in time.[16] Stephen would

George Bonga and two brothers helped establish the American Fur Company post at Grand Marais. George spent two trading seasons there. Courtesy of the Minnesota Historical Society.

later receive annuities as an enrolled member of the Fond du Lac Band.

George and Stephen followed their father's footsteps in being Anishinaabemowin-English interpreters. Their father, Pierre, served as an interpreter at Fort William.[17] His sons George and Stephen were later employed as interpreters at treaties between the federal government officials and Anishinaabeg, with some of their Anishinaabeg relatives present. Stephen served as a translator for the 1837 Treaty of St. Peters, which dealt with much of central Wisconsin and a part of central Minnesota. It was Stephen and Patrick Quinn's job to translate from English to Chippewa while another set of interpreters translated from Chippewa to English. One observer described Stephen as a principal interpreter, as his partners were "not being able to speak intelligibly in either language."[18] George served as an official interpreter for the 1847 Treaty with the Pillager Band of Chippewa Indians.[19] Being an interpreter also meant vouchsafing what was said, but not recorded, during treaty negotiations. An interpreter's integrity was tested with his kinsmen and also with his employer. Depending on how the treaty was received by traders, they might not want to employ Bonga or another interpreter again. On the other hand, it was difficult for interpreters not to be viewed with suspicion by some Anishinaabeg. More commonly George interpreted for a short term or as needed, for example, when he served as an interpreter for the Protestant missionary the Reverend Edmund Ely.[20]

Stephen returned to the North Shore in the mid-1850s, when he was the guide for artist Eastman Johnson, who painted Grand Portage Anishinaabeg.[21] Stephen died in 1884 in Superior, Wisconsin. George and Jack eventually lived in the Leech Lake area, where many of their descendants live today.

What did the isolated crew think of the Bongas' unusual background, half Anishinaabeg and half black? Early in their lives the Bongas defied some racial categories we might assume were in play. On the borderlands, there were few blacks to trigger racial categories set elsewhere. One contemporary would later describe George Bonga as "the first white man that was a negro that ever traded at Leech Lake."[22] But George appears to have had some racial categories in his mind when he wrote complaining about one post employee: "But certainly Mr. Aitkin's is rather unreasonable of not sending me a Frenchman instead of the half breed."[23]

Grand Marais was at this time an American frontier, occupied by an outlier of a corporate entity that valued men who could get along in the woods, trade, and speak Anishinaabemowin. The three African American–Anishinaabeg men were not (yet) put in racially demarcated categories of established society. Many of American society's "rules" had not made it yet to the North Shore. Or as one scholar put it,

> the Bongas actually lived in a society that was in an Indian world, rather than a British [or American] colonial world. Social and political customs, including diplomatic protocol and religious rites, were determined by Indian rules and practices. Therefore, the Bongas were not caught in a rigid system of slavery and sphere of identity formation that was based on Anglo-American notions.[24]

For Chapman, George Bonga was his go-to guy. He could speak Anishinaabemowin, was strong and determined, and knew his way around the country or could figure it out.[25] There was no evidence in Chapman's journal that he considered the Bongas subservient to others; in fact, it appears they were crucial to Chapman's efforts.

Racial categories on the frontier were not as rigid as in the East or South, but they were changing. Bonga did not consider himself black or Anishinaabeg, while he clearly was both. Despite being of mixed heritage, George Johnston did not see himself as an Indian or Métis. Instead, he saw himself as an educated and thus a civilized observer of Indians in a tumultuous time. Johnston made observations in which he implicitly separated himself from his Indian trading clients or even those living near a government agency. He wrote:

> It is now near seven years since I first landed at this place [Grand Traverse Bay], and during that period I have closely watched the progress of civilization among the band of Indians inhabiting this region, and I am sorry to say that there is little visible, of moral improvement, they certainly were a more innocent people in their natural state, and they then professed a certain pride of integrity & honesty, but at present this is all vanished away from them, leaving them as they are now are, relics of depravity, debased from their original position.[26]

Johnston's negative attitude toward Indians was similar to that held by Anishinaabe historian William Warren. Both realized that "that identity is not determined merely by descent, but by upbringing and culture, by where and how one lives."[27] While being protective of his mother and thus indirectly acknowledging his Indian ancestry, Johnston consciously chose to identify as an elite and as well educated, and not Indian or Métis.

He identified strongly with his father and followed his father's lead in feeling superior to others. John Johnston wrote:

> The Canadians and half-bloods all over the country are very numerous, and from want of instruction are, if possible, more the slaves of sensuality than the Indians themselves. In fact they know not what is meant by morality or religion, and from the idea that they are good Catholics, would make the task of reforming them arduous indeed, for the prejudices attendant on ignorance are ever the most difficult to be conquered.[28]

Chapman, too, had disparaging words about one "half-breed," Boucher, who was supposed to be his guide. Instead Boucher turned out to be exasperating and even overtly challenged Chapman's leadership. Chapman's frustration with Boucher perhaps led him further to castigate a fellow Fond du Lac clerk, the French man Pierre Cotte, who did not choose Boucher to accompany him. In Chapman's reports, Boucher was responsible for some of his trading failures; in one entry he accused Boucher of losing "five pack[s] because of bad conduct."[29]

The idea of "half-breed" had only recently entered HBC parlance.[30] It was not a fixed concept at the time; it was changing. Throughout Johnston's, Chapman's, and Bonga's lifetimes, racial categories and dominant mores were hardening. As a young man, Johnston's "mixed-descent" heritage was still an asset, and yet by his older years he had become, in the eyes of the growing number of Yankees, a "half-breed" and not an equal to whites. For example, in 1825 at Sault Ste. Marie, a controversy arose about whether "mixed-blood" men such as Johnston should be permitted to vote, since any Indian blood could disqualify him. And as one scholar noted, by the 1830s marriages to mixed-bloods or Indians were no longer socially acceptable.[31] This problem was particularly acute for the aspiring Henry Schoolcraft, as he was married to George's sister Jane.

Ambrose Davenport Jr. was twenty-two years old when he accompanied Chapman and the Bonga brothers to Grand Marais. He worked for a Yankee (Chapman) and alongside the African-Anishinaabeg Bongas and the French Canadian Boucher. He grew up on Mackinac Island, the oldest son of a military hero from the War of 1812, who, along with his wife, hailed from Virginia. Ambrose Davenport Sr. gained renown after Michilimackinac fell to the British. Davenport and others became prisoners in their own village. After the garrison fell to the Redcoats, he refused to swear an oath to the crown to the British officer in charge, and he and two other American soldiers were sent to a British prison in Detroit. In other words, the elder Ambrose fought against John and George Johnston. In 1814, Ambrose Davenport Sr. became a guide and led American soldiers attempting to retake Mackinac Island and garrison.[32] He eventually became a farmer on Mackinac Island.

Ambrose Jr. and his younger brother, William, left their parents' farm and worked for the AFC at various posts. It appears Ambrose was yet unmarried when he ventured up the North Shore. But only a few years later he married Susan O Ge Ma Quay Des Carreaux, a granddaughter of an Anishinaabe ogimaa, Misquabunoqua.[33] Years later, a Quaker newspaper would report: "She is a Chippeway Indian from beyond Lake Superior. . . . She is also highly valued for her arts in healing, knowing all the mysteries of Indian 'medicine,' and having the nerve and the faith to apply them."[34]

Ambrose Davenport worked for the AFC for many years. And ironically, in 1832, he was the clerk in charge of an AFC post at Grand Portage.[35] Apparently he was an enterprising clerk, as in 1834 he was one of the best-paid clerks of the AFC, garnering five hundred dollars per year.[36] We also know he played the fiddle, probably on the long winter nights.[37] But in Grand Marais, almost ten years earlier, he was new to the trade.

Fur trade families often intermarried. Years after their time in Grand Marais, the Davenport and Johnston families were entwined. Ambrose's younger sister married George Johnston's younger brother, William Miengum Johnston. After decades with the fur trade, Ambrose became a "fish inspector" and then a lighthouse keeper late in life in 1853. Three of his sons

Ambrose and Susan Davenport. Ambrose Davenport was one of Bela Chapman's men at Grand Marais when the American Fur Company post was established. He worked many years for the American Fur Company at different posts.

would also become lighthouse keepers on Lake Michigan—a life-style that kept them on the fringes of civilization.[38] Davenport died on November 4, 1879, at Mackinac, at the age of seventy-nine.[39] His wife, Susan, outlived him by more than ten years.

Given the makeup of the men, what language would have been spoken at the post? English was spoken, but perhaps with the south-ern drawl of a Virginian descendant mingled with a Yankee dialect. The Bongas were fluent in English, Anishinaabemowin, and likely French as well. With their grandfather's and father's long association with the British garrison at Michilimackinac, perhaps they spoke with some British military colloquialisms. Johnston, too, spoke in English, French, and Anishinaabemowin. With their schooling in Montreal, Bonga and Johnston were literate, as was Chapman. Johnston liked to display his familiarity with classics and wrote in an overtly refined style. Perhaps Chapman's group of men spoke French or Anishinaabemowin so as to not be understood by Chap-man. Boucher, Chapman's antagonist, would likely have spoken in French. Chapman was probably learning Anishinaabemowin while speaking with his wife. Thus, many of the men were trilingual or at least bilingual. All the Anishinaabemowin speakers at the post, in-cluding their wives, spoke a different dialect of Anishinaabemow-in than those they traded with. Thus, in the trade storeroom, there could have been plenty of opportunity for misunderstanding, ridi-cule, and alternately good-natured jesting while negotiating prices for furs or the value of their credits.

What did they talk about on the long winter's nights in the men's quarters? How did the Yankee, son of a Virginian soldier, the French Canadian, and the African-Anishinaabe Bongas get along? Did they haggle about the topics of the day, politics, or food in addition to making their way in a difficult place? How did their differences clash or fit together? Chapman thought highly of his men, except Boucher, suggesting all but the French Canadian were contributing to their collective efforts. Did Chapman's stiff Yankee disposition push the French Canadian Boucher to the point of trying to subvert their collective effort? Was there a symphony of complaints—in any language—voiced in the men's house when Chapman or Johnston was absent? What did the men think about Chapman trapping marten himself? Was it Yankee resourcefulness or an act of desperation? As hired men—with a set wage—they did not equally share Chapman's goal of trying to make a profit and thus impress Morrison and Aitken. Johnston, for his part, appears to have uniformly disdained and felt above his men. Would he have associated with them, given his opinion?

One relief to the stress of cramped, cold quarters was likely Ambrose Davenport's violin. Maybe he had learned the jigs and lively reels that were popular with voyageurs and were customary at posts.[40] And could anyone play another instrument to accompany Davenport? Often an informal pecking order was established among the men, with the clerk the head, and a formidable employee such as George Bonga as second in the informal social order.[41]

Turmoil and "low spirits" engulfed the AFC men as the depth and struggle of winter bore down on them. Chapman, fearful early on of being short on provisions, sent off two men to Fond du Lac to overwinter. Losing two men out of handful must have foreshadowed hardships and changed dynamics among the men. He justified his decision by noting his superior's instructions: "As you directed me two men is as good as four here." It is unclear which men left, but there was no mention of Stephen or Jack Bonga in his journal.[42]

In contrast, Johnston claimed two of his men deserted from their post. He wrote:

> I begin to apprehend some unforeseen accident has happened to Tasack & L'Equier, this being the eighth day since their departure and have not yet arrived. 5th I make preparations to go in search of them but blowing too strong from the North west prevented me from starting. I left this the ensuing day with a severe cold &

headwind. I however managed to reach salmon trout river, But could not proceed any further owing to our old canoe filling with water (having no gum) as Tasack took the whole of what we had. 7th I returned and with difficulty reached our houses & on my arrival the men told that L'Equier & Tasack had each of them taken two shirts & 2 pr Mitassens, & the latter a bowel and soap, that being sufficient & evident proof of their desertion to Fon du Lac.[43]

Desertion to Fond du Lac was particularly tempting, as Johnston's men were traveling to Roche de Bout, just shy of halfway there. Johnston exaggerated his desertion claim, as they did not desert but returned to Fond du Lac. Desertion in fur trade parlance usually meant disappearing (and thus trying to erase one's debts) or more commonly missing one's canoe brigade when it was just setting out westward. When competition was fierce among companies, they sometimes offered a signing bonus that made desertion particularly tempting as a man could hide nearby his home. Desertion was a serious charge, as it implied lack of obedience to Johnston and not living up to their contract. However, we are unsure of the nature of L'Equier and Tasack's contractual agreement with the AFC. Both the "unauthorized absences" of L'Equier and Tasack and the challenge to Chapman's authority by Boucher underline the harsh conditions, the often poor or inadequate food, and perhaps even the low pay the men experienced.

The Old Northwest and the American Fur Company in the 1820s

Nationally, rapid change was afoot when the AFC post was established in Grand Marais. Indiana and Illinois had just become states, and Michigan Territory, which then included the North Shore, ran (on paper) from the present Michigan state boundary to the Mississippi River. Settlers poured out of the East to locate and farm new lands in the Ohio valley, Michigan, and Illinois. Some of the land seekers were ex-soldiers, as the military contracted in numbers from 62,000 during the War of 1812 to fewer than 10,000.[44] In 1819 the first American troops arrived at what became Fort Snelling, at the confluence of the Minnesota and Mississippi Rivers. Henceforth there were American troops in what would become the state of Minnesota. The goal of the outpost was to win the allegiance of Indians (such as the North Shore Anishinaabeg) away from the British and to stop the Dakota and Anishinaabeg warfare, which was dampening trade.[45]

Great change also swept into the region. In 1823, the first wheat was harvested outside of Fort Snelling, foreshadowing future rich agricultural production.[46] In the 1820s, most Americans were small farmers and fond of hard spirits, and this would not change for many decades.[47] Both Chapman and Johnston might have wished to have canned goods along; at this time they were first patented for preserving food but not available on the frontier.[48]

Unbeknownst to the AFC men at Grand Marais, a hung-up presidential election ran on from November 2, 1824, to February 9, 1825, when the disputed election went to the House of Representatives for resolution and the House elected John Quincy Adams president over Andrew Jackson, despite Jackson having won the plurality of both popular vote and Electoral College.[49] Any stray thoughts of Washington, D.C., however, were eclipsed by its distance, more than a long, hard month of traveling by canoe, schooner, canal boat, and carriage. Nor would the small colony of traders at Grand Marais know that the U.S. War Department created the Bureau of Indian Affairs in March 1824. Ironically the new Indian Office was run by a Quaker interested in Indian education and assimilation.

A parade of technological changes swept in with the 1820s. A sawmill perched on St. Anthony Falls—the future site of Minneapolis—cut white pine into planks beginning in 1822. The felling of Minnesota's pinery followed in subsequent decades. A year later, in 1823, the first steamboat made it up the Mississippi to Fort Snelling. Elsewhere in the 1820s the first practical application of the steam engine locomotive took place. By the end of the decade the first railroad was operating in the United States. The opening of the Erie Canal in October 1825 unlocked the way for an expansion of water transportation and commerce on the middle Great Lakes. A traveler could now go by water transportation from New York City to Detroit on a scheduled basis. There the same traveler might have to wait days for a sailing vessel to tour the upper lakes, Lakes Huron and Michigan.

The effects of Jay's Treaty in 1794, according to which Britain had to withdraw its economic activity—largely fur trading—north across the border, required the inland headquarters of the NWC to be moved from American soil at Grand Portage to the Thunder Bay area.[50] Though the War of 1812 was fought eastward of Lake Superior, it created much chaos and uncertainty in the region. A number of Anishinaabeg fought with their British allies. Hoping that the British and their Indian allies would prevail, the NWC partners anticipated that one consequence would be the removal of John Jacob Astor and his South West Company operation from the upper lakes. And when the Fort William detachment helped easily seize Michilimackinac, the news gave the partners grounds for optimism for their plans.[51] While they had moved their inland headquarters to Fort William, they continued to run smaller but lucrative posts such as at Fond du Lac and others south of the border, ignoring Jay's Treaty.

When the Treaty of Ghent of 1814 ended the war, the British agreed to remove from Michilimackinac north across the traditional water route. The Americans then moved back into this advantageous location. The British treaty negotiators had originally called for creation of an independent Indian buffer state in the Great Lakes region but gave this up early in negotiations.[52] They eventually did little for their Indian allies living in the American Midwest. The defeat of Tecumseh and Indian allies in the War of 1812 conceded the young United States' hegemony over the region. There would no longer be a significant, large-scale threat of Indian warfare in the Upper Midwest.[53] The North Westers also lost three of their four large Lake Superior vessels used to haul freight. These consequences of the War of 1812 and other subsequent changes—often orchestrated by John Jacob Astor—created an opening for his AFC.

The end of hostilities was marked by year-long frigid weather. The region plunged into grim cold, or what was known as "the year without summer."[54] The 1815 explosion of an Indonesian volcano kept the sun's warmth from penetrating the atmosphere. The next year in Quebec snow fell in June, and there was a heavy frost in July. The summer of 1816 was 3.6 to 5.4 degrees Fahrenheit cooler around Lake Superior than average. No one understood at the time why it was so cold or knew if it was a harbinger of some strange phenomena to come.

For the Anishinaabeg, another, incomprehensible harbinger was treaty negotiations for their homeland—negotiations that were conducted in Europe. But the Treaty of Ghent did not fully resolve the international boundary in the canoe country west of the Pigeon River mouth, then still misidentified on official maps and in treaty language as "Long Lake." In the 1820s an international border commission, with surveyors from British Canada and the United States, arrived in the region to survey and suggest possible lines along the contested border. Not surprisingly, no Anishinaabeg were included or officially consulted about how their homeland was to be divided. But ironically a few Indians and Métis became guides to the border surveyors. The AFC traders, who needed more practical advice on where the border was located, had largely assumed the border would be along the customary route from Grand Portage to Rainy Lake and Lake of the Woods. Still, much uncertainty persisted in official circles, such as exactly where the headwaters of the Mississippi River originated (particularly how far to the north) and if and how the headwaters intersected the international border, as was supposed by some.

Beginning in 1822, British and American survey parties traveled up and down customary waterways from Grand Portage, Fort William, and Fond du Lac to Lake of the Woods to survey and draw accurate maps. Survey parties canoed throughout the area until 1825.[55] Survey maps were eventually used by competing commissioners to fashion geographical arguments for where the border should be located. Most of their maps were prepared by 1826, but the border commission did not officially resolve the location of the international border until 1842. David Thompson—a veteran fur trader and geographer who had often traveled these lakes and portages—led the British surveyors. Arriving at Fort William in 1822, he sent the British border commissioner a map and description of the route in a letter composed from his memory.[56] Supplementing his survey with geographical information solicited from area Anishinaabeg, a year later he completed a map of the customary route from Grand Portage to Saganaga Lake.[57] At the same time, the British began a full-fledged effort to chart Lake Superior under the command of Lieutenants Henry Bayfield and Philip Collins. The two had already charted all of the lower Great Lakes and began on Lake Superior with the HBC brig *Recovery*, leased to the Royal Navy for that work. Johnston met Bayfield and Collins while they were surveying on the south shore.[58]

The American surveyors, their British counterparts, and Royal Navy men worked separately. For some time the American border delegation—of surveyors and official commissioners—were assured that the border ran up the Pigeon River along the customary voyageur route. Their "comfort" with the old route reinforced American traders' belief that any country south of this line was indeed American territory.[59] However, the British calculatingly disputed the commonly accepted border, and it was not formally resolved until the 1842 Webster-Ashburton Treaty. The dispute created some nagging uncertainty for traders and allowed some creative forays back and forth, although the traders seemed more certain of the boundary than their respective official survey delegations.

The AFC men never met any of the survey teams. The surveyors' fieldwork wrapped up in early fall prior to the AFC arriving at Grand Marais. However, there was a good deal of contact between the American and British survey teams and their HBC hosts at Fort William. The American surveyors purchased food and quarters, sent and received mail, and acquired canoes from the Fort William post. And yet, the American surveyors did business with Robert Stuart and the AFC in Michilimackinac. However, in 1823, the presence of the first true American government officials, Stephen Long and the American surveyors—James Ferguson, George Whistler, and in one summer Lieutenant Joseph Delafield—had a noticeable impact on the HBC. Suddenly, the HBC clerks observed there was a burst of American presence, some with obvious military connections. The shadow of the War of 1812 still loomed in many people's memory. Fostering a sense that Americans were truly moving into the area, some AFC officials became customs inspectors at key locations. Swiftly it seemed, the HBC was not the only English-speaking mercantile and political force in northwest Lake Superior.

The American Fur Company

John Jacob Astor enjoyed legendary success with the American Fur Company. A onetime poor German immigrant in New York, he began and ran one of the most profitable businesses in America. His business skill lay in his ability to understand and manipulate the unique conditions of the fur trade.[60] Morphing his business acumen from the fur trade to New York real estate, he reportedly became the richest man in America. His strategies led to large profits and growing power in America. While leaving much of the management of his Great Lakes enterprises to other men, he amassed a 90 percent profit from "the Northern Department." And he made considerably over 100 percent profits from his purchases of trade goods.[61]

To safeguard his success, Astor shifted a good deal of the risk to the individual trader rather than assuming it himself. Astor or his company sponsored an "independent" trader with "outfits" but with an exclusive option for the AFC to buy their furs. And if poor luck, "dismal [trading] country" such as Grand Marais, or poor management drove the trader out of business, the trader's assets became the AFC's, including Indian debts.[62] Astor's system was different from the share system of the NWC and the salary-based system of the HBC.

But Astor was not just rich. He was powerful, particularly in the unsettled fur trade margins of America. For example, he bankrolled efforts to establish an American colony on the West Coast, or Astoria. The War of 1812 foiled his continental-wide gamble. Sixty-one men died in this enterprise, but it hardly slowed down Astor.[63] His power could also be expressed more modestly; for example, it included the AFC issuing an 1824 warrant for arrest through the Michilimackinac, Michigan, circuit court.[64] His most decisive deed to insure his fur trade success was to kill the U.S. factory system of trading with Indians. The government factory plan of supplying Indians with trade goods began in 1796 but floundered, in part, because they did not provide alcohol to Indians and their merchandise was of inferior quality.[65] Meant to be a government responsibility, the factories were to protect Indians from unscrupulous private traders and the degrading effects of alcohol. These "factories" were to trade goods to Indians at cost and thereby wean them from trading with British traders.[66] Despite these intentions, by 1822, Astor's influence with American politicians had stopped the government factory system.

Astor's collusion with certain U.S. politicians was mutually advantageous. Through the rise of Astor's empire and favorable laws, the United States removed British influences from the Midwest. For example, in 1808 Astor received a letter from President Thomas Jefferson saying that the U.S. government would confer "great advantages" to American traders in order to "oust foreign traders, who so much abuse their privilege by endeavoring to excite the Indians to war on us."[67] Astor was also in the habit of loaning money to the government. He helped finance the War of 1812 and lent money to important politicians, such as James Monroe, to whom he gave $5,000.[68] Congress returned these favors to Astor. Congress passed a law on April 29, 1816, that provided that "licenses to trade with the Indians . . . shall not be granted to any but citizens of the United States." British traders, such as the NWC at Fond du Lac, had to remove across the border.[69] Astor used this law to force his British partners in the South West Company (and also partners in the NWC) to sell their interests to him. He then renamed the South West Company the American Fur Company. Additional lucrative NWC outposts south of the border were then given up.

But a problem arose with a strict interpretation of this law because the French Canadian voyageurs were still essential to the success of the fur trade. As Ramsay Crooks, the AFC's senior manager on the upper lakes, said,

> these people are indispensable to the successful prosecution of the trade. Their places cannot be supplied by Americans, who for the most part are too independent to submit quietly to a proper control . . . 'tis only in the Canadian we find that temper of mind to render him docile, patient, and persevering, in short they are a people harmless in themselves whose habits of submission fit them peculiarly for our business.[70]

Through Astor's efforts, Canadian boatmen continued to be hired, but British posts could no longer be placed on American soil.

The preferential treatment that Michigan territorial governor Lewis Cass showered upon the AFC has prompted some scholars to speculate that Cass was indebted to Astor. Indeed, some believe Astor bribed the former U.S. army officer, future ambassador, and presidential candidate.[71] One allegation suggested that Astor bribed Lewis Cass with $35,000 to "see things his way," but no hard evidence has yet been found to substantiate this rumor. It was true, however, that Cass directed one Indian agent to "afford every assistance" to the AFC at Mackinac, to the degree that few other competitors received licenses.[72] Astor and his men were willing to use laws and administrative fiat to promote the exclusiveness of their trade.

Still, there were limits to how far Astor's government "friends" would go. For example, the American government chose not to become involved when Lord Selkirk endeavored to punish NWC agents and Métis who reportedly killed twenty-one Scottish settlers on June 19, 1816, in Rupert's Land (near where Winnipeg is now located). Selkirk had sponsored these settlers as a philanthropic effort to aid impoverished Scots. In retaliation for the killings and in addition to seizing the NWC's Fort William, Selkirk directed a brigade of mercenary soldiers "of nine canoes with about forty men" to invade the Fond du Lac department of the South West Company and seize goods valued at several thousand pounds. At Fond du Lac, clearly on American soil, Selkirk's men arrested James Grant and his clerk, William Morrison, who had played a part in the hostilities for the NWC.[73] At Fort William, they detained another clerk working for Astor, Eustache Roussin. While the brutal fight was between Selkirk's HBC and the North Westers and largely on British lands, Astor demanded that Washington send a military force against Selkirk from Michilimackinac, Prairie du Chien, or Green Bay and recapture the seized goods. But Washington chose not to become embroiled in a serious international incident only because of the loss of merchandise. And yet the loss was significant. William McGillivray of the NWC, who owned half of it in shares, estimated the fur trade returns at Fond du Lac to be worth $25,000.[74]

Astor did not just use powerful friends to accomplish results. He also used monopolistic business practices. For example, in 1815 he "cornered" the source of highly desired twist tobacco. Grown in Brazil, it was the favorite of Indian trading partners, and without it a company was at great disadvantage.[75] Many Indians were accustomed to gifts of good twist tobacco as a means of demonstrating good will prior to trading.

As a final step in gaining competitive advantage in what today might be called implementation, Astor's senior manager for the Northern Department, Ramsay Crooks, worked to have AFC agents become custom house officers, "in order to keep our opponents on their own side of the boundary."[76] And in one case, an "independent" customs collector at Mackinac owed Astor $4,000 and thus became partial to Astor's interest, and some have suggested he allowed much of the company's goods to pass into the upper lakes duty free.[77] The Indian agent at Michilimackinac, George Boyd, was so pliable that in July 1819 he authorized William Morrison to seize goods illegally brought within Fond du Lac and the outlying region.[78]

To fully compete with the HBC, Astor grew the AFC into a mercantile empire, with its Great Lakes regional hub at Michilimackinac. Taking on the British from Mackinac, the AFC lugged large quantities of goods and supplies westward, including to the border country, to compete with the HBC. It was a fierce competition.[79] With all the advantages Astor could muster, the AFC grew to over seven hundred employees by the War of 1812. It likely expanded thereafter.[80]

All three dominant fur trade companies, NWC, HBC, and the AFC, were merciless toward smaller competition. Indeed, George Johnston, likely with the backing of his father's Sault Ste. Marie–based fur trade business, suffered the brunt of the HBC in the border country just prior to joining the AFC as a clerk in Grand Marais. As one Rainy Lake HBC clerk concluded, the region was too poor to support both the HBC and the AFC, so the best way to oppose the Americans was to trap as many animals as was possible to drive them off.[81] An onslaught on fur bearer populations in the border country would disproportionally hurt the smaller American outfit with less cash reserves.

During the winter of 1821–22, Johnston established two posts near Rainy Lake, at Crane Lake and at Lac des Mille Lacs, north of the customary border. Johnston, in turn, hired two clerks to operate these posts. One clerk, Joseph Cadotte, was initially successful and purchased a great deal of wild rice, which the HBC was used to acquiring and using. Johnston's men also sought to oust the HBC from their post at Crane Lake—clearly in American territory. But the HBC was stronger, and Johnston's men were driven off. Meanwhile, operating from a small outpost at Basswood Lake, an HBC clerk temporarily seized the outfit of an American trader traveling toward Red River, saying he seized the goods under the pretext that the trader was going to transport and then trade alcohol.[82] At Lac des Mille Lacs, two of the American men were killed, and the remaining men fled back to their post at Crane Lake.[83]

In part to crush the opposition, HBC governor George Simpson appointed the resolute Dr. John McLoughlin as the man in charge of the Rainy Lake district. Better supplied, McLoughlin took advantage of the poor wild rice harvest—poor for all traders and Indians alike—to oust the Americans. However, with no rice, Indians would reduce their "hunt" for furs.[84] Johnston's men had retreated to a new post on Vermilion Lake deep in American territory. But the HBC also had a post on Vermilion Lake.[85] Johnston's men were starving, and it was reported "they eat a few of their furs." In January 1823, McLoughlin had provisions given to the Johnston men on Vermilion Lake, hoping to keep them in business long enough to forestall any interest of the larger AFC moving into the border country. True, Johnston's men were starving, but McLoughlin now realized it was better to have a small independent trader nearby than the AFC.[86] But while providing food, McLoughlin's HBC men ran into an AFC trader at Vermilion Lake who was also an American customs agent. Realizing they were now facing the full force of the AFC and the American government, the HBC men retreated from Vermilion

Lake. They did not want to face American penalties for trading in American territory nor unintentionally intensify competition with the AFC. For Johnston, however, the appearance of the AFC and just across the border the HBC was too much. He fled the border country as an independent trader.

But the hard competition merely shifted to a more direct confrontation between the HBC and AFC at Rainy Lake in the summer of 1823. A member of the British survey team quoted an HBC clerk:

> The two or three houses you see form a fur-trading post of John Jacob Astor, the great merchant of New York. The man is one of his agents. He is fishing for a dinner. If he catch nothing he will not dine. He and his party are contending with us for the Indian trade. We are starving them out, and have nearly succeeded. . . . The expedients for preventing a rival from entering a rich fur country are sometimes decisive. Every animal is advisedly exterminated, and the district is ruined for years.[87]

If an individual trader could survive, the profits were very high, but it was risky business. When Indians took fall credits, sometimes the interest on these debts was as high as 100 percent. However, the full interest was rarely paid off. Indeed, it was calculated that it would rarely be paid in full, but it engendered a sense of indebtedness. Traders were surer of their success if a group of Indians was indebted to them and there was little option for them to go elsewhere. Most commonly only half or a third of debts were paid off. Still the economic return was enormous.[88]

The year 1824 was a very profitable one for the AFC:

> In October, 1824 the company announced that the . . . greatest quantity of furs ever before offered for sale at one time in the United States, will be put up at auction, in the city of New York

on the 11 instant. . . . It consists of 12,500 lbs. of beaver, 120,000 muskrat skins, 72,000 Raccoon ditto, 60,000 hare and nutria ditto and 10,000 buffalo robes from different regions.[89]

Clearly the company that posted Bela Chapman and the next year George Johnston in a little outpost on the North Shore was, in the larger picture, an economic and political force ready to contend with its British rival to the north.

The American Fur Company in the Region

The AFC was subdivided into departments, with the Northern Department focused on the Great Lakes. The center of the AFC effort was Michilimackinac, roughly where Lakes Superior, Huron, and Michigan intersect. It was a buzzing entrepôt, with near a thousand employees converging there in the hectic summer months:

> This island is bold and rugged, as seen in the approach to it, and on all sides, except the north-west, there the hills incline gradually down to the shore. . . . Below this is another terrace, about four hundred yards deep, of nearly level ground, and just under the hill on which the fort stands. On this the town is built, and the gardens are cultivated, in which are about fifty trees. . . . The houses are, with the exception of those owned by the American Fur Company, all of logs, and small: most of them are covered with bark, and nearly all are going to decay. The Fur Company's buildings are extremely valuable, and well adapted to the purposes for which they were built.[90]

At the height of the summer season, Michilimackinac was teeming with fur trade brigades made up of a mixture of people clad in a wide array of clothing styles and colors and speaking French, Odawa, Chippewa, Iroquois, and English.[91]

Much of early Michilimackinac "society" was made up of people of mixed descent. Catholicism was a vital part of this world, and the Bongas were participating Catholics. The many Métis who lived or once had homes there had family networks spreading out to much of the region.[92] The Métis society had many of their own customs, made afresh from older customs from the Old and New World. For example, one scholar noted, "the French-Métis observed their winter holidays in familiar ways, paying little or no attention to their English-speaking neighbors and employers. Much of their holiday celebration focused on their children. Métis families commemorated Christmas with religious ceremonies, followed by drinking and dancing, but they did not exchange gifts until the New Year."[93]

Many traders had married Indian women—"in the manner of the country"—and had raised Métis children. Métis families at Mackinac and Sault St. Marie, like the Johnston children, were not stigmatized by their origins in the first two decades of the nineteenth century. However, this changed, particularly in the late 1820s and 1830s. Protestant missionaries and military officers with white wives arrived at Mackinac, and power shifted from Métis and Catholic to Yankee and Protestant. Among those who became a devout Protestant was Robert Stuart, head of the AFC in Mackinac. The coming of Americans and Protestant missionaries also started a change beyond Mackinac.[94]

Social conditions in Minnesota were similar to those at Mackinac, though different in their smaller scale:

In 1820 Minnesota country was still a world unto itself, with a culture that was foreign to the settled parts of the United States. Scarcely a soul in the region was not related to the Dakotas or Anishinaabe—or sometimes to both—either by birth or through marriage. After generations of intermarriage a single individual could conceivably trace a lineage that included Scots, French, and American, Dakota, and Anishinaabe forebears among his extended relations. English was scarcely spoken, French was the lingua franca of the region.... Within a decade, this familiar way of life would be well on its way to extinction.[95]

A Scot immigrant like so many traders, Robert Stuart was the AFC's senior manager in Mackinac from 1817 to 1834. Stuart was under contract with Astor alongside his countryman and friend Ramsay Crooks. They both worked on salary and for a small percentage of overall profits. Stuart was an imposing and "imperious man," while Crooks was quieter but also hard-nosed. Stuart's reputation was well known, particularly for physically knocking down drunken or blundering employees.[96] Stuart was in charge of the Northern District of the AFC, including the Fond du Lac post and thus Grand Marais and Grand Portage. Indeed, Stuart was at the height of his influence in the AFC—evidenced by a promotion in salary and increase in percentage of overall profits—exactly when the fledgling outpost was being established at Gichi Bitobig.

The Minnesota Arrowhead at this time was within Michilimackinac County, a part of Michigan Territory. But in reality it was unorganized American territory. Territorial governor Lewis Cass appointed Stuart county treasurer and associate justice for Michilimackinac County during the years Chapman and Johnston were in Grand Marais.[97] Despite the border competition in the 1820s, there was a feeble American presence on the North Shore. The most significant American presence by far, even if relatively light, was the AFC.

North Shore Anishinaabeg's long-term alliance with the British was scarcely shaken by the arrival of Chapman, Johnston, and other AFC men. Participation in the 1812 warfare had created strong bonds between area Anishinaabeg and the British, particularly for participants such as Espagnol. For many decades Fort William served as the principal trading location for the North Shore Anishinaabeg. The Americans knew they had to make inroads into this alliance. Further, the British had a long-standing tradition of distributing presents to Indians living along the border, but the Americans did not. Sought-after British presents might have included blankets, calico cloth, stroud (wool), ribbons, thread, needles, scissors, twine, fish nets, fishing line, kettles, knives, flints, gunpowder, and tobacco.[98]

In 1822, Governor Cass made an effort "to interdict" the visits of the upper Great Lakes Indians to the British posts, but few Indians habits were changed. When all was said and done, American Indian agent Henry Schoolcraft had little funds to keep up with the gift giving of the British.[99] The long-standing alliance between the British and Anishinaabeg was difficult to budge.

The 1821 merger of the HBC and the NWC had another impact in the region: there were lots of unemployed clerks and men in the fur trade country. Those clerks who were fortunate to stay on with the new HBC often received reduced pay.[100] David Thompson noted "the new order of things, has thrown these wilds into a state of wretchedness and it will require some time before they settle down into a state of quiet poverty."[101] Another consequence was the rise of the Red River settlement, where Métis, often former HBC and NWC employees, moved after the merger. Métis and others established farms, made pemmican, and collected buffalo wool (in one scheme), and a small settlement grew. The trickle of Métis to Red River escalated in 1823 as the HBC made it policy to send "half-breed" orphans to Red River under the care of Catholic missions or Protestant establishments. A limited number of "old servants" and families were transported to Red River.[102] Red River became an "alternative" place for Métis to go if they sought to, or had to, leave the trade.

But Red River was not a paradise for retired or unemployed Métis. Rumors swirled around its survival. For example, HBC clerks at Rainy Lake reported that "several freemen [Métis?] have been killed by the Sioux," and upwards of nine hundred lodges of Sioux prevented buffalo from coming near the Red River settlements. The implicit objective of the Dakota was to try to starve out the Métis and remnants of Scottish colonists and regain control of this area.[103]

A month and half later, the same clerk noted that the report that "the Americans brought here some time ago, about the Scioux Killing the Freemen of Red River are all false."[104] Despite these rumors and the unsettled nature of life in the region, Red River grew in the coming decades.

During the 1820s, the type of furs trapped for the North American trade changed. Profits remained high for the AFC, but the species they sought were shifting in response to a change in market preference.[105] The golden era of beaver and marten furs—of the NWC period—was in decline. During the early 1820s, only half as many beaver were trapped as a few years before. The years just preceding the establishment of the Grand Marais outpost saw some of the best marten trapping on American soil. But numbers fell off dramatically during the experiment at Gichi Bitobig. The 1820s were also relatively low years for harvests of otters and wolves.[106] In those areas of the United States trapped during the early 1820s, there was a steady increase in the trapping and trading of muskrat, foxes, and mink.[107] Muskrat trapping exploded in numbers—if not in value—in the years following the Grand Marais operation. Trapping of lynx also increased but followed the cycle of lynx increases in response to the periodic peak of hare populations. And then lynx numbers fell during the ebb of hare populations. One September Espagnol brought "nine summer cats" to the HBC.[108]

While the kind of animal species trapped was changing, the technology was not. Traps were largely still made by hand, mostly of wood, by the Indian trappers and women snaring small game or furbearers. Heavy, handmade metal traps were used to trap beaver in Upper Canada as early as 1743.[109] Later, by 1797, traps were baited with castoreum, the secretions of beaver scent glands, and beaver were trapped in greater numbers. In the words of Thompson, "all of them were infatuated with the love of Castorum of their species, and more fond of it than we are of fire water. We are now killing the Beaver without any labor."[110] The AFC was purchasing handmade steel traps made in Montreal in the 1820s, and some made it as far as Fond du Lac. They were extremely valuable, worth eight dollars per trap, but were very heavy and rare. Some were made poorly. It is unlikely these pricey trade items, sometimes loaned out, would have been employed at Grand Marais. More likely they were used where there were predictable high returns.[111] Elsewhere, owning a steel trap or two was a sign of great wealth and was rare. Indians were still "trapping" beaver by busting their dams and thus emptying the pond and then driving them out of their lodges to be clubbed, so as not to ruin the pelt by spearing or some other means. In upstate New York, Sewell Newhouse began to mass produce traps in the mid-1820s, but few had made their way west at the time of the AFC operations in Grand Marais.

Fond du Lac

The Grand Marais post was dependent upon Fond du Lac. Indeed, during the stark days and nights the young clerks must have thought fondly of Fond du Lac. To the men huddled at Gichi Bitobig, Fond du Lac stood out as a livelier, larger, more established post with better food and more supplies and warmer winter quarters. But in fact, there had been a succession of fur trade forts along the St. Louis River. The North Westers operated Fort St. Louis from August 1793 to 1811, three miles upriver from Lake Superior. The South West Company—under both NWC's and Astor's ownership—ran the post from 1811 to 1816, but it was relocated eighteen miles upstream, closer to the lucrative posts on the Mississippi River.[112] More persistent than the fur trade companies' tenure, an Anishinaabeg and small Métis community thrived along the St. Louis River.[113] The succession of Fond du Lac posts was described in 1820:

> About 5 miles up we passed an old establishment of the N.W. Co's which they deserted during the late war. We reached the S. W.

Co's establishment an hour before sunset where we encamped, 21 miles from the m. of the river.... This place was first occupied 3 years since, during which several buildings have been erected. It is pleasantly situated on the brow of a high hill and at the head of several small Islands formed in the river. A spot of land of 3 or 4 acres from which the timber had been cut for fires, is tilled, and is now bearing very fine potatoes. The soil is a rich black mould. The Co. with great difficulty have transported to this place 3 horses, 3 cows, one yoke of oxen and 4 bulls. They also have the implements of husbandry. It was a great treat to obtain milk at this distance in the wilderness.... A young crane about 3 ft. high had been tamed and was running around here.[114]

The AFC station was made up of six or seven log buildings, the majority with chimneys. Each log structure was covered with bark on the roof and on its sides. Above the log structures was cleared ground bounded by wooden fences. In one area potatoes were growing, and wheat in another. "Indian corn" and squashes of immense size were also grown.[115] Nearby were two small graveyards, one for whites and a smaller one for Indians. Indians often encamped on a small island adjacent to these structures.[116] Another trader later recalled that the Fond du Lac buildings included a blacksmith and carpenter shop, icehouse, root house, stables, and "retail store."[117]

The AFC manager Robert Stuart had early and high hopes for the Fond du Lac post.[118] It became a regional hub for the AFC, so by 1826, its various outposts produced 150 packs, or $35,000 worth of furs.[119] Still, the North Shore contribution to that total was slight. Grand Marais was typically the smallest of the eleven AFC posts serving Fond du Lac.[120] Its function, clearly, was different than some of the higher-paying posts. But at the time when Chapman started trading at Grand Marais, its potential returns were yet unknown.

Ramsay Crooks, head of the AFC's Northern Department, hired William Morrison to run Fond du Lac during the first half of the 1820s, when Chapman and Johnston were at Grand Marais. Morrison was an experienced and sought-after trader. He also spent much of his career at Fond du Lac so he knew a great deal about its district—its outposts to the west and north in particular. In the words of a competitor, "Mr. Morrison stands high in the Opinion of all those who are Acquainted with him as an Indian trader. He was well known to the Indians of Rainy Lake."[121] His fur trade "vitae" was extraordinary: he had worked for the XY Company, the NWC, and now the AFC. He even was made prisoner by Lord Selkirk's hired men.[122] Hence, he probably was no fan of the HBC. He was "Canadian" born, became a naturalized American, and then retired to Canada.[123] He was married three times, two of them country marriages to Native women, and the third to the daughter of a distinguished fur trader. Morrison's first wife, an Anishinaabe woman, Shaughunomonee, died sometime during the period Chapman and Johnston were at Grand Marais.[124] Soon thereafter Morrison retired from the fur trade and moved to Montreal.

The details of Morrison's contract with the AFC are well known, and he assumed much personal risk in the financial success of the district. On November 24, 1821, the AFC entered into a four-year contract with Morrison for a salary of $1,400 per annum to oversee their trade in the entire region of northern Minnesota. This contract, written by Crooks, is, in part, as follows:

> And in addition that you will regulate and conduct the trade of all such Posts or Places as may be established by the American Fur Company in the country North of the Fond du Lac Department, say in that region extending from the old Grand Portage on Lake Superior to the Lake of the Woods.[125]

From 1822 to 1826, Morrison operated the Fond du Lac district posts on "halves," or half of the district was run at his expense and risk.[126]

In 1826, William A. Aitken succeeded Morrison at Fond du Lac,

William Morrison was Bela Chapman's and George Johnston's superior in charge of the AFC operations in northeastern Minnesota and northwestern Wisconsin. Courtesy of the Minnesota Historical Society.

also working on a "halves" basis.[127] However, prior to this time he worked alongside Morrison, and thus some of Chapman's and Johnston's journal entries are addressed to him as well. Aitken, too, married a fellow fur trader's daughter and an Anishinaabe from Sandy Lake.[128] Eventually, sparring with Crooks and charged with mismanagement, he quit the AFC abruptly in 1838.

In Grand Marais

The interjection of an international spat—precluding foreigners from trading in British Canada—recommenced with the British government retaliating against American posts in Upper Canada. The AFC was forced to close posts it had operated on the shore of Georgian Bay in Lake Huron. As early as December 1821, AFC managers were scheming about how to "oppose" the HBC on the Minnesota border. Hiring Morrison at Fond du Lac, the region's hub, was one step to set the plan in play. Eventually, the AFC opened three new posts close to the Canadian border between Grand Portage on Superior's northwestern shores and Lake of the Woods.[129] Crooks knew a post on Rainy Lake should have more men, at least twelve to fifteen, to adequately challenge the HBC.[130]

For much of the summer months as Chapman and Johnston labored at Fond du Lac, they did not know where they were going—to which post—or when. Only by July 31, 1824, did the AFC tell Indian agent Schoolcraft that there would be a small post at Grand Portage.[131] Aitken received a license to "be used in his trade with the Indians at posts of Grand Portage, Vermilion Lake, Rainy Lake, and Pembina." Even after Chapman and Johnston had left, it was not clear if someone would follow upon their efforts. However, George Berketh was next employed to run the post at Grand Portage in 1826–27. Records of this effort have not been located. But like Johnston, Berketh was of mixed Anishinaabeg descent.[132]

In reality there was a succession of AFC traders on the North

Shore from Chapman until the larger-scale fishing "experiment" began in 1836, based primarily at Grand Portage, Isle Royale, and to a lesser degree at Grand Marais and Isle Encampment. Even after the secret business agreement of 1833, when the HBC agreed to pay off the AFC not to contest their border trade so as to regain a monopoly, there were American traders on the North Shore. In fact, the only years for which we do not find records of a small AFC outfit, or in one instance an unnamed trader, was the winter of 1825–26 and 1835.[133] Contrary to the presumption of no traders on the North Shore, we know that the AFC was firmly entrenched in posting their men there for almost two decades. Unfortunately, we do not have much documentation of these other traders, their locations, or details of their trade. It was likely Morrison and then Aitken became more realistic about what profits could be made at Grand Marais and Grand Portage. Armed with this knowledge, clerks after Johnston must not have agonized as much over the minimal profits, until AFC commercial fishing began in 1836.

The isolation at Grand Marais distressed both Chapman and Johnston. No mail route was established to Fond du Lac. Thus, unlike the clerk at Fort William, once in place they did not receive any coaching or strategic thoughts from experienced men on how to get the better of the HBC. They were, in a very real sense, isolated for seven to eight months. Their heartfelt feelings of isolation, almost that they were abandoned for no purpose, was ironic because of the luminaries in the area, especially to the north of them. The American border survey crew worked during the summer months of 1823, 1824, and 1825. The British surveyors, too, traveled through Fort William en route west. The American Army major Stephen Long and expedition men left Fort William on September 15, 1823, for Sault Ste. Marie, just a few weeks before Chapman arrived in Grand Marais.[134] An HBC governor traveled through Fort William. And finally, just a month or so after Johnston left the North Shore, in May 1825, Captain John Franklin went through Fort William on his second arctic

1823–24	AFC at Grand Marais (Bela Chapman, clerk)
1824–25	AFC at Grand Marais (George Johnston, clerk)
1827	AFC at Grand Portage (George Berketh, clerk)
1828–29	"Americans" (likely AFC) at Grand Marais (clerk unknown)
1829	"Americans" (likely AFC) at Roche de Bout, forty-five miles southwest beyond Grand Marais, possibly Shovel Point or Palisade area (clerk unknown)
1830	AFC at Grand Portage (Duncan Ross, clerk)
1830–31	AFC at Grand Marais (clerk unknown)
1831	AFC at Grand Portage or Grand Marais (clerk unknown)
1832	AFC at Grand Portage (Ambrose Davenport, clerk)
1833	AFC at Grand Marais (clerk unknown)
1834	"Americans" (likely not AFC) at Grand Portage (clerk unknown)
1836	AFC at Grand Portage (Pierre Cotte, clerk?); start of commercial fishing
1837–40	AFC at Grand Portage and Grand Marais (Pierre Cotte, clerk); fishing only, no dealing in furs
1840 or 1841	Cleveland Company at Grand Portage (clerk unknown)

American fur traders on the Minnesota North Shore, after 1821 and before 1841.

expedition and thus did not meet the Americans. From the men's perspective, the little Grand Marais outpost was in a forgotten corner of Lake Superior.

As early as the fall 1821—a few months after the merger of the NWC and the HBC—the AFC was ready to test the reorganized HBC and attempt to win the trade in the Minnesota border lands. The upstart was ready to challenge the Walmart of its day.[135] We do not know who devised this plan. At one point Johnston implies that establishing the AFC post at Grand Marais was a mistake made by an AFC official beyond Aitkens and Morrison at Fond du Lac. Johnston, writing to Aitken and Morrison, lamented, "those who put you up to again establish this post, [should] suffer all the bitter pangs of the distressed in mind."[136] Was it Crooks or Stuart, or less likely Astor, who devised this plan to challenge or "wall-off" the HBC from more lucrative areas to the south? Or maybe it was Crooks or Stuart trying to please Astor. By 1823, Astor was largely disengaged from the day-to-day business of the AFC, or if he was engaged, it was only when a major decision was afoot, such as the opening of an AFC operation in St. Louis. Crooks (and to a lesser degree Stuart) was left in charge of the Northern District, and he in turn decided that Morrison should take the lead in contesting the border trade. Crooks offered a contract to Morrison for trade in "the old Grand Portage."[137] Crooks wrote of this plan to Stuart:

> You are already aware that Morrison will establish some new posts along our northwestern border. The old Grand Portage is allowed to be within our line, and there the N.W. have always had a good little post, since they retired to Fort William. An outfit from Fond du Lac department should be sent to that place under some active men; and in order to keep our opponents on their own side of the boundary, our clerks or traders are to be made customhouse officers, and as an additional security against the interfering with our Indians, the new station should be located as far from the boundary line as may be possible, have a due regard to the interest of the trade; and this will lessen the temptation which the rum of our adversaries would always be sure to create where our houses so near to theirs.[138]

A retired trader later summarized this challenge: "William Morrison was chosen to manage that Department employing many clerks to assist him in carrying on the trade and opposed the Hudson Bay Co as strong as possible on the line of the British & American territories where Swords, Knives & Guns had to be used in their desperate fight for a few Rats & Mink skins."[139] The Americans knew that Fort William was being increasingly emptied of its supplies and downgraded in importance. For example, the British surveyor David Thompson observed that by August 1823 Fort William was being poorly resupplied with trade items, but they still had plenty of provisions and, sadly, alcohol.[140]

Alcohol

Alcohol flowed particularly freely along the border country, despite some attempts to control it in Indian country. Its use and abuse are perhaps both the most misunderstood and calamitous part of the fur trade. Its use ranged from "ceremonial" in the sense of recognizing stature or good hunting or showing reciprocity between trader and Indian, to destructive and sometimes violent binge drinking. Both the HBC and AFC clerks doled out large quantities of alcohol, including to the HBC employees at Fort William.[141] For example, the Fort William clerk calmly noted, "The men drinking and fighting this afternoon."[142] We do not, unfortunately, know how much alcohol Chapman, Johnston, and their men were imbibing or further whether their alcohol consumption had an impact on their trade.

One scholar has demonstrated that alcohol was a means of developing trust between trader and Indian clients to the point of developing a "metaphorical kinship" between them.[143] This ephemeral relationship nonetheless led to greater trade and a reccurring trade partnership and became an essential fur trade custom. This relationship between trader and specific Anishinaabe is solemnized in one entry at Fort William:

> Old Mad[dam] La Graceaux, old lady of about 100 years of age died on the 12th. Also a daughter of one of our principal Indians (L'homme du Sault) was drowned on the 20th Ultimo. A girl of 12

years of age. Gave out 5 gallons rum amongst all the Indians with the plug tobacco and 1½ bushel Indian corn to make a feast.[144]

Contrary to the stereotype, alcohol was often given to Anishinaabeg as a gift to "send a band off," not as a method of swindling Indian trading partners. Gifting alcohol had become a routine custom in much of Indian country and was particularly common where competition was acute. Despite being longtime traders, the Johnston family loathed its use. George Johnston's father, the Irishman John Johnston, wrote in his journal:

> Whiskey is the great object. Their love of this poisonous draught is without bounds. A taste of it can be likened to nothing but the bite of the tarantular [spider]. It inflames them all over, and they become distracted for more. If more is given, it but increases their rage for more. . . . When drunk, like their white brothers, they have no control over their passions and is in drunken frolics that their murders are chiefly committed.

Elsewhere John Johnston called it "evil rages" and repeatedly cited its "degrading effects."[145] His son did not articulate his feelings in his journal toward this practice except to slip in once that he was "under the necessity of giving them Half a Keg Liquor."[146] Chapman was blunter, recording "all drunk," and "the Indians drink rum as free as water."[147] As was typical, there was no self-reflection about his role in "freely" dispensing alcohol.

Chapman and Johnston were undoubtedly coached to dole out alcohol to try and cement connections to their Indian trappers. And they were provided with ample alcohol supplies to do so. Their superiors had vivid memories of the disastrous yearlong experiment in which the AFC did not have alcohol on the border during the 1818–19 season, and their fur returns plummeted. In this one case, it was the HBC, not the NWC, that took advantage of this situation to lure "American" Indians to trade with them.[148] A few years later, a letter from Lewis Cass to Indian agent Schoolcraft confirmed the legal use of alcohol among Indian traders working along the border: "You are therefore authorized to permit the introduction of whiskey in such limited quantities as you may think circumstances will justify, into the Indian [country] on our boundary west of Lake Superior, and adjoining the trading posts of the Hudson's Bay Company."[149] AFC traders competing on the border formally retained this liquor privilege through 1827. In July 1822, Stuart requested from George Boyd, the agent for Indian affairs at Mackinac, the right to import liquor into the Indian country for the particular use of the boundary trade.[150] In 1823, Stuart complained that the HBC used whiskey to buy Indian food and starved out an AFC trader. A year later when Aitken presided at Fond du Lac, he was granted a permit to bring two barrels of liquor to the northern frontier.[151]

The scale of alcohol use was staggering, leading to a common comment at Fort William: "The Indians still drinking but not troublesome."[152] In 1824, the Northern District of the AFC had increased its annual volume to 8,000 gallons of whiskey and 2,000 gallons of high wine.[153] And the HBC was liberally dispensing alcohol as well, particularly as a reward for bringing in valuable furs. For example, a group of Indians arrived "and brought amongst them all 196 skins including Attineau's fur which they brought in. Gave the Indians 3 gall[on]s high wines."[154] When HBC governor George Simpson or other luminaries passed through, the Fort William clerk gave out alcohol more freely to recognize Anishinaabeg leaders and the HBC's relationship to them. According to Chapman, the prodigious use of alcohol in the country led to the outcome that a small keg of liquor could customarily be found in an Anishinaabeg's wigwam.

Competing with the HBC

One example of the "dirty tactics" one fur trade company used was evident after the 1816 tragedy at Red River.[155] During Lord Selkirk's invasion of Fort William, he acquired a copy of an "Indian Manifesto" that the NWC tried to convince area Anishinaabeg to assume, profess, and act upon. The manifesto avowed that the HBC—or "English"—were losing "their footing" at Red River and the Anishinaabeg had many "reasons for driving away the English," such as they allegedly put poison in their rum, brought smallpox to the country, and drove away cattle and "spoilt our lands." While not particularly effective, the HBC cited it as "a speech to put into the mouth of an Indian [that] shews the villainous falsehoods the Nt. Wt. Co. endeavour[ed] to spread respecting the HBCo."[156] Or, as one participant succinctly put it, the companies used "force and fraud" to make a profit.[157]

The AFC clerks at Grand Marais were at a great competitive disadvantage compared to their HBC opponents. The Fort William clerk was able to feed forty to fifty Indians during the winter of 1824–25. They provided "whitefish, potatoes, and a little unhulled corn. By these acts we gained their good will."[158] The HBC operation was bettered supplied than the AFC operation. The HBC clerks had more options in the variety and quantity of gifts to give away to trading Anishinaabeg. Chapman and Johnston had a hardscrabble existence with few provisions to share and less stock to provide gratis, as was customary in the trade. Nor did they know if an Indian became indebted to the AFC clerk at Grand Marais if the AFC might recoup any of those debts in following years. Both clerks presumed their efforts would be the last of the AFC in the area—or so both hoped—but it was not to be.

Fort William employees had greater access to food, regular fish runs in the Kaministiquia River, agricultural products such as milk, chicken, and beef, and established relationships with area Indians. Unlike a number of HBC men, the AFC men were not married to area Anishinaabeg and thus had no kinship relationships to draw upon. Johnston's mother's clan was Caribou, common among North Shore Anishinaabeg. But there was no evidence he identified himself as related to the Caribou clan to potentially utilize his kinship ties to better his business results. Unlike the Anishinaabeg, AFC men did not have extended kin networks to draw upon when food ran low.

The HBC enjoyed a further competitive advantage as they were still willing to trade for "country produce" from Indians. Thus, they credited Indian women and men at the following rates:

Canoe birch bark, bottom piece, 1 shilling, 6 pennies
Canoe birch bark, side piece, 9 pennies
Gum or pitch, 1 pound, 1 penny
Snow shoes, pair, 2 pennies
Caribou skin dressed large, 1 shilling 6 pennies
Caribou skin dressed small, 9 pennies
Sugar maple, 1 pound, 4 pennies[159]

Anishinaabeg could thus trade a wider range of items than merely furs, such as the produce harvested locally by women, including maple sugar, watap, gum for sealing canoes, berries, and canoe bark. The AFC men did not have the means to trade for country produce.

The experienced workforce of the HBC (and "freemen" residing nearby) was another advantage. Their location alongside the largest river in their territory gave them diverse fishing options. They knew how to set seine nets in the river to catch thousands of whitefish and knew the locations of the best fishing grounds in Thunder Bay. They knew the locations of individual Anishinaabe hunting grounds. They were experienced in locating a cached canoe (often along Lake Superior) as a means to find the start of an individual's or family's trail inland. By holding on to experienced wintering servants and having freemen occasionally work for the HBC, they maintained a knowledgeable workforce.[160]

HBC employees, in turn, were veterans of harsh competition. But the HBC clerks at Fort William were worried about the Americans. They repeatedly went "looking out for Americans."[161] One clerk wrote, "being uneasy about the Americans I set people to watch about the old Grand Portage, until the ice began to take in the lake."[162] Two months later, the same clerk wrote he was nervous about losing trade to the Americans. The HBC men also sought to figure out the Americans' strategy. To do so, they sought Indian intelligence about whether the Americans had arrived and how many men were part of the outfit—to gauge the investment and thus commitment to the enterprise.[163] Ironically, the HBC clerk had assumed they would establish a post at Grand Portage, rather than Grand Marais; thus, it took two months longer to realize the Americans had landed and had begun trading.

Both the HBC and AFC men likely used typical competitive measures, such as "running down their oppos[ition] with lies in the opinion of Ind[ian]s . . . and telling them they will do so and so to us."[164] And the HBC went to great pains to cut off the potential threat from the Americans by establishing a small "guard," sometimes called a "watch tent," at White Fish Lake. A Mr. Grant and HBC men at Petite Peche on White Fish Lake were to insure a "road" was not established by the Americans to the area and to report on which Indians were trading with the Americans.[165] But both companies had a problem: they sought to trade with Indians who trapped furs on "the other" side of the uncertain border.

For anyone living in this time and region, any AFC establishment at Grand Marais would unavoidably be negatively compared with its competitor Fort William. In 1823, Lieutenant Delafield, head of the American border survey team, described Fort William:

Sunday, July 6 [1823] Fort William is a very large establishment in decay. It is contained within pickets enclosing acres and at each angle of the square has a block house, some bastions included for artillery pieces. Two or three small pieces were mounted.... Since the coalition of the Hudson's Bay and North West Companies, this post has become very insignificant & fast going to ruin. Mr. Stewart is the present agent about to be relieved by a Mr. McKenzie. Both gentlemen meet me at the landing & pay me the compliment of hoisting their flag in the fort upon my arrival.... Breakfast and dine with Mr. Stuart and mess, in their large hall. We were 6 or 8 at table in a hall that was large enough to dine 300.... There is a handsome square of ground neatly leveled, &c. within the pickets, the hall on one side facing the entrance, and empty warehouses and useless offices on the other three sides.[166]

But even in decline or decay the fort still impressed a visitor. There were all the furnishings—a long cherry table, tools, countless jars of medicines, light streaming in the sets of windows on the many buildings, what was left of the fine dishes, and trade goods in relative high numbers compared with the ragtag presence of the AFC at Grand Marais. The schooner *Recovery,* iced in on the Kaministiquia River during the winter of 1823–24, certainly underscored the different level of investment of the two companies.[167]

After Chapman left Grand Marais, it was likely that the Fort William HBC men burned the few, small AFC buildings at Grand Marais. It was a safe and anonymous way to "hurt" the opposition, particularly if they came back. Most North Shore Anishinaabeg hoped that the AFC would return and thus would have been likely to have left the vacant buildings alone. On the other hand, if they were indebted to the AFC and worried about it, they perhaps would have thought that burning their small establishment would hinder their return and extinguish those debts.[168] The HBC, however, had more enticement to burn the AFC outpost, and it was easy to do in the summer months.

The HBC workforce knew the region well, as many of their employees had lived there a relatively long time or had married North

Shore Anishinaabeg women and gained knowledge through those relationships. Chapman and Johnston knew little about the country, and sometimes their endeavors were handicapped by that lack of knowledge. Only rarely did they engage a North Shore Anishinaabeg to guide them. If they had engaged Espagnol, for example, they would have benefited from his extensive knowledge of the North Shore. British surveyor Thompson noted:

> While at the SE end of the Carrying-Place [Grand Portage], a respectable and intelligent chief, call the Spaniard and his band came to us; their country and hunting grounds are near halfway to the river St. Louis, and about the irregular ridge of land that produces the head waters of the rivers to Lake Superior ... I conversed part of two days with them, they gave me the names of fifteen considerable rivers, from the St. Louis to the Pigeon River inclusive; all of whose head waters, approximately to those of the head waters of the Lake of the Woods.[169]

This knowledge was so far-reaching that Thompson elected to "skip" the field work of the survey of much of the Pigeon River and rely upon his memory and Indian maps of the area made in charcoal on birch bark as the basis for his maps to be submitted to the British Border Commissioner.[170] And yet with the Americans and British still debating the border and geographical knowledge precious, area Indians became reluctant to share this information. As they had been left out of the treaty negotiations, they had little incentive to now assist the surveyors. Thompson noted that "very little satisfactory information can be obtained from the Indians in a journey: especially as their jealousy is already awakened by our examination of their country."[171]

Chapman and Johnston felt immense pressure to make a profit, prove themselves, and contribute to their superiors' financial gain. They were also well aware that their superior, Morrison, was working on "shares," so making a profit would be especially warmly received. A good showing would mean that they might get a more lucrative posting the next winter. But Morrison and Aitken also knew, especially through years of trying, that profits were less likely to be made at Grand Marais. The pressure to trade well led both Chapman and Johnston to frustration and a sinking feeling. They increasingly wrote gloomy names for Grand Marais, starting with "wintering ground" and shifting to "Fort Misery" and "the Devil's Own Country."

Both companies charged dearly, to Indians and employees alike, for the transport of goods to their inland posts. The value of goods traded varied by the distance from market, be it Montreal, Albany, or New York City. For example, some prices at Fort William were twice as expensive as at Michilimackinac. Wanting to economize, American surveyor James Ferguson proposed bringing deer skins to make shoes, as others wore out. He reasoned his government support was meager, and they would be a long distance from any resupply.[172] Prices also varied slightly through time if there was competition nearby and distance from a supply source. In 1820 at Fond du Lac, a beaver skin was estimated as worth two dollars. A two-and-a-half-point blanket was sold for four beaver skins, or worth eight dollars at the point of sale. One small or half-axe was worth one skin, or two dollars. One fathom of stroud was worth four skins, or eight dollars.[173]

Prices could also be translated into muskrat skins. In 1828, a local Anishinaabe might trade fifty muskrat skins for a three-point blanket or cloth for a capote. A Montreal gun was worth one hundred muskrats, while a beaver trap was worth thirty muskrats, and a muskrat trap was worth fifteen skins. Anishinaabeg would recognize the term "plus" to mean one beaver skin, or the most basic measure of trade in the country.[174]

In some posts, the trader or Indian might try to strong arm their trading "partner" to control the terms of the trade. When traders had the advantage, they might even try to steal furs, such as John Tanner experienced on the Grand Portage.[175] But the opposite was sometimes also true. For example, the Reverend Edmund Ely re-counted: "It is a common thing for some stubborn Inds. To endeavor to intimidate the traders [by] drawing their knives, & the only way is for the trader to show them that he is not afraid of him, as an appear-ance of fear would more embolden them."[176] There was no record of intimidation at Grand Marais, though it might have occurred. Grand Coquin did test the boundaries of what the AFC might provide free-ly for him and his family. While Espagnol was more circumspect, because of his position (and success as a trapper), he was given valu-able objects to try to win his favor.

Espagnol's Dilemma and the Anishinaabeg

E spagnol knew the American traders were coming. As the pri-mary leader of the Anishinaabeg, he would travel widely out of the traditional territory, to Fond du Lac, for example, to consult with other Anishinaabeg leaders, perhaps AFC men, and even more rarely American government officials.[1] Whenever possible, he inter-cepted relevant news and hearsay. Back home he listened intently to news from band members, traders, surveyors, and others. It was particularly up to him to assemble this information quickly and to foresee how it might impact the North Shore Anishinaabeg. To be a good leader, he needed to anticipate great change and have a pru-dent response. Espagnol must have watched the Americans build their small post with unease. Obviously it meant a turn of fortune, but would it be for the good of his people, or would they suffer from the hands of the Americans? Their arrival propelled the question of which company was best for the small band. The North Shore Anishinaabeg had strong ties with the British, and during the War of 1812, Espagnol had fought alongside them. How would he handle the allegiance many of his band had to the British, including some in his family and clan, so it did not preclude possible benefits from the Americans' arrival? Now forty years old, he was an experienced trader and knew ways to bend the trade to benefit his band. Still he must have wondered whether the Americans' arrival was a sign of unwelcome change ahead or an opportunity to shift advantageous trading terms back to band members. And there were great risks involved. If he sided too much with the Americans and they then left, the HBC men might retaliate and make future trading more unfavorable. Or if too many of his band traded with the Americans, the HBC could conceivably shut down Fort William, as it was no longer a linchpin in the HBC's trading network or plans. No HBC traders would mean greatly reduced trading options, and the American trading terms would likely ratchet up unfavorably, as he had seen the HBC's do.

Espagnol was tall and a powerful individual. Whites would call him "respectable and intelligent" as well as "well shaped." HBC governor George Simpson, impressed by Espagnol, remarked that he had "the air of a prince," had a remarkable memory, and was a good orator.[2] Simpson would regularly recognize Espagnol in council and then direct the Fort William clerk to provide him gifts of tobacco, flour, butter, clothing, hulled corned, and alcohol. Espagnol, in turn, would distribute much of these gifts to his band.

In Anishinaabemowin he was known as Aysh-pay-ahng (it is high/heaven), though traders preferred either the French name Espagnol or the Spaniard in English.[3] He was the emerging leader at the time, surpassing the limited role of Peau de Chat, the elder. The leaders were related by marriage, and their two bands would often travel and camp together.[4] Father Francis Xavier Pierz's belief that Aysh-pay-ahng's father was a Spanish trader probably means he was a French Canadian with Spanish blood or who spoke Spanish, rather than a true Spaniard, who surely would have been noted in fur trade journals. According to Pierz, Espagnol was born at Grand Portage to a "savage mother"; thus, he was the only major protagonist in this account born in the area.[5]

There is conflicting evidence about whether Espagnol was of mixed descent. Only two statements declare he was of mixed descent, or "half-breed" in the words used by HBC factor George

Keith. Father Pierz asserted that Espagnol was "the son of a Spanish trader and an Anishinaabe mother.[6] However, in his baptismal records, Pierz does not record that Espagnol's father was a Christian, which he carefully does for the few others with non-"pagan" parents.[7] Other celebrated Anishinaabeg leaders had parents of mixed heritage, such as Little Pine or Shingwaukonse from the Garden River/Soo area.[8] But what was remarkable about his supposed mixed descent was that the succession of HBC scribes did not comment on his heritage like they did for so many others, nor did the observant David Thompson or Governor Simpson.

During his lifetime Espagnol witnessed great change, often lurching and tragic change. Just born, he was a survivor of the smallpox epidemic that raged through the Anishinaabeg of border country. Scores of North Shore Anishinaabeg died, particularly elders and young children. Later he would learn that he was also born the year of the Peace of Paris, in which the American and British subdivided his band's traditional territory. He grew up during the height of the NWC's operation at Grand Portage, when more than a thousand men celebrated rendezvous during the midsummer. He knew what it felt like for his band to be outnumbered each summer by canoe men and a handful of fur trade dignitaries. Grand Portage was swarming with canoe men camping along its shores, scouring everywhere for firewood and carousing. Later, as he became the family provider of meat, he had the misfortune of having the hunt become harder as big game animals became scarce. The accelerating of trade and more traders hunting led to diminished numbers of big game, especially of caribou and moose. Beaver numbers plummeted as a result of unrelenting trapping. Even the location of the NWC post changed in his teenage years, when the headquarters moved to the mouth of the Kaministiquia River. Grand Portage was largely vacated, and only a few buildings remained.

Espagnol was married and with his wife had at least two daughters and at least two stepsons. His wife, Josette Otakaki-on, was five years older. No fur trade records have been found to date that mention Espagnol had sons; thus, he did not have a son to potentially inherit his leadership position. The fact that Espagnol's stepson Patisckquseng was married to Peau de Chat's daughter meant that he was related by marriage to Peau de Chat and thus even to Grand Coquin. A little over a year after Johnston and men left, Patisckquseng died.[9] Espagnol's then sole stepson, "Maymushkowaush," subsequently became a leader at Grand Portage.[10] Family tradition asserts that the "Maymushkowaush" family was from the Chicago area and then became a numerically dominant family in Grand Portage in the nineteenth century.[11] Espagnol likely attended the Fond du Lac Treaty in 1826, but none of the leaders from "Old Grand Portage" were signatories.[12] He died sometime after the fall of 1843 but before the 1844 negotiations for the Isle Royale Compact. Joseph Peau de Chat (the younger) succeeded Aysh-pay-ahng as the "principal chief."

There are no images of Espagnol, as there are of Attikonse, another contemporary leader.[13] Written descriptions of Espagnol are few and biased, but they are all we have. In 1830, Frances Simpson, the young wife of HBC governor George Simpson wrote: "In the course of the morning we were visited by an old Indian Chief called the Spaniard, who came to present his Furs. He was the most lively, good-tempered looking Indian, I had met with; appeared both surprised & pleased at seeing me, and shook me very cordially by the hand several times. . . . He was accompanied by his son-in-law, who was dressed in a similar style, tho' his clothes were of plainer colors—he was a young Man, and paid great deference to his Father."[14] Governor Simpson described meeting Espagnol in 1841, when he was in his midfifties:

> During the interval occupied in preparing the Canoes, I had an interview with a party of Chippewa Indians, who were encamped near the Fort, awaiting my arrival. The audience chamber was a large empty floor in the Store, in which I and my fellow travelers

took our seats on one side and the Indians, about 40 in all, on the other, the Gentleman in charge Mr. Swanston and Collin, a servant, acting as interpreters; all strangers except Mr. Cameron, a Missionary, were carefully excluded. The ceremony of shaking hands all round having been performed; the Indians were called upon to open the proceedings, when their chief, by the name L'Espagnol, stood forward in the centre of the room. He was the remains of a fine tall man, but somewhat advanced in years but still upright and strong; his dress consisted of a scarlet cloth coat, decorated with gold lace and epaulettes, and bright brass button, but in the hurry of his toilet he had not removed the paper that was wrapped round many of them; without unmentionables or other nether garments, the tail of his shirt answering the purpose of a kilt, and suspended round his neck was large silver medal.

Having again shaken my hand, he commenced his oration in a loud, high tone of voice, and was exceedingly fluent; the purpose of it was, to tell me that he and his followers had wandered from the British territory and crossed the lines to the Americans, but that upon serious reflection they thought they had acted wrong as they had been always well treated by the Hudson's Bay Company and were now returned penitent, and if permitted by the company they would settle near the Fort, and the smoke of their wigwams should thence forth rise only among the forest of the British; he concluded, by requesting that as they were all Catholics, a priest might be sent to live with them.[15]

Despite this pledge, Espagnol was born in what became American territory and had spent a good deal of time in his birthplace. HBC clerks mentioned he had to be "indulged" because he hunted in American territory.[16] We know that his band regularly tapped maple sugar trees in the Grand Portage and Grand Marais areas, likely returning to his wife's or his mother's sugar bush. He also would sometimes resort to Grand Marais in the fall "to pass fall fishing trout." Occasionally he would dry and cache his catch nearby.[17] He also often overwintered "inland" along the border lakes and sometimes nearby Grand Marais. One time he "hunted during the winter near Fond du Lac."[18]

His home territory was extensive: from the rocky bluffs of Arrow Lake and rice beds of White Fish Lake, along the border lakes westward toward Basswood, south along the shore to Palisade, and northward to the Kaministiquia River and Fort William. He fished in waters virtually everywhere in between. He caught sturgeon in the Pigeon and Kaministiquia Rivers, speared whitefish in Pigeon Bay, and with his family quickly erected "gill nets" to ensnare hundreds of migrating passenger pigeons. He also tracked and hunted caribou, sharing the meat with his family, clan, and then band members, and sometimes brought choice "cuts," such as caribou tongue, to the traders. Espagnol was a good trapper and brought a great deal of furs to be traded. For example, in April 1824, Chapman desperately tried to trade for his "7 bears, 1 moose, 4 Rein Deer, 100 martins and 150 castor [beaver]."[19]

Like other Anishinaabeg leaders, Espagnol sought to understand traders and the few other whites he had met. What was their source of power? Was it akin to the spiritual power of Anishinaabeg? And what was the role of whites' spiritual beliefs, of Christianity, in creating or maintaining that authority and influence? Was Christianity one key to understanding the gichi-mookamaan, or white person?[20] During the summer of 1838, Espagnol traveled as far as Manitoulin Island in Lake Huron to consider and eventually be baptized as a Methodist. Later, on September 30, 1838, he was rebaptized by Catholic Father Pierz in a full church service held in a cedar-bark-clad chapel in Grand Portage. Many other Anishinaabeg in Grand Portage and Fort William had already been converted by Father Pierz that summer, including his stepson Paul "Memaskawas" on August 10, 1838.[21] It is unlikely that Espagnol fully converted to Catholicism. More probable was that the differences between Christian denominations were insignificant to him, and he likely maintained many of his traditional beliefs. He did not, for example, take the next step and become a godparent to other Catholic converts, as many of his band did. His efforts to understand Christianity were likely driven by the fact that he was an ogimaa with the purpose of trying to understand the foreign spiritual power in their midst and discerning whether that understanding might help his band thrive.

As a leader and an acknowledged powerful individual, Espagnol was called upon to do tasks other band members did not. When a windigo threatened the lives and social fabric of the North Shore Anishinaabeg, Espagnol was elected to dispatch him, a very dangerous and disagreeable task. Windigos were grisly creatures that had killed and eaten human flesh. They were thought to be supernaturally strong and cared not who they might kill next. Their hearts were made of ice. Anishinaabeg would most often flee windigos, as they were a horrible threat. Even rumors of windigos nearby put all on edge. Among the few courageous enough to have fought a windigo, some had died. Instead of fleeing, Espagnol made the long trip to Basswood Lake to hunt and kill a windigo couple. As Basswood Lake was on the western edge of his traditional hunting area, he knew the way. Locating only the man, Espagnol killed him.[22] The greatest threat over, his band were relieved.

During Espagnol's childhood, the overall leader of the Grand Portage, Vermilion, and Rainy Lake Bands was Nectam. As a powerful leader, Nectam was recognized as the premier ogimaa of multiple bands. Coming from the Rainy Lake region likely during the midsummer rendezvous at Grand Portage, Nectam would occasionally be on the North Shore. Hence, as a child, Espagnol likely observed him. The Rainy Lake and Vermilion Lake bands were more numerous than those of the North Shore, but many Grand Portage women had married into those bands, and thus they were closely related, making Nectam's overall leadership more possible. And yet it was rare for a leader to rise above his own band and provide accepted leadership to others. But his overarching leadership did not last long. Nectam died when the NWC post was still in Grand Portage, before 1803. His economic alliance with the North Westers undoubtedly bolstered his regional leadership.[23] To honor him, the NWC had his remains erected on a scaffold east of Grand Portage Creek to be near the large fur trade establishment. When the North Westers moved to Kaministiquia River, Nectam's remains were moved to the new location.[24] After Nectam's death, there was an overall leadership vacuum along the North Shore. No single ogimaa led the North Shore Anishinaabeg until Espagnol was recognized almost two decades later. Instead, clan ogimaa, such as the elder Peau de Chat (Skin of the Cat), fulfilled leadership roles.

By the late 1820s, Espagnol was recognized as the principal leader of the North Shore Anishinaabeg.[25] "There is one principal Chief to whom the others in a great measure look up—the only name he goes by, even with the Indians is 'Espagnol.'"[26] Father Pierz recognized him as "the chief" and provided him weekly tobacco to develop rapport. As befitting his standing, Espagnol was generous, sharing the tobacco with his men. British and American surveyors, priests, and especially the AFC and HBC traders recognized him as the primary ogimaa. He had grown from being the leader of an extended family group, a clan-based group, to a leader of other family/clan groups on the North Shore. Father Pierz mentioned that he became a leader "because of his great talent . . . for war and hunt."[27] Members of the band recognized Espagnol through a process of consensus, because of his bravery, experience, and knowledge. It is not likely he became the primary leader through inheritance, as his father may have been a white man; if his father was Anishinaabe, he was never named. Instead, he became the leader through his own merit. In addition to being a good hunter and warrior, he was a skilled orator, generous, and brave—all traditional traits of an Anishinaabe leader.[28]

Espagnol joined the British side during the War of 1812. He would certainly have been encouraged by traders to do so as they assembled a company of men to fight along with the Redcoats.[29] Distinguishing himself in warfare would have also been an alluring draw for him and other warriors. And he received medals and gifts from the British recognizing his role and actions.[30] Espagnol may have also received a Union Jack flag, as flags were given to important chiefs. One of his forebears inherited an older British flag—without the cross of St. Patrick, before the Union Jack—which was handed down in the Maymushkowaush family.[31]

Espagnol was a discerning trader and practiced orator, often marshaling whatever he could to tip his advantage. For example, he reminded the HBC clerk that he had other trade options to the south if the price seemed too high:

> The Spaniard with twelve other Indians arrived and was treated in the usual way but on the whole did not appear altogether to his mind, in being disappointed of a small keg of wine which he says Mr. C. T. McIntosh promised to give him and says he were to arrive at the American fort, the table would be garnished with wine, brandy, and shrub. Whereas you have only that poor stuff whiskey to give me.[32]

He frequently "worked" the fur trade competition so that favors were extended to him and his band:

> Michel Collin and two men went off this morning with a supply of provisions and advances for the winter to the Spaniard to the Grand Marais, which is the place he appointed to meet our people.[33]

But just as commonly, Espagnol became hard to find, despite significant efforts of HBC men to locate him "inland" in midwinter. In essence, he kept the HBC guessing where he was and how well he was doing, and sought to preserve his trading options at Fort

William and Grand Marais by being unfindable. And when there was no AFC presence in Grand Marais, on at least two occasions HBC men traveled with gifts and food as far westward as Arrow Lake to find Espagnol and insure his continued relationship with the Fort William traders.[34] The traders sought out information of his whereabouts and often engaged a "guide" or an Indian, who would be rewarded for his efforts to help locate Espagnol.[35] When traders found his winter camp, he had fewer stratagems to make the best trade, and the traders would have fewer gifts for him and his band.

If possible, he often waited until late in spring to trade his furs, thus giving him an advantage of knowing what the values of pelts were at each trading post and adding anticipation to how many furs he and his band might bring in. The trader was more likely to be anxious to bolster his trading results. Another technique he employed was to split the family's winter furs among different companies. His stepsons traded with the Americans at Gichi Bitobig, but his larger packet of furs he took to Fort William. This pattern was noted by an HBC trader at Lac La Pluie: "the Spaniard was always honest at least. At least I found him so while I was at Fort William. But his Young trade one Year with [unintelligible] who came in the spring along the south side of the Lake from the Sault to Roche de Bout."[36] Just as the traders had their methods, so did Espagnol and his kinsmen. They and their predecessors were shrewd traders, exchanging items for at least a century. By watching and learning, he obtained the best bargain possible.

Although Espagnol encouraged his stepson to trade with Chapman, he himself severely limited his trade with the AFC. Espagnol, and most mature men, continued to trade with the Fort William HBC. The majority of Chapman's trading partners were younger men, sons of noted hunters. Ten younger men traded and took credits from Chapman, while only three mature men did.[37] Did Espagnol have a hand in this strategy, or were the young men experimenting and parting from the norm? Whatever the reason, it permitted

Espagnol and other noted hunters to maintain their relationships with the HBC, while slightly encouraging the AFC to remain in their midst. Splitting the returns kept both companies in play.

But trading for him was more than an economic transaction. As the recognized leader of the North Shore Anishinaabeg, trading had larger consequences for Espagnol than for the Grand Coquin. Trading furs was also an act of creating alliances and cementing strong relationships with the HBC and AFC and their respective leaders. With a strong relationship he was able to push trade more favorably and sometimes push their alliance. He would, for example, sometimes assist the HBC traders, as when two arrived at his camp "so much emaciated" that they were immediately fed and assisted with the best route back to Fort William, going to Lake Superior and then using Espagnol's canoe to return. Other times he would gift or provide sturgeon to the HBC men or provide them with valuable reconnaissance, such as assistance with the start-up of the AFC fishing operation at Isle Royale in 1837. On occasion he would also assist traders such as Chapman by relieving them of their customary obligation to feed Anishinaabeg such as Grand Coquin and the band. In one instance, Espagnol, "who has had mercy enough," reprieved Chapman by leading Grand Coquin away.[38]

Having a well-recognized (and carefully managed) alliance with the HBC meant greater gifts, recognition of Espagnol as a leader worth listening to, including at meetings with HBC dignitaries passing through, and the ability to shape interactions with newcomers to the area. What some traders thought was merely an economic relationship was much more nuanced and prone to relationship making than some Europeans recognized. Thus, HBC factor John McLoughlin could cursorily state to his counterpart at Fort William, "I do not think he will be worth the trouble and Expense of Keeping [as a trading partner]."[39] But for John Haldane, Espagnol was the central player in the decision by the Anishinaabeg to remain allied with the British or the Yankees, or to move to another location. Or as a young HBC clerk remarked, "This is certainly an expensive band of Indians to the company, but they hunt on American territory and require indulgence."[40]

North Shore Anishinaabeg

Each Anishinaabeg band's means of sustenance was finely tuned to the specific resources in their area, particularly reliable concentrations of edible resources. Thus, some bands relied heavily on wild rice, others on big game, and some on squash and corn. Even more so than many of their kinsmen, North Shore Anishinaabeg were "fish people." Fish were their most reliable and nourishing food. And the Anishinaabeg used a variety of ingenious methods to catch fish, including using gill nets, setting weirs in streams, spearing through ice, using hooks and line from canoes and off the edge of ice on Lake Superior, and seining in the Kaministiquia River. They caught fish of all kinds: sturgeon in the Kaministiquia and Pigeon Rivers; suckers in streams in the springtime; river-running whitefish in the "Kam" River in the spring; lake trout by "flambeauing," or spearing by firelight, in Washwaunongong Bay; and "jack fish," or northern pike, through the ice on White Fish Lake and other inland lakes.[41] Loche, or burbot, were speared through the ice on Thunder Bay in the depth of winter.[42] Gill nets were commonly used on Lake Superior to catch lake trout, whitefish, and some herring. Anishinaabeg technology permitted the catching of siscowet trout, or what we call "fat trout" today, in relatively deep waters.[43] Siscowets were a welcome supplement to an Anishinaabeg low-fat diet. And siscowet oil could be used in an amazing number of ways—as a lotion, as grease in canoe gum, for making leather pliable, and as a medium for medicines.[44]

Fish could be caught in almost every month, in open water or under the ice. But the spring and fall spawning "runs" were most important as then fish could be caught in the greatest quantities. Fish were frozen and smoked to preserved them for the long and often hungry winter months.[45] To dry fish, they were hung on wooden racks over a small (and thus relatively cool), smoky fire. Much of the fishing and all of the preserving of fish was done by Anishinaabeg women.[46] When the ice was thick enough, men would use spears and lines at Thunder Bay, Pigeon Bay, Gichi Bitobig, and wherever sheltered waters had sufficient ice, even at small locations such as Good Harbor Bay west of Grand Marais.[47] Spearing was typically done by men and could produce modest numbers of fish, but they were fresh food at a critical time.

North Shore Anishinaabeg harvested wild rice, or "wild oats" in some traders' terminology, but they had access to few first-rate wild rice lakes compared with their kinsmen to the south and west. The country immediately west (in the Lake Superior basin) had few wild rice lakes. White Fish Lake was the most important wild rice lake in the area. Evidence of the relatively low production of wild rice is the fact that little rice was traded as country produce to the HBC at Fort William. In contrast, wild rice was a common trade item at Rainy Lake. One ogimaa, Little Rat, from nearby Lac des Mille Lacs, even led his band more than 140 miles (one way) to Rainy Lake to harvest rice, returning in the first part of October.[48]

Wild rice was not mentioned by Chapman or Johnston. Both arrived after the harvest would have been concluded, and they do not mention trading for it nor Anishinaabeg using it. We cannot discern if the 1824 wild rice failure at Rainy Lake due to fall "flooding" also occurred on the North Shore,[49] nor can we confidently assume that the "good" wild rice harvests of fall 1823 at Rainy Lake extended to the North Shore, as wild rice conditions are especially localized.[50]

Contrary to some assumptions, North Shore Anishinaabeg did not hunt a great deal of big game at this time. There was little big game to be had other than the widely dispersed woodland caribou, or what the traders called "rein deer." Moose and white-tailed deer were virtually unknown in this region. Traders were not impressed by the overall fertility of the rocky North Shore:

It may not be improper to observe here that the tract of country which extends to the westward of this Establishment [from Ft. William] in the direction of Fond du Lac is very poor in large animals & rabbits, beaver and all other fur bearing animals, excepting Martins are not numerous but the natives cannot attend to the trapping of the latter during the three severe months that the Winter generally last, because it is impossible for them to find the means of subsistence in that inhospitable region during the above said period; hence it is only in Fall & Spring when they can get fish in the Inland Lakes to support them that they can attend to the Martin hunt.[51]

With big game regionally depleted in this rocky and not biologically fecund area, North Shore Anishinaabeg hunted the few caribou and bears. One consequence of having fewer big game animals was a lack of leather for the Anishinaabeg to use for clothing. Instead, parchment and factory-dressed leather were traded and used by the Anishinaabeg to make snowshoe webbing and moccasins.[52] In fur-rich areas, big game often became depleted first, making food harvesting during the trapping of furbearers a stressful time. With little access to moose and deer, Anishinaabeg turned to other types of meat, including beaver trapped for furs. HBC clerks began to note that each man had his own trapping and hunting grounds, useful information for traders to know when traveling to hunting and trapping grounds to trade.[53]

That the Anishinaabeg relied on traders' cloth, rather than dressed skins, to make clothing is particularly borne out by Chapman's journal, which records that half of the trade was in clothing, ribbon, stroud (wool), and thread. This trade follows a fur trade pattern of fabric and particularly woolens (blankets, capots or jackets, leggings) being the most commonly traded commodities. Common cloth commodities were molton (cotton) and stroud. Hardware such as knives, axes, fishing spears, and files were also commonly

B. F. Childs, "Chippewa Lodges, Beaver Bay," circa 1870, part of his *Gems of Lake Superior Scenery* series. Note the cooking tripod between the two birch-bark lodges, called *wanagekogamig* in Anishinabegmowin. Courtesy of the New York Public Library.

traded. Surprisingly, there is no record of area Anishinaabeg trading with Chapman for a gun.

North Shore Anishinaabeg moved frequently in a year, most often to take advantage of concentrations of food but also to trap furs. One NWC trader in Nipigon country described some of this seasonal movement:

> Indians seldom remain above five days at the same place hunting all they can find in the vicinity, and then move on in search of more game.... They seldom move more than three leagues [nine miles] at a time, on account of the children.... They dry all their meat and, sometimes, their fish, both to preserve it and to make it lighter of transport, as they have a great number of portages to carry across. The man carries his canoe, his gun and his medicine bag, the women and children must carry all the rest of their lumber, which consists of kettles, axes, bales of dried meat, a drum or two ... bag wherein they have their knives, files, the bones and scrapes to dress their skins and leather, powder, shot and ball,

tobacco, some cloth, their furs (if not hid somewhere) and their birch rind covering.[54]

A North Shore Anishinaabeg family moved from their inland winter trapping grounds to their traditional sugar bush in March. There were often other families maple sugaring nearby and doing the never-ending work of harvesting enough firewood to keep the sap kettles simmering. After boiling up the sap into maple cakes or caked sugar, they moved alongside major streams and rivers in the spring for runs of spawning fish. Sturgeon and whitefish would be running up the Kaministiquia by mid-June, providing a much appreciated surplus of food. By July the river whitefish had "disappeared." Also in June, they peeled, or "raised," birch bark for myriad purposes (canoe building and repair and making containers, or mukuks, and winnowing trays for wild rice).[55] The return of waterbirds to hunt—geese in particular—was most welcome and a harbinger of spring. In midsummer through August, families traveled to harvest berry crops in recently burned over areas.[56]

By late August or early September, North Shore Anishinaabeg had trekked to the wild rice lakes—Whitefish, Gunflint, Rose, Northern Light, and South Fowl—to harvest, dry, and winnow wild rice. Also, caribou rutting season began in late August, making them more vulnerable to hunting. The Anishinaabeg would then return to Gichi Gami to their traditional locations for the fall fish runs of trout and whitefish in particular. Their location along the lakeshore was critical for their success. They sought out places close to reefs where some trout would spawn early, and then would perhaps move again to locations yielding later-spawning trout and whitefish. For example, in early October large trout would begin to spawn at the craggy Shagoinah Islands off Thunder Cape. A little later, whitefish would also spawn there.[57] In less than two weeks their spawning run was done. Fishing in more open water prone to rougher seas endangered both one's life and gear, but the risk was offset by the bounteous concentrations of fish available to gill net, especially large trout and whitefish.

In late fall, after freeze-up, the North Shore Anishinaabeg took their fall debts and "necessities" from traders and returned inland to hunt and trap and fish through the ice, for pike on White Fish Lake, for example. Sometimes the men left their families to travel to a distant trapping area. Women provided small game for their families, particularly by snaring rabbits not far from their camps. When food stores were low in the depth of winter, jack fish, or northern pike, were caught with hook and line through inland lake ice. And if the wind was calm (and thus the exposure tolerable), they might try spearing or netting the suckers that were abundant near the Welcome Islands in Thunder Bay in mid-January.[58] When it was extremely cold, trappers and their families would hunker down in their shelters to stay warm. Once or twice during the winter, an adult family member, often a woman, snowshoed to Fort William or to the AFC posts to trade and pick up additional supplies. They most frequently returned immediately, if conditions permitted.[59]

It is tricky to gauge the population of North Shore Anishinaabeg at this time. One problem is fluid tribal boundaries; for example, does one include smaller "bands" such as at Lac des Mille Lacs and Saganaga Lake? Further, there was much movement to distant trapping opportunities to the west and shorter migrations—as made by Grand Coquin and family—along the border route. Nonetheless, one 1805 count observed there were 332 Anishinaabeg in the area (including those living along the Kaministiquia River, Lac des Mille Lacs, and Dog Lake). The 332 Anishinaabeg were made up of 70 men, 84 women, and 178 children.[60] Johnston's conservative census in 1825 stated there were only 61 total at Grand Portage.[61] But Grand Portage was not a major residential area at this time. These are some of the highest and lowest population estimates. Perhaps more important to note is that the population of Anishinaabeg immediately to the west, what scholars call the Boundary Water Anishinaabeg, tripled between 1821 and 1871.[62] It is likely that some growth in the North Shore Anishinaabeg population occurred during this time.

For the Anishinaabeg, Lake Superior was the major transportation route, it being easier to travel than across the rocky terrain. Movement was up and down the shore and occasionally across to Minong (Isle Royale). Traveling on Gichi Gami sometimes required skill and nerve. For example, on a harrowing journey from Grand Portage to Thunder Bay in 1838, Father Pierz described the canoe plunging down and laboring up and over waves so large they reminded him of the steep roofs of his home.[63]

What we today call the border route was also a major aboriginal trail. This heavily used travel corridor intersects with the Lake Superior route, pinpointing the center of the traditional territory of the Anishinaabeg. This core area included the bifurcation of the border route into the northern route along the Kaministiquia River and Lac des Mille Lacs and the southern route to and from Grand Portage along today's international boundary. Rivers were an extremely important part of their traditional area because of the availability of fish and their use of them as travel routes in summer and winter (if the ice was trustworthy). The borders of their traditional use area were fuzzy and not strongly asserted. For example, Fond du Lac Anishinaabeg would sometimes hunt northward up to Encampment Island on the North Shore, an area typically recognized as used by Anishinaabeg living to the north.[64] The border to the west, along the border route, was also quite fluid, and Anishinaabeg living along the route were more or less associated with kinsmen to the east (North Shore), west (Basswood and Rainy Lake), and south to Vermilion Lake (by Ely).

Gichi Bitobig was off center of this core area. The difficulty of cross-country travel from Gichi Bitobig to the interior caused one veteran trader to remark:

> the Americans are at the latter place [Grand Marais] and it is forty miles south of the Grand Portage—the Country they are to pass

is very thick wooded and Mountainous and so difficult to travel through that I never Knew an Indian coming from the South of the Grand Portage in the Winter unless the lake took and it did not take [freeze] this year.[65]

In hindsight, Gichi Bitobig's location on only one traditional travel corridor, Lake Superior, and not in the core use area of the local Anishinaabeg made it a less than ideal choice for an AFC post.

Chapman did not make any reference to maple sugaring, and Johnston made only one reference to Maangozid and family going to the sugar bush. Does this mean there was little to no sugaring done in the sugar maple "belt" above Gichi Bitobig? Both traders were on the North Shore during sugar maple sap runs. Maple sugaring was keenly noted in the Fort William journals, and occasionally some of the traditional areas were identified. One clerk observed: "the greater party of the Indians have left there [White Fish Lake] and gone as usual to pass the Spring near the old Grand Portage." And another clerk wrote: "Spaniard and band were going to make maple sugar toward Grand Marais."[66] Fort William was at the northernmost range of sugar maples, and the sugar made from the sap was provided to posts out of maple sugar range.

Why weren't the AFC traders—or their women—making maple sugar? Was it was deemed women's work and thus escaped any mention by the AFC clerks? Or did the traders' women—not from the area—respect the rights of the "owners" of each sugar bush and thus did not sugar? More likely, though there is no evidence whatsoever, the Anishinaabe or Métis women along with the traders did make maple sugar, but it escaped documentation, like so much of what they did. Given the fact that both Chapman and Johnston were hungry and Johnston later ate a great number of leeks to survive, they likely did make maple sugar, particularly since the most frequently noted women's activity at Fort William was making it. And it was so important to the Fort William diet that even men assisted in cutting wood for boiling sap. In the spring of 1833, the "women of the fort" made over a thousand pounds of maple sugar, likely boiled down to its crystallized form.[67]

The role of North Shore Anishinaabeg women was not spelled out in early historical documents with their decidedly male bias (reliant on male authors). Yet what women did and contributed was essential to living in an Anishinaabeg camp, at the AFC post at Grand Marais, and even at the larger, entrenched Fort William. Women set up camp, hauled camp goods to the next location, made snowshoes, and sewed and gummed canoes. Even when traveling in the winter months, women put up all the lodges and cut all the necessary firewood.[68] At the posts they repaired canoes with watap, or split spruce root, and produced the sap, grease, and charcoal that made the gum to make canoes watertight.[69] They mended and set gill nets and built the fish weirs used in small streams.[70] When food was scarce in winter, women snared rabbits, the last reliable food. Snowshoe hare were of such importance that snaring them was one of the few women's activities noted at Fort William: "Their only means of supporting life consists in catching Rabbits, which they snare with great dexterity and in fish."[71] Grouse were also a precious but lesser winter food source. Women and men both snared marten. Women made moccasins and the webbing on snowshoes with tanned leather.[72] To preserve fish, women smoked them on racks to dry and froze them whole, or if salt was available—as it was at Fort William—stored the fish in salt brine in barrels.[73] They were the primary harvesters of plants—berries, wild rice, and maple sugar.[74] Women quite often traded furs and "country produce" with the HBC clerks at Fort William. For example, Peau de Chat's wife and daughter brought eighty-three pounds of gum harvested at Grand Portage for trade.[75] They might also bring in significant qualities of canoe birch bark—the best-quality bark—to trade to pay down their debts.[76]

Grand Coquin

Grand Coquin, or Great Rogue in English, was not from the North
Shore. He and his extended family came from Rainy Lake country.
He, then, was hunting and trapping in an area used by other Anishinaabeg. Some hunting territories were recognized as belonging to a
man, such as those of La Bete and Le View, and thus Grand Coquin
would have to receive "consent" to hunt or trap in these individual
territories.[77] He would have sought permission from another Anishinaabeg, or perhaps even Aysh-pay-ahng, to fish along the North
Shore. It was also quite possible that Grand Coquin's request went
through his older brother, Peau de Chat. He then would address the
appropriate person. Rarely did anyone object to trapping or hunting
on his territory, especially if asked appropriately.

Despite, or perhaps because, Grand Coquin was from another,
but related, band, he was the Anishinaabe who most frequented the
Grand Marais post. Learning much more about Grand Coquin is
difficult, because *Coquin*, or "Rogue," was a generic and disparaging
term used by traders for Indians who were acting in an unexpect-
ed way, such as driving a hard trading bargain or relying on traders'
food stores more than the traders liked. For example, one HBC district report for Lac La Pluie identified three Indians as "Coquin,"
but only one was labeled "Grand Coquin." As one clerk pronounced
when searching for "an Indian of the name Grand Coquin, he is not
only so by name, but by nature."[78] Fortunately, there was only one
"Grand Coquin" in the region, the area that runs from Rainy Lake
to the North Shore.[79] His Anishinaabemowin name was Waw Waish
e Kabow, translated by one clerk to mean "Handsome Figure."[80] He
also appears to have been particularly knowledgeable about Rainy
Lake geography and spent much of his adult life there.[81] Rainy Lake
fur traders identified him as being of the Lynx clan.[82]

The Rainy Lake–Grand Marais Grand Coquin was the younger
brother of Peau de Chat (the elder), or brother of "Skin of the Cat."[83]

Peau de Chat was a member and leader of the Fish clan.[84] Thus, Grand Coquin was related to a prominent Anishinaabe ogimaa living along northwestern Lake Superior.[85] In Anishinaabeg culture full brothers would be of the same clan, the clan of their father. That Peau de Chat and Grand Coquin appear to have been brothers but of different clans suggests they had different fathers but the same mother. Or, alternately, perhaps the clerk at Rainy Lake who noted their clan membership had one or both of their clan identities wrong.

Grand Coquin knew the border route, as he had been employed as the guide that led a party from Lac La Pluie to Fort William in 1820.[86] This meant he could find his way through dozens of lakes and portages by memory of past experiences, instruction, signs along the way, and his ability to read the landscape for clues, such as portage locations. His mobility along the border made it more plausible that he might "try out" another location such as Gichi Bitobig.

Grand Coquin stayed on the North Shore for only thirty-one months or perhaps less. By April 1, 1825, he was back trapping in the Lac La Pluie post area, where he then resettled.[87] His likely strategy was to "try out" each company. He tried them all, first the HBC and then the NWC—both at Rainy Lake—then the HBC again, then the AFC at Grand Marais, and the HBC again at Rainy Lake.[88] He was aiming to gain competitive trading advantage by trying out new clerks and hopefully obtaining new prices. Perhaps, too, his prior debts at a post might be scrubbed clean in an effort to win him back. His search for a competitive edge with traders compelled them to note that he was "a staunch friend to the Americans" and "this Indian was for the Americans last year and have proved unfaithful to them, he this Fall could not get his wants from them, so it is most likely they the Yankees will have a look for him as he is on their Territory."[89] His goal to find better trading terms wherever he could led one trader to remark that he and others were "so spoilt that they think themselves entitled to get advances a matter of right and that they pay merely because they are willing so to do."[90] Or perhaps Grand

Coquin sought to advance his reputation and thus gain prestige, resulting in traders providing more gifts:

> Grand Coquin & sons with one of the Crapeaus arrived. They
> brought amongst them all 460 Rats, 2 otters, 2 beaver, 1 bear, and
> two martins. Being as good as a spring hunt as they generally
> make. The first part of the winter these Indians really did noth-
> ing. And to encourage him for the future the Grand Coquin got
> a Chiefs clothing—with a keg of drink which was certainly more
> than he expected.[91]

Despite the challenge in "dealing with Grand Coquin," there was still money to be made by the fur companies. But more fundamentally, both sides needed one another for food. And Grand Coquin was a good hunter. One winter when moose were hard to find, he killed two. When he had moose meat, he shared some with the Lac La Pluie HBC men. But when trapping (and not hunting), he and his family were vulnerable to starvation. Much as the HBC men were dependent on some food provided by Indians, so too were the Anishinaabeg trappers and their families dependent on traders' food. "The Grand Coquin & family arrived—they must have starved hard for they are reduced to skin & Bones. . . . They brought 8 lynxes. I gave them a load of potatoes, some corn & pounded sturgeon. These starving families will ruin us."[92] Five weeks later, the Rainy Lake clerk commented, "The Grand Coquin's son came for more Provisions. Luckily we have wheat, other ways the Indians or we would starve to death. There is no doubt there were Indians along the river who are [not] dead are now."[93]

Chapman's trading entries noted that local Anishinaabeg (La Bete's son, Espagnol's stepson, and Espagnol) took debts for fishing-related supplies, but Grand Coquin did not. Yet Grand Coquin and family ate a great deal of fish caught by traders—140 by Chapman's count in mid-November. Both clerks became fed up with Grand Coquin, prompting the sarcastic outburst from John-ston, "No danger of his leaving this when the others started."[94] Grand Coquin would rely upon the customary provisions from the Grand Marais traders as long as this "method" worked. Willing to push the limits and experiment, Grand Coquin was the first to trade and take debts from Chapman.

Chapman's and Johnston's journals record Indians "starving" a number of times.[95] While at Saganaga Lake, surveyor David Thomp-son recorded "all in a starving state."[96] Tough winters, no access to fish, and little to no big game made for hungry times. For Anishi-naabeg, "starving" could mean they were literally on the brink of col-lapsing, but it could also have a metaphorical meaning.[97] Johnston's statement "as is customary in this quarter, all starving is the com-plaint" suggests an additional meaning. It was customary for Anishi-naabeg to say to their hosts that they were, indeed, hungry and they would appreciate their hosts' hospitality.[98] Or as one Lac La Pluie trader observed, "nothing pleases an Indian more than in giving him something to eat immediately on his arrival. It is the grand Etiquette of Politeness amongst themselves."[99] Only a few years later, School-craft provided an account of how a statement of starving might also include a customary component:

> Mongosite (the Loon's Foot), a noted speaker, and Jossakeed, or Seer of Fond du Lac, arrived in the afternoon, attended by eleven persons. He had scarcely exchanged salutations with me when he said that his followers and himself were in a starving condition, having had very little food for several days.[100]

Additionally, Anishinaabeg might report to Chapman and John-ston that they were starving to explain why they trapped so few furs. Essentially, they were diverted from trapping to find and procure food.

Maangozid, or Loon's Foot

An aspiring but young leader at Fond du Lac, Maangozid, or Loon's Foot, also decided to try out a new trapping area, perhaps because, like Grand Coquin, he had clan relations or some connections to North Shore band members that made such a venture more welcoming. For whatever reasons, the thirty-seven-year-old Maangozid and his family canoed to Grand Marais to trap furs for the AFC operation.[101] He was already deeply familiar with the AFC, having resided at Fond du Lac much of his adult life. He had married the daughter of Zhingob, a Fond du Lac ogimaa. But Loon's Foot, the younger son of noted Anishinaabe ogimaa Katawadidai, or Broken Tooth, grew up at Sandy Lake, Minnesota. His father was the principal leader at Sandy Lake until 1832, even while Loon's Foot was on the North Shore.[102] Loon's Foot inherited one of his father's medals and received two of his own, medals being a sign of prestige and recognition. It was rare for an Anishinaabe man from Sandy Lake to move to the North Shore. And it was also unusual for a Fond du Lac band member to do so. The ties (marriage, travel, and even clan makeup) between these bands and North Shore Anishinaabeg were comparatively weak. Instead North Shore Anishinaabeg had many clan relations with Anishinaabeg living westward along the border route and would frequently travel there and intermarry with them. Loon's Foot was related by marriage to prominent fur traders, as one of his sisters was married to Captain Charles Ermatinger, and another to Samuel Ashmun. A third sister was married to Shebagizi (Hole in the Day), a great Anishinaabe leader.[103]

Maangozid became a prominent leader of the Fond du Lac Band after his time in Gichi Bitobig. He was a signatory to a span of treaties from the 1820s to 1850s, including the treaties at Prairie du Chien and Fond du Lac, the 1837 treaty, the 1842 Treaty of La Pointe, and the 1854 treaty.[104] Some local Anishinaabeg feared he was too ready

After his trapping and trading efforts with the American Fur Company at Grand Marais, Maangozid, or Loon's Foot, became an important leader of the Fond du Lac Band. Courtesy of the Kathryn A. Martin Library Archives and Special Collections, University of Minnesota Duluth.

to cede lands to the United States.[105] As a gifted speaker and politician, he "displayed considerable skill in parlaying his pro-American stance into a position of leadership acknowledged by both Americans and Ojibwas." However, his rival Nindindibens, son of the old chief, became the principal leader of the Fond du Lac people.[106]

Like a number of Anishinaabeg leaders, Maangozid was deemed a religiously powerful individual, being both a practitioner of Midewiwin and also a "Jossakeed," or "seer."[107] His clan, the Loon dodem, were keepers of a copper plate and thus strongly connected to the powers of copper as part of traditional Anishinaabeg religion. In the Presbyterian minister's words, Maangozid was a "pagan."[108] After investigating Christianity with the Reverend Edmund Ely and briefly converting (like Espagnol), he would within a year reject it and return to the traditional religion. That Maangozid might seek out a "synthesis" of religious beliefs was beyond the zealous Reverend Ely's comprehension.[109]

Maangozid's relationship with the AFC varied. At one point he was nearly an employee, and at another he was an energetic, independent trapper. His trapping effort did not go well initially as he did not know the territory. However, a few days later, his son brought in a beaver. At one point he brought in nineteen marten to trade.[110] But on at least two occasions, Maangozid accompanied George Bonga in an attempt to locate Anishinaabeg camps in the interior.[111] Both from Fond du Lac, Bonga and Maangozid knew each other prior to this time and may have preferred to "team up" their efforts. Maangozid and his family remained in the area long enough to make maple sugar but do not appear in the Grand Portage spring census conducted by Johnston. We do not know when Maangozid returned to Fond du Lac.

Anishinaabeg Clans

Invisible to many non-Natives and understood by fewer yet, clans, or dodems, were an organizing principle for the North Shore

Anishinaabeg. Some traders, for example, knew about clans but did not fully understand them. In their simplest role, clans defined who Anishinaabeg could and couldn't marry (they had to marry outside of their clan). And most typically the woman went to live with her husband's family.[112] Clan membership descended through the male line, so Grand Coquin's children would be of the Lynx clan, and Peau de Chat's children of the Fish clan. Dominant clans at Grand Portage were the Fish (including Bullhead and Catfish subclans), Crane, Caribou, Moose, and Marten.[113] The Bear clan, particularly the Kadonce family, lived outside of Grand Marais, and other clan members lived at Beaver Bay.[114] Multiple clans inhabited a village. But certain clans were more numerous in different areas. For example, some clans were particularly common among the northern Anishinaabeg residing in Canada but were comparatively rare among their southern kinsmen in the United States. Caribou clan members were common on the border lakes to the west, but they were joined by Fish clan members, who commonly canoed out to Minong (Isle Royale).[115] Clan members extended hospitality to traveling fellow clan members, as they were related to them:

> All those who are of the same mark or totem consider themselves as relations, even if they or their forefathers never had any connexion with each other, or had seen one another before. When two strangers meet and find themselves to be of the same mark, they immediately begin to trace their genealogy, as which they even beat my countrymen, the Highlanders, and the one becomes the cousin, the uncle or the grand father of the other, although the grand father may often be the youngest of the two.[116]

For the Anishinaabeg, clan membership created "obligations" and thus a social net. Clan members were obligated to help out other clan members, to provide food, or to help with a sick child. They shared food, such as the wild rice harvest, with clan members in particular.[117] Clans were essentially extended family groups in their territory but with connections and obligations to clan members who lived elsewhere. On the North Shore, during the period of AFC at Gichi Bitobig, clans were a de facto economic group. They also were the base for leaders, usually men who were effective leaders and good speakers. Clan leaders often strategized about where to move next, what resources to seek, and how to minimize the uncertainty of food gathering. Clans functioned in a number of ways. They structured social relationships, they were often defined economic groups—the family members who might trap together—and they served a limited political function in dealing with outsiders, such as fur traders and other village leaders.

If Espagnol's father was European, his clan would have been one of a non-Anishinaabe parent, perhaps Eagle. It appears that May-mushkowaush, his stepson, was a Crane clan member. If Maymush-kowaush had been Espagnol's son, he would have been of a same clan. Espagnol likely began as a clan leader, then graduated to being the overall ogimaa of the North Shore Anishinaabeg.[118] Ironically, two other Anishinaabeg who figure prominently in the journals— Grand Coquin and Maangozid—were members of uncommon or minor clans on the North Shore (Maangozid was Loon clan, and Grand Coquin was Lynx clan). They were not yet recognized as leaders in their tribes. They most likely were "trying out" new locations and new clerks to see if they liked the country, to gain additional experience and knowledge, and to prove to traders they could and would go elsewhere. They were also trying out new opportunities on a lesser-used section of the North Shore Anishinaabeg's traditional use area.[119] If Grand Coquin and Maangozid were compelling speakers, assisted other leaders, or were adept politically, they could create important alliances between themselves and other ogimaag, such as Espagnol, while they were on the North Shore. Their experiences on the North Shore would eventually give them a wider perspective to draw upon when they returned home.

4

"Fort Misery"

Much of Chapman and Johnston's writing was focused on their dim hopes to escape failure. There was a sense of falling into an abyss, even in their chosen names for the place: Siberia, Fort Misery, or just Misery. Johnston, as usual, was the more dramatic of the two:

> We started early this morning & mounted our snow shoes. We walked all day and at last lost the road owing to the severe fall of snow on the mountains. We consequently could not find the Old Villain. Returned the ensuing day and reached the Lake. The waves were running mountains high, we were obliged to leave our canoe & started on foot along shore. I was glad enough to reach this on the 17th I have only to Remark that it's the Devil's own country, as Cats and dogs would be hardly able to extricate themselves out of it.[1]

And during the customary time to celebrate New Year and be optimistic about the years to come, he added:

> May we all be able to see many of them, in health & happiness is my sincere wish, as also good returns from every quarter, to cover the losses of this place, for I can see no prospect of making any thing here whatever. Never was I more lonesome in any place,

or had a more earnest wish of doing something to the benefit of those by whom I am employed.[2]

Chapman, too, bewailed his predicament:

I have seen hard times since my last epistle, we have had a very refreshing shower of rain from the north east which lasted three days beginning on the 3rd last and ending on the 5th every thing has been wet through + through but as bad luck will have it I have no Peltry to get wet. My buildings are worse than any hog pens, I am entirely cast down to see my returns, we are now arrived at spring and nothing done, to say we live would be false only stay and hardly that since March began we have taken no fish until this day the boys have speared a dozen small trout, times are dubious.[3]

A "lonesome" and worried Chapman turned to trapping. He largely failed: "I am every day at hunt but kill nothing. I have made 2 rows of traps but trap nothing."[4] Johnston in a letter to his brother-in-law Henry Schoolcraft characterized his time on the North Shore: "I wintered [in] one of the worst and most horrible country I ever saw without exception. I lived poorly all winter and this spring more so, living on leeks for a whole month"[5]

Both clerks lamented the forlorn effect of the ever-present wind. Chapman was repeatedly windbound, while Johnston's goods were soaked by waves caused by high winds. Winds and deep cold occasionally prevented the men from traveling to inland Anishinaabeg camps for trade. And during the depths of winter, winds kept firm ice from forming in the Grand Marais harbor, thus preventing the AFC men from harvesting fish. Without firm ice, their spears could not be used nor could hooks and line be dropped off the edge to lure fish to bite. Further, without firm shore ice, their travel up and down the lakeshore was impeded. Their ever-constant and largely maddening companion wind become a metaphor or an abbreviation for a suite of forces that handcuffed their success.

Given the troubles Chapman and Johnston and men experienced, the vexing question remains: why was the AFC determined to have a post on the North Shore during this time? We know, for example, that their fur profits were very meager and likely a loss. Surely the difficulty of feeding men at Grand Marais became clear, especially without access to fish in the late winter and early spring months. Both men struggled mightily to establish a post and left feeling a failure. Why would first William Morrison, then William Aitken, and perhaps Ramsay Crooks continue to pursue such a dismal prospect and send Johnston back up the shore the next year and then his successors? A few years later, according to an HBC clerk, the AFC had not made many inroads: "there are twelve [Anishinaabeg] men, eleven women and twenty one children on American Territories and frequent their establishment at the Grand Marais. None of whom are good hunters with the exception of the Spaniard and Stepson and an Indian called the Bete."[6] But for a number of successive years, there was a small AFC wintertime establishment on the North Shore, either at Grand Marais or Grand Portage.

Why did the AFC persevere? AFC traders likely had a handful of reasons to continue to make a go of it. One reason was simply to block the HBC men from making trading incursions across the border. Perhaps they thought a clerk like Johnston who could speak Anishinaabemowin would have better results. Or perhaps they knew it would be a long-term enterprise and it was OK to take some short-term losses and incur some debts from North Shore Anishinaabeg. But neither Morrison nor Aitken informed Chapman or Johnston that the AFC was there for the long-term and thus the clerks should try to develop greater loyalty among some Indians so they would trade with them. On the other hand, fur trade intelligence continued to confirm that Fort William had been downgraded and was no longer an anchor point for HBC aspirations and economics.[7]

It was no longer even on a main supply route. It was thereby more vulnerable through time to a well-financed and patient challenge.

Or was it that a handful of AFC men had a vendetta against the HBC stemming from Selkirk's clash with their employer at the time, the NWC? Was this vendetta their motivation? Remember that Morrison was briefly taken prisoner when Lord Selkirk—the majority owner of the HBC—took over Fort William from the North Westers. And did Morrison purposely choose the Bongas to accompany Chapman to Grand Marais knowing that their father had been imprisoned at Fort William by Selkirk and the HBC? Ambrose Davenport, too, may have harbored ill will toward the British, as they had imprisoned his father and threatened to hang him during the later years of the War of 1812.[8] Maybe there were scores to settle. And perhaps Astor, too, had a grudge against the British generally, having lost a great deal of money, men, and some would say prestige at Astoria in the War of 1812. And in the long run Astor had lost profits through competition with the HBC and NWC. Astor and his senior managers also knew that expansion, and better yet an economic expansion that was virtually a monopoly, would eventually pay off handsomely. AFC growth, even into marginal areas, might have been worth it to the company's future. Or maybe Astor, in effect, simply enjoyed declaring that he was not intimidated by the HBC establishing the border posts, particularly where the mighty NWC had its summer headquarters (from his perspective, the difference between Grand Portage and Grand Marais was slight). Or the whole operation was seen as so economically insignificant that Astor, Crooks, and Morrison may not have thought much about it at all. They may have simply thought it worth a try to see if the "Old Grand Portage"—where lots of furs had come through a few years before—could regain some of its old glory. Likely all of these reasons—some economically blind, others economically astute, and others personal—played a role in the AFC's decisions.

Or perhaps Chapman and Johnston's bosses hoped that they might find some niche or the promise of one that would make their experiment worthwhile. For example, dozens of canoes were made at Grand Portage and then Rainy Lake for the NWC and then supplied to other posts. At the time of the HBC-NWC merger, Fort William canoe makers were "to get ready" fifty canoes.[9] And Fort William regularly supplied some agricultural produce, such as butter, to other posts. Could Grand Marais furnish some commodity of use, beyond furs, for the AFC? A few years later, the AFC did profit from having persevered at Gichi Bitobig and posts along the border. In 1833, trader Aitken signed an agreement with the HBC governor for the AFC to cease trading in the border region in exchange for the HBC paying the AFC three hundred pounds sterling annually. The agreement lasted for fourteen years, thereby cutting off North Shore and Rainy Lake Anishinaabeg from access to a competing fur trade company.[10] It was good money for doing nothing except posing a previous threat.

Chapman's New Year's salutation to his bosses was ironic. Chapman wrote, "may peace happiness and prosperity attend you throughout the same and all your lives may you reap the fruits of your labours in a continuous harvest in all season and lay up a goodly store." And he woefully concluded, "I am all alone," as his men were off trading.[11] Chapman would not experience any of these good wishes in Grand Marais, no fruits to his labors, no continuous harvest, no peace. Indeed, the stress of his situation led to two outbursts in his journal, one a diatribe about Boucher and half-breeds, and the other a raw description of his predicament. Both clerks were desperate to succeed but did not. This was Johnston's second failure in Minnesota but Chapman's first. But neither were posted in opportune circumstances nor assisted during their isolation for much of the year.

Fur trader society was, in effect, a very small "world." When Johnston and Chapman resided in Sault Ste. Marie, they would regularly cross paths. Sometimes this small world would lead to strained events. Chapman would go on to narrowly defeat James Schoolcraft (younger brother to Henry, who married Anna Maria Johnston, who was George Johnston's younger sister) for a seat in the territorial legislature. This two-vote loss fueled the impulsive James Schoolcraft's grudge against Chapman.[12] Another example of the families intermixing is that Ambrose Davenport's wife (not likely with him when he was in Grand Marais) and Johnston were first cousins and in-laws. Their grandfather was the celebrated Anishinaabe ogimaa Waubojeeg. And apparently Chapman and Davenport both admired Andrew Jackson, as both named sons after the president.[13] We can only guess why they did so. Was it because Jackson was a frontiersman, a non-elite, or because he extended votes to all white men? Ironically both men married women of mixed descent. How does this jibe with Jackson presiding over the 1830 Indian Removal, in which so many Choctaw, Cherokee, and Creek Indians died?

From the vantage point of today, it is surprising that the first sustained American enterprise at Grand Marais was corporate based and managed as part of an aggressive international business. Moreover Gichi Bitobig, or "Fort Misery" in Chapman's words, was both a solitary fort for the Americans and economic misery. For the first Americans, it was a demanding place. For the few Anishinaabeg who traded there, it was a short-lived economic opportunity, part of a succession of fur traders with whom they exchanged furs for valuable and time-saving material culture. Through the years after the AFC era, the same hardscrabble country surrounding Grand Marais ultimately protected it from rampant transformations, such as through a boom in settlement or a grid of roads.

But the AFC was not a benevolent business. Astor raked in profits while many of his employees made a trifling wage. Clerks braved hardships. Some of the routine fur trade actions were quite cynical. For example, alcohol was provided to Anishinaabeg to create a further demand for its availability and use, thus creating incentives to trap a greater number of valuable furs. And the HBC plan to trap the border country hard just to "hurt" their competition essentially produced a scorched-earth policy toward furbearers.

While neither clerk left journals with much ethnographic detail, Chapman's journal entries are particularly void of descriptions of Indian life in the area. This was mirrored in Chapman's limited references to specific Anishinaabeg—he mentions only Espagnol and Grand Coquin by name. And he clumsily "gets rid" of Grand Coquin and family, who linger for days at Grand Marais. Johnston mentions only a few others, such as Little Englishman, L'homme du Bois Fort, Crapeau, and of course Maangozid, but he does not tell us much about them. Chapman recognizes only one chief—Espagnol.

North Shore Anishinaabeg reticence to trade much with the AFC suggests they viewed them as newcomers, perhaps even upstarts, and as relatively weak in terms of men committed and resources brought to bear. For example, the AFC men had little food to share, their post was tiny in comparison with Fort William, and they had fewer trade items than the HBC. The question that must have dogged Espagnol was, were they a one-shot phenomenon, or were they committed to coming back year after year? Were they truly an alternative to the HBC? Espagnol must have watched with alternating amusement and then concern as Grand Coquin tested them by receiving dwindling food from the AFC and not doing as they wished. But were they coming back? Even the clerks didn't know. A few younger Anishinaabeg were indebted to the AFC, but there is not much evidence of any deep "loyalty" to the Americans. Perhaps the Anishinaabeg were hopeful that if they did not come back, any debts would be wiped clear.

Chapman must have been a relative jolt to Espagnol and band—a real Yankee, likely with Yankee values as much as those of a trader (less likely to give goods away to create a bond of good will with his trading partners). Chapman's journal was focused on problems with his men, and he says very little about the Anishinaabeg. He also focused on Grand Coquin but more to vent his frustration than to record any trading insights he might have learned from him or other Anishinaabeg. Chapman and Johnston were noticeably different than the HBC in that they were not trading for country produce (maple sugar, birch bark, watap [spruce root], or choice cuts of caribou meat). But the AFC at Fond du Lac was trading for country produce. For example, Anishinaabeg could trade forty pounds of maple sugar in mukuks for four skins at this time.[14] And what did Espagnol and Grand Coquin make of Johnston's extravagant wardrobe, refined speech, and proud ways?

The Anishinaabeg also noted that the AFC was like the HBC in some ways. Their boatmen were similar and were as likely to speak French and some Anishinaabemowin, as well as English. The AFC seemed to follow many HBC tactics, for example, trading with Anishinaabeg at their camps, and sending men to encampments at Grand Portage and White Fish Lake (called *en derouine*). The AFC also largely based their fur trade calendar around Anishinaabeg subsistence pursuits, such as fall fishing along Lake Superior. However, they also pressured Anishinaabeg to trap in harsh winter months, which aggravated the already difficult task of securing enough food. The AFC and HBC gave away similar gifts. Aitken wrote in 1834, "Indians of the Region have received ammunition & tobacco gratis for 15 years," including those years at Grand Marais.[15] The primacy of gift giving, especially of tobacco and smoking a pipe, continued as a fur trade custom for both trader and Indian.

A number of pressures were coming to bear on North Shore Anishinaabeg at this time. There were insistent but covert pressures on North Shore Anishinaabeg to centralize their leadership in fewer and more tractable men. Fur traders, government agents, missionaries, and surveyors all sought a dominant leader who could direct his people in a hierarchical manner, rather than the egalitarian society of traditional Anishinaabeg. It was more difficult and time consuming for whites to deal with the many clan leaders. Treaties would further reinforce this covert pressure for more hierarchical leadership.

While some inroads were made toward recognizing "fur chiefs" or those particularly compliant with fur traders' wishes, North Shore Anishinaabeg society remained strongly egalitarian.

Contrary to this pressure to become a more hierarchical society was great fluidity in membership in the North Shore Anishinaabeg. Members were coming and going in significant numbers. Grand Coquin came to the North Shore from Rainy Lake. Maangozid came from Fond du Lac to test trapping and trading conditions with the AFC. Espagnol's son, or stepson, Maymushkowaush and his family came from the Chicago area. The Caribou clan that settled in Grand Portage moved there from the Lake Winnipeg environs. A number of prominent families came from the Soo area, including Garden River and eastward into Lake Huron. Others came from Nett Lake to Grand Portage.[16] The movement and closing of posts through time, particularly after 1821 and the shrinking of Hudson's Bay Company operations at Fort William, impacted this group.

There was also some out-migration, according to HBC trader John Haldane in 1824: "The Indians about Fort William are not as numerous as they were some years ago—some having gone to Nipigon, others to Fond du Lac, and a small part to St. Mary's."[17] North Shore women marrying Anishinaabeg from elsewhere often moved away to nearby bands, especially the Nipigon and bands along the border route. North Shore Anishinaabeg would also trade, travel, or intermingle with a number of other Indians groups that lived in the greater region. Lord Selkirk, the primary owner of the HBC at this time, observed this about Crees, with whom the Anishinaabeg intermingled:

> The Crees or Kinstineaux, are of the same great family as the Algonkins, Sauteau or Chippeways [Anishinaabeg] & speak a language nearly the same. They formerly occupied all the country West of Lake Superior but their numbers being extremely thinned by smallpox, which about the Year 1780 spread thro' their

country like the plague they abandoned the less desirable country near Lake Superior & concentrated themselves in the more
fertile plains to the Westward of Lake Winnipic & also spread
themselves to the Northward, into countries which had been less
exhausted of game than their own.[18]

Mobility in and out of the area was widespread. This fluidity in
band membership may have contributed to Nectam's leadership being extended to a relatively distant band from his own, and explain
why the band did not have a recognizable fixed name. They were
Fort William Natives when the post was at Fort William, and Grand
Portage Natives when the post was there. They were never called
the Kaministiquia Anishinaabeg, after the dominant river and lake
in their area (like the Nipigon or even Fond du Lac Anishinaabeg).
This fluidity in membership may also have slowed movement toward a more hierarchical society.

Another pressure that was contrary to moving toward a single
leader (of a single band) was the impact of the border. Border-related
issues only increased in treaty and post-treaty and annuity times. As
the HBC traders increasingly noted, the "American Indian," "favors"
the Americans, or hunting lands south of the border. Essentially,
the North Shore Anishinaabeg were forced to split into two even
smaller groups. For many Anishinaabeg, where their traditional use
areas were, north or south of the border, determined if they "became" Canadian or American. By 1848, the presence of a resident
Jesuit mission had resulted in the segmenting of traditionalists from
Catholic converts. Fervent Catholic converts settled in Fort William.[19] Instead of creating fewer leaders, by the 1840s and 1850s the
border had fractured the group and increased the number of leaders.
Some now met with British Canadian officials, and other ogimaag
met with Americans. And yet some leaders continued to cross the
border for political and economic purposes.

Despite these contradictory forces, the group coalesced under Espagnol. Both North Shore Anishinaabeg and traders recognized Espagnol as a primary leader. He demonstrated, after all, many characteristics of a traditional Anishinaabeg leader. He was a very good hunter. In 1823, he traded sixty beaver and a "good many Otters and Martins" with the HBC. In 1834, he and his stepson "brought about 100 skins, chiefly martins." A year later he, his stepson and some of Peau de Chat's band brought in "350 skins of good furs chiefly martins, beaver, and otters."[20] His power and confidence led him to investigate the religions of whites (both Catholicism and Methodism), as did other Anishinaabeg leaders at the time. He was energetic. He traveled widely within the territory, from Fort William to Grand Marais, from Grand Portage to Arrow and White Fish Lakes, and further inland and to the west. And if Espagnol was of mixed descent, there was no evidence that North Shore Anishinaabeg recognized him as less of a leader because of his possible ancestry.

The North Shore Anishinaabeg were able to maintain much of their traditional way of life despite these pressures and changes. They moved freely throughout this area, made their own choices about where to go, and traveled widely. Through Espagnol's and others' leadership, they maintained political control of their group, despite the Americans and British ignoring them in ongoing border deliberations. Perhaps the North Shore Anishinaabeg had this in mind when they attended but did not sign the 1826 treaty in Fond du Lac. They maintained their traditional religious beliefs while exploring those of the Gichi-mookomaan—white person. Espagnol exhibited traditional Anishinaabeg values when he shared tobacco, food, and trade goods he received gratis. Even his role in killing a windigo at Basswood Lake, who threatened the group, was a traditional act of protecting the band. The North Shore Anishinaabeg maintained their language while also learning French and English. Indeed, Espagnol's successor, Joseph Peau de Chat, wrote a letter in French in the 1840s and, like so many others, was trilingual.[21] But the journals detail that Espagnol and others worked hard to maintain some level of economic independence from a single fur trade company. While economically reliant on some trade goods, they still maintained an interdependency with the companies. The HBC needed them as they needed the HBC. The AFC were a hopeful, but also not a dominant, economic option.

Gichi Bitobig was part of the North Shore Anishinaabeg's fishing, trapping, plant gathering, and maple sugaring territory. It was also a welcome sheltered place for stopping when traveling along Gichi Gami. It was an important place for fall fishing and the trailhead to maple sugar groves held in possession by families. But it was neither in the heart of their territory nor on the extreme periphery. Grand Marais was a bit "off the main stage." It is tempting to suggest that because it was slightly off center stage, it was a place where a "newcomer" such as Grand Coquin might go. There, away from the core territory, he was perhaps less likely to create friction with Anishinaabeg over established fishing, maple sugaring, and perhaps even trapping locations. Yet with the aid of his brother, the elder Peau de Chat, he could request and gain access to many favored spots. The new and fluid situation created by the AFC at Gichi Bitobig seems to have fit his economic and geographical experimentation.

North Shore Anishinaabeg territory, especially away from the dominant river—the Kaministiquia—was relatively unfruitful and unforgiving land. The territory of the North Shore Anishinaabeg was comparatively large for their small numbers. On the south shore, two estimates suggest that 29 or 30 square miles was needed for each Anishinaabe to subsist.[22] But Cook County alone is 3,300 square miles, which would mean a hundred Anishinaabeg could have resided there during the fur trade era. We know, however, that the North Shore Anishinaabeg territory was three to four times the size of modern-day Cook County and perhaps a maximum of 250 lived in this area. In short, the rocky landscape of this country did not produce as much readily available food, keeping numbers comparatively low compared to the Nipigon, Fond du Lac, and Rainy Lake bands.

The presence of the AFC probably led to increased trapping pressure in the area, although few records spell this out. Certainly, the mere AFC presence in Grand Marais meant more hunting pressure near there than was likely before. Furthermore, along the border it was a common fur trade tactic to encourage Indians to trap the area harder to reduce its attractiveness for the competing company.

By 1825, the HBC was changing its overall policy to reduce summer hunts of beaver, as the furs were less valuable and this method obviously cut down on the population. A year later, the policy was further articulated to discourage summer hunts except for along the American borderlands.[23] In short, the fledgling conservation policy did not extend to the border country, where different rules applied. Traders tried to influence Indian trappers in other ways. For example, they sought to have traditional hunting grounds recognized by fellow Anishinaabeg. Otherwise it led to a situation in which "many Indians have no hunting grounds which they can call their own, they therefore go about poaching on the Grounds of others, hence those who have Beavers kills them at all Seasons, rather than they should fall into the hands of those roaming Poachers."[24] Their role in changing the traditional division of lands and resources—some of which were communal, some family, and some individually recognized—is difficult to judge.

Why is this story important? What does the moment of Chapman and men paddling into Gichi Bitobig mean to us today? Awareness of this story, better yet its retelling, changes Grand Marais's origin story, transforming most area residents' knowledge. Today Grand Marais is not commonly thought of as a "fur trade town" or Anishinaabeg place. Nor is it thought of as having a corporate origin. The battle of two giant corporations—the AFC and the HBC—shaped Grand Marais in the 1820s and 1830s. Awareness of these "corporate" influences has not been as strong as it might have been had the presence of the AFC and HBC continued into the 1854 treaty and settlement period. If the location of the AFC post were known, the site could help engender a sense of a fur trade past. History tends toward simplification and one story line. But what we know about the Bongas and their presence in Grand Marais—their speaking Anishinaabemowin, English, and French, and George Bonga's education in Montreal—reminds us that the past can be more complex and cosmopolitan than we might have assumed, surprising us in its richness.

The current narrative of early Grand Marais history stresses its hardships. What the AFC men experienced at Grand Marais is consonant with later stories of its being a tough place to make a home. The AFC traders were unconditionally tested in Grand Marais. Food was scarce midwinter. Johnston was reduced to finding leeks in the springtime. They thought of themselves as deserted, forgetting the Anishinaabeg amid them. It is intriguing to speculate about how they might have lived better. Arriving earlier and being settled sooner would have helped them, as would proximity to alternative food sources in the winter.

The most obvious impact of the AFC tenure was on the fauna of the area. Moose were a target because they supplied a tremendous amount of meat, and thus they were hunted to virtual extirpation.[25] It was a number of decades before moose numbers rebounded. Woodland caribou were much sought after during the lengthy fur trade era, resulting in lower numbers in the area. Beaver were trapped hard during the AFC period and earlier. They, too, were virtually gone from this country at this time. When beaver hats went out of style (mostly in Europe) and their importance diminished, their numbers recovered.

The continued AFC operations at Grand Marais, beyond the years of Chapman and Johnston, may have had an unintended consequence for the settling of the international border. A year after Johnston left Grand Marais, the American and British border commissioners were in a squabble about where the border line should be drawn. The British in a strategic ploy proposed the border be fixed along the St. Louis River northward until it met the Vermilion River and then into Rainy Lake.[26] If the British had prevailed, the Arrowhead region including the Iron Range, would have been part of British Canada. The American border surveyors were aware of the AFC operations as they communicated with Ramsay Crooks and Robert Stuart. Perhaps this information was passed along to the American commissioner General Porter.[27] Having Americans on the ground, on the lands at question, could have substantially helped the argument that the border should be along the traditional water route, or the border we have today.

The country immediately surrounding Gichi Bitobig has the biological faults of its virtues—or what we appreciate today. It was and is a rugged, rocky country with little topsoil that does not predispose itself to agriculture. As Douglas Houghton in 1840 stated upon first examining Grand Portage, "The soil of the surrounding country is mostly rocky & barren."[28] And it was not very productive trapping country compared to the country to the west beyond the height of land of the Lake Superior basin. Furthermore, the Sawtooth "Mountains" thwarted easy access to the west to travel along major rivers such as the Pigeon and Kaministiquia. The area's rocky terrain, few travel corridors, and lack of productive soil made it less of a magnet for trading. As the AFC's experience confirmed, it was not a trading Shangri-La. It remained a frontier decades after places in the southern part of the state. But these attributes—its rugged lands—have also kept it from being transformed by an influx of people and the trappings of modernity.

The AFC story at Grand Marais was lost for more than a century and half. Prospector George Cannon found two small deserted log houses there in June 1843. His party used the door of one of the houses as a dining table without knowing for what purpose the cabins had been built.[29] The physical presence of the AFC post was ephemeral and did not lend itself to incorporation into the origin story of Grand Marais.[30] But when we graft it onto what we know of Grand Marais today, we have a richer and more inclusive story, which in turn makes it a more accessible and recognizable story to more visitors who come to enjoy it.

The Journals

Three diverse "journals" are the primary sources for this book. Each is different in outlook and history, and none is exactly a journal as we might think of one. Each one is in fragile condition, and conservators limit access to the original documents. The two American Fur Company journals (really, a logbook and letter book) are filmed and thus can be read in the original script through a microfilm reader. The Fort William post record has been available through a typed transcript. Fortunately, the ink of both AFC journals remained steadfast and readable prior to their conservation care. George Johnston's writing was relatively easy to read today, while Bela Chapman's script was more difficult. As he was undoubtedly writing in a cold and drafty log cabin or sometimes in a tent, his script sometimes elongates, complicating its readability. There are many run-on sentences in the AFC journals. Neither writer was particularly fond of periods; in fact, there are few punctuation marks, and there is more commonly a gap or a dash than a period. Sometimes it is difficult to discern where one thought ends and another begins.

Both writers abbreviated a great number of words and phrases, much like the language style of texting today. The meaning of some abbreviations is obscure. In quotations, I added the rest of the abbreviation in words and phrases where I think the meaning may be difficult to discern. As would be the case with a journal I might keep, there are plenty of misspellings, inconsistent grammar, and British Canadian spelling throughout. The Fort William journal was written every day and is more mundane in content, while Chapman's and

Johnston's entries focus on what they believe are key events; they jump days or sometimes weeks at a time. The Fort William clerk was much more likely to name the Anishinaabe man with whom he was trading. Chapman and Johnston named only a few.

Much remains unsaid in these journals; just as with an iceberg, so much remains unseen. Following the custom of the day, neither clerk mentioned the number of women present—or even their wives. Both clerks exercise the power of the pen, and many of the recorded failures were deemed those of their men and not themselves. Mundane things, such as what they were eating, were not mentioned. Occasionally they detailed the dubious character of one or more of their men, with one sometimes rising to the level of a scapegoat. Their superiors, who would eventually read all or most of these entries, were wise to many of their excesses and projections, but they were still interested to read which employees were particularly hard-working and would discern if the young clerks had gained the ability to control their men and master tough situations. Their superiors were eager to receive firsthand information about the country, Indians, and their competition at Fort William.

Both AFC clerks were relatively ambitious when they wrote these entries, particularly Chapman, who was trying hard to make a good impression on his superiors. Accordingly, they wanted to demonstrate their efforts and prove they were men of prudent action, particularly if their results were failure. Their trading success and these journal entries might influence where they would be sent next—whether a busy and lucrative post or one in a backwater. Predicting early and then explaining their failure were ways to assert it was not their fault but the circumstances they were placed in.

Both clerks were the last to leave Fond du Lac for a posting, or, as Johnston said, "last on the list." Perhaps this was why they appear to have had an improvised group, thrown together at the last moment. The Fort William journals tell a very different story of a stable crew, even supplemented by "freemen" or residents of mixed descent. And while the AFC chose not to post any men at Grand Marais during the summer months, the HBC was busy with routine agricultural pursuits detailed in great lengths in the journals.

Each clerk's writing style illustrates some of their differences in personalities. Chapman wrote with a plainer style and was more faithful to the expectations of writing a daily log, while Johnston sprinkled his writings with literary allusions and longer entries and used letter-type conventions. Chapman was comfortable addressing his bosses as "Dear Friend," while Johnston was more apt to write "Dear Sir" or "Sirs." Chapman wrote more directly to his bosses, acknowledging his role as a subservient employee. Johnston, on the other hand, occasionally questioned his bosses' decisions (particularly why they wanted to reestablish a Grand Marais post). More commonly, though, Johnston showed a great deal of deference to his superiors. The HBC journal is even more conventional than Chapman's, and the roles of named individuals assume a fixed hierarchy among the men.

Both Chapman's and Johnston's journals have a sense of exploring unknown geography, unfamiliar competitors, and even novel natural phenomena. For both American clerks, this was terra incognita. They did not know the geography well enough to find important Anishinaabeg in their hunting grounds. Further, they convey a sense of expansionism—of Americans using lands and resources that they assumed were theirs to inhabit. In contrast, the HBC journal reported on the geography in a matter-of-fact tone: it was well known to them.

Johnston was writing to two different audiences, and his entries were more for a copybook than a journal. He was writing to Messieurs Morrison and Aitken, and a few drafts of letters appear meant for his brother-in-law Henry Schoolcraft. Through the years, Johnston regularly provided Schoolcraft with information about "Ojibways." Both obviously employed the language of the day. Chapman frequently referred to his daily entry as his "epistle." Johnston referred to Grand Marais as Siberia, and Schoolcraft called Sault Ste. Marie "the Siberia of the American army."[1] Both used customary closings, including highly formalized phrases such as "your obedient servant" and "I am your obedient servant." This was abbreviated to "I am, etc." Another common and longer closing was "I remain, Sir, your faithful and obedient servant," which was abbreviated to "Your obt. Svt." Chapman often also signed off with the humble "good night."

The journals and allied documents are sometimes difficult to read. A few of the words and, more rarely, letters are undiscernible. For example, Chapman wrote of having taken hogs up lake to Grand Marais. He also wrote of "hogs" metaphorically to refer to, in his estimation, greedy Indians. His elongated letters made it impossible to be sure if the *h* is a *b* and if the *g* is a *y* for *boys* instead of *hogs*. Or could it be *dogs*, rather than *hogs*? But no, he brought hogs (in his canoe or bateau) along with dogs. Fortunately, only a few passages are undecipherable. The journals can also be difficult to read because some of the language used that was common to the time is offensive. In order to preserve the authenticity of the historical documents, they are transcribed and reproduced here unaltered.

Many fur trade journals have been lost. The availability of the Chapman and Johnston journals begs the question why they survived when so many have vanished. We can only speculate. The Chapman logbook is found among the Henry Sibley Papers at the Minnesota Historical Society. Sibley was first an American Fur Company trader, then a businessman. Eventually he became the delegated congressman for the territories of Wisconsin and Minnesota and finally the first governor of the state of Minnesota. It is not surprising that his papers were saved, especially given the AFC connection between Sibley and William Aitken. Although it is speculative, when William Morrison retired from Fond du Lac, the journal likely moved to his successor, Aitken, who held it until he was fired in 1838. Sibley then likely acquired it, and indeed he did acquire other papers from Aitken after his firing, as Sibley was then the senior AFC official

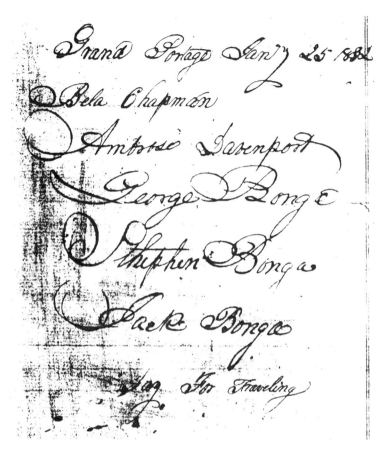

Cover of Bela Chapman's logbook. The original Chapman logbook is held by the Minnesota Historical Society in St. Paul, Minnesota. Photograph by the author.

in Minnesota.[2] One reason the journal may have been kept and handed down among fur company men is that journals were often used by traders during treaty payments to substantiate their claims against various Indians. According to the traders and their journals, if an Indian "owed" the trader and had never fully paid, the traders would likely be reimbursed for those debts during treaty payments. Perhaps the Chapman logbook survived because it had an odious future purpose, that is, to be used as a record of debts owed the AFC from North Shore Anishinaabeg in forthcoming treaty settlements.[3] It could have become the means by which traders could intercept monies originally meant for Anishinaabeg. However, since the AFC collapsed in 1847, years before the 1854 treaty, the debts were not recovered by former traders. Further, the 1854 treaty did not permit annuity payments to be redirected to debtors or supposed debtors.[4]

We can be more confident about why Johnston's journal survived in the Henry Rowe Schoolcraft Papers in the Library of Congress in Washington, D.C. In short, it was useful to Schoolcraft as it provided him information about the AFC and an area to which he had not yet traveled. Further, we know that Johnston actively provided historical, linguistic, and ethnographic information to Schoolcraft for his many publications about American Indians. After Schoolcraft's death, his widow donated his papers to the Library of Congress, in part to ensure the prestige of the family name. Johnston's journal of his time in Grand Marais would have been particularly instructive to Schoolcraft because it provided rare information about conditions near the international border just as parties from both governments were surveying (and later negotiating) its final disposition.

Additional historical records that provide comparative perspective on what the men and companies were doing came from the international border commission records. The U.S. surveyor team's records are in the National Archives at College Park, Maryland, and include the first American maps of the border route drawn from firsthand experience. The maps are exquisite and were drawn before topographic lines had been invented. Serendipity and much googling sent me to the Maine Historical Society website, where they had posted online David Thompson's letters from the British survey team. It is a wonderful historical irony that the lead British surveyor's letters, written to advocate for a drawing of the international border favorable to the British, ended up in an American institution. Thompson's letters, born of much experience in North America, greatly enhance information in Chapman's and Johnston's writings.

Johnston's journal ends unexpectedly, although he and his men likely stayed in the area a number of weeks longer. Perhaps because he was *en derouine*, traveling to trade with Indian camps, he stopped writing in this journal. He resumed writing in this journal on August 4, 1825, when he was in Sault Ste. Marie. A year later, while attending the 1826 Fond du Lac Treaty, he would again come into contact with a "delegation" of Anishinaabeg from the "Old Grand Portage," those he had sought so desperately to trade with a short time before.[5]

Also found among the Schoolcraft Papers is a "List of the Total Number of Indians at Grand Portage and Its Vicinity in the Spring 1825." All evidence suggests Johnston provided this information to Schoolcraft, who had not yet been to Grand Portage. Johnston even stated in a letter on July 13, 1825, that "I will have in your office a statement of the number of Indians inhabiting old Grand Portage where I wintered." This census provides the first name-specific census (of men) for Grand Portage and, indeed, the North Shore.[6]

The forty-eight-page Fort William post journal survived in a humbler way: it was kept at the HBC post until it closed. Thomas Richard, the last clerk at the post and the one who oversaw its closure, appears to have given the beat-up and coverless journal to prominent Thunder Bay citizens, and eventually it was donated to the fledgling Thunder Bay Historical Museum Society more than one hundred years ago. The journal and other fragments kept by a succession of Fort William clerks thus made their way to the local historical society. Instead of ending up at the HBC Archives in Winnipeg with other post records from North America or being lost, like most such records, this and two other journal segments stayed in Thunder Bay.[7]

It is unclear who wrote the Fort William post record. Since the handwriting appears to change, it probably had more than one author. Two of three possible authors, Alexander Stewart and Roderick McKenzie Sr., were not present for much of this time. This is confusing, as Stewart's family appears to be present at the fort, but he appears to have left before the journal begins.[8] Similarly, McKenzie was still at Lake Nipigon for much of the diary entries and thus is not likely its primary author. According to HBC records, John Haldane became chief factor of the Lake Superior District in 1823, but according to the journal, he was there as early as October 1823 and leaves in June 1824—a period of time that covers much of the writing. His duties for the entire district would take him as far east as Michipicoten and Sault Ste. Marie. Ironically, the journal entries refer to a "Mr. Haldane" while he was present at Fort William. So if he were the unlikely author, he was writing about himself in the third person! He was succeeded by McKenzie in June.[9] The journal entries end in September 1825, or roughly when Johnston arrived in Grand Marais. McKenzie probably concluded the writing after he arrived from his long stint at Nipigon, where he was known as the "Captain of Nipigon." All three of the possible authors (Stewart, Haldane, and McKenzie) were born in Scotland, worked first for the NWC, and eventually became HBC senior managers. Of the three, Haldane was the most likely author of the first part of the journal, while McKenzie could have written the last few months. Or perhaps there was an unnamed clerk who worked under Haldane and then McKenzie who was the author or even just substituted authorship on occasion. A few years after the journal was written, Haldane's career ended prematurely, as he "scrapped" with HBC governor George Simpson. According to Simpson, Haldane was "self-indulgent and [had] a propensity for intrigue."[10]

The Fort William post journal is topically different from Chapman's and Johnston's journals. The most significant event is the hosting of her majesty's "naval survey party" led by Lieutenant Bayfield. The outfitting of the *Recovery*, its travail getting over the shallow bar at the mouth of the Kaministiquia River, and its return are covered in detail. There is not a sense of isolation in the Fort William records, which documents the arrival and departure of national and international parties. But the dominant entries in the Fort William journal are about the routine employment of the HBC men. Thus, there is much detail about the fall fishing in the river and at fishing stations on the perimeter of Thunder Bay. The summer entries are replete with details about agricultural work such as planting potatoes, cutting hay, harvesting crops, and the first frost. Early fall entries document the butchering of oxen, cows, sheep, and pigs. Winter entries devote a good deal of attention to men cutting firewood, Native women snaring rabbits, and the arrival and departure of the winter express bringing mail and news from posts to the east and west. Maple sugaring is the focus of early spring entries. Throughout the journal there is much detail about area Anishinaabeg and dutiful notation of their successes and failures. All in all, the Fort William journal emphasizes well-trodden routines and the completion of habitual tasks. Not so in the AFC journals, in which there is a sense of surprises and ad hoc getting along.

Perhaps the most extraordinary find is a rare and dusty copybook at the Bayliss Public Library in Sault Ste. Marie. This is not a microfilm copy but the real thing, George Johnston's bound letter book. Opening Johnston's journal in a glass cubby of the library, I discovered brittle, faded plants still pressed between the pages. Some of these flowers could have been collected on the North Shore more than 190 years ago. What compelled a young Johnston to collect and then care for these pressed plants? Clearly he must have thought they were rare and worth this preservation. But he also nearly starved in the spring of 1825 on the North Shore, surviving on wild leeks. These and other marvels make his, Chapman's, and Espagnol's stories more poignant and not so remote from today.

The Log of Bela Chapman

Grand Portage Jany 25 18?2

Bela Chapman
Ambrose Davenport
George Bonga
Stephen Bonga
Jack Bonga

Log for Traveling

Sept 23rd, 1823 Lac Superior

Dear Sir: We encamped here at the Portage.[1] Late, I found things not in the best order &c my biscuit was all spoiled or eat. I know not which. My whiskey barrel was empty and the kittle of lard you gave me broken and I covered with double cloth well served that it should not be subject to opening. I found the covering all in pieces and the lard more than half gone. The pork I had in bag perhaps the dogs eat &c I wish you a good nights rest. B.[ela] C.[hapman]

Sept 24 Knife Island[2]

Sir: I have made a good day considering the late hour we embarked this morning. My foot is very painful. I suppose owing to the cold &c. Nothing new. good night.

25th Island of Encampment[3]

Dear Sir: We have been wind bound here all day, wind south. There is appearance of good weather tomorrow. good night, I retire to rest early. B.C.

Sept 26 Lac Superior

Dear Sir:
I have had a good day today. The wind has been north west we have sailed some and rowed some and we are encamped on the beach about two leagues north east the river Baptism.[4] It is now late and so farewell till tomorrow.

27 Sept

Sir: The wind has changed to the south and I am windbound here at 2 Rivers.[5] I am apprehensive for my foot which grows worse. hope for the best. Yours ob., B. C.

Sept 28th Lac Superior

Dear Friend:
I get along but slowly and yet I loose no time that we can march.
The wind is south and blows hard. I have made a small piece of
road this day, part encamped at the River called Entm[6] etc...
Yours ob[edient]. B.C.

29th Lac Superior

Dear Master:
I have committed one great error this day I put into the River of
Gilead[7] so called this morning in a large sea of the Lac. The sea
continued running all day but no wind and I have remained here.
My men say there is 4 leagues of rocks [ahead] and no encamp-
ment, so good night

30

Sir: I have not yet left this place. The wind has been south all day
and blows hard. What this morning will bring to pass is yet not
know[n]. I wish you again might rest and a happy return of the
morning. B.C.

Oct 1st

My friend the sorrows have placed _____ in me. I am still wind
bound in this river of Gilead. I have almost considered to build
and winter here. We make good fishing farewell, B.C.

Oct 2nd

I am still here and about to lay me down the fourth time in this one place to pass the night. The wind is north east. We shall probably be wind bound some days. Good night.

3rd Oct. Lac Superior, Grand Marrais

Dear Friend:
Here I am. The wind has been west the day past and we have had a fine last encamped very early here. We found the first Indians since we left Fond du Lac. The chief is here and the Grand Co-quin.[8] They have just arrived from Fort William. All drunk and we have set our netts and all is well so good night.[9] B.C.

5th Oct, Lac Superior

Dear Sir: For two days past I have been in [the] commissary with the Gentlemen of this place. I have consulted the chief as to what place it will be best to winter. and they all say that this is for the best that there is no Indians, etc [at] the other side of the Portage. [A]nd the fishing is better here than there. the weather is cool and the fishing good. I have closed the commissary and the peltries, etc.——good night BC

6

Sir: I have concluded to winter here and have begun to build. nothing new. Yours, ob BC

7 Oct

Dear Sir: This has been a fine day and we have put up the body of our store house. I have had [the] first addition to my family this winter[10] BC

12 Oct

Dear Sir: Excuse if I write not every day for we are all employed and the weather from my last [note] has been foul. Our fishing is good &c I am still making nets we have 5 in the water at this time and I have the 6th almost done.[11] continue building. Our store has fall down. I have miserable men to build. Fare you well, BC

Wintering ground, Oct 23rd 1823

My Friend:

Since I last wrote my time has been making nets fishing putting up fish etc. We have had beautiful weather for the season. I got rid of all the Indians on the 13 last. We have good fish[ing] as yet all trout, whitefish we have not yet taken at all. My men get along with building very slow. They have this day finished my house if it can be called a house for it has more the appearance of a hog pen. I could have done all the work that has been done myself in half the time tomorrow I go into it etc. Wish you a good night rest.

Wintering Ground 28th Oct

Sir:

Since I last wrote my time has been taken up in plastering my house over or rather in plastering it, for it could not be said to have been plastered before.[12] Beautiful weather. fishing fair. no new[s] from any quarter. Your most ob. BC

Fort Misery Oct 31st

Dear Sir

I intend soon to write you daily as soon as I got settled we had a heavy rain last night and every thing got wet for it rained more in the House than out this has been a cold day, snows some.[13]

Very affectionately yours, B

Fort Misery Nov 8th

Sir:

The weather has been fine since I last wrote. We have news from the Indians this day. All starving. Fishing [inland] is over. Yours ob BC

Fort Misery Novb 13th all in the _____

Sir:

I have concluded to send off two of men for fear of being short in provisions. As you directed me two men is as good as four here. We have made no white fishing at all. We have lost 2 nets and our lines which is the fault of that famous good man Boucher that you would send here.[14] Good night. BC

Misery 20 Nov.

Sir:

I have very unwelcome visitors the whole band of the Grand Co-quin have arrived starving to death.[15] My fish I have counted and put under key. I have 12 hundred in all. we have had a variety of weather since I last wrote you. Ob BC

Misery 27th Nov

Dear Sir:

Since I last wrote I have been all in the horrors. I have tried to send off my men to White Fish Lake but have failed for want of a guide, my famous Boucher knows no more of the country than George, I have sent the Indians [adrift ?] this morning in my wrath. Hope for the best, Yours Bela

Misery Dec 11th[16]

Sir:

My hogs have all come back. And cheat me and steal, the devil is not a match for him. pleasant for the season. 6 feet snow in land (Indian's news) it is a pity such Indians should have a trader forev-er being my provisions low.[17] My health good, my foot has healed up sound at last, no further news. Yours Obt Servt, BC

Fort Misery Decb 20th

To W. M. sir:
This morning I sent off a long drove of hogs. The lord send them as pleasant passage may they never return. Continues fine weather for the season, no appearance of ice. BC

Decm 24th

Sir:
Say unto you, what shall I say or what will you think when I tell you I have got rid of all my hogs, we have had two earthquakes since winter commenced and we shall shortly have a third or some other phenomena will make its appearance so I bid you good by. BC

January 1st 1824 Fort Misery, an evening

My good Friends all:
I wish you a happy new year, may peace happiness and prosperity attend you throughout the same and all your lives may you reap the fruits of your labours in a continuous harvest in all season and lay up a goodly store of that wealthy which finish with not for the world to come that in that great day we may not be found wanting. I am all alone. I have sent my men off two days past to White Fish Lake with one hundred skins,[18] &c farewell BC

13th Jan eve[19]

Sir:

My men arrived this morning have not found the Indians. The conduct of Mr. Boucher begins to shine forth in bright colours have it not been for George he would have returned from old Portage but George would not return so he was oblige to proceed. Since the 3rd I have had more boys to feed. Yours, B Chapman

Fort Misery Jany 19th Evening

Dear Sir:

This morning I sent off my men to Burnt river[20] to see if they could find an Indian that winters there. Continues pleasant. We have had the earthquake as I prognosticated, yours, BC

Jany 23rd Eve

My men return find the Indians. [And get a] good returns. Agree to wait for them again ten days hence, two packs at the Least, mostly beavers.[21] I must prepare to send [men] back immediately so good night. BC

Fort Misery 28th Jany Eve

My Dear Sir:

I have not been able to send my men away this morning owing to the wind. As I wrote you in my last that I should send back immediately the day has been extreme pleasant and fine for marching, and as I am now at Leisure I will write you daily until the return of my men BC[22]

29th

Sir:

This has been another good day. The Lake has been as calm as a bottle as the French say. I have my tenth marten[23] and this time I have said something of my hunting I am every day at hunt but kill nothing. I have made 2 rows of traps but trap nothing. It is snow showering as you may say. I have 10 martens old

30th

Another fine day for marching. The wind has been north, my men have had a good time this is the third day they have had time to go to the River Tourt[24] where the Indian provisions are, if he stands be oblige too have where they left him

Fort Misery Jany 31 eve

Dear Sir

This has been another good day for men to march, no wind, but note no further news. Ob

Febry 1st

The last night has been the coldest we have yet had the small lake[25] froze over but there has been a tempest blowing from the west all day and still continues to blow there was no ice to be seen at 9 o'clock. I have never seen such seas in the Lake before although the wind has been off land &c

2nd

The wind has blown all night and still continues to blow hard. cold and good night.

3rd

My men have just arrived and no Indians. There shines forth, the inestimable worth of your famous Boucher would to God, you had him with you. I have already expressed myself about him but I cannot but believe otherwise than it was a contrived plan among you for any man that will give employ to such man after knowing him as you all know him must be blind to his own Interest. If Boucher is such a famous why did not Cote[26] that great friend of half breeds, take him with him for I demonstrated having him with me from the beginning and I can now say in ___ that I have lost five good pack[s] by his bad conduct, etc. As for my other men I am much pleased with them. I will here make this one remark that all that bear name with the man are the best. I have found it by experience. Excuse sir my harsh expressions.

Good night, Yours, etc. B.C.

Fort Misery Febry 4th, 1824

My Dear Friend
Sir this has been the coldest day we have yet had there is appearance of the Lake freezing. The small lake is froze over and in all probability will not break I wish that might not for we are in want of ice to fish.

5th

Continues cold the wind is west and no ice to be seen what a pity there is appearance of snow warm weather. good night BC

6th

This has been a warm and pleasant day for the men are rather in low spirits Ob BC

7th

Morning snow, wind North East at night I will write you another line, etc, good bie—it has been a blustering day snowy and windy and still continues to snow wind North East etc. The time rolls slowly as my provisions are almost spent I have all my hogs to feed and of all Indians. He is the most troublesome I ever saw, I could fill my book up if I would give full scope to my thoughts but I forbear for it would be wasting paper and ink one thing I must make commission for & ask pardon in looking over my letters I have found in that of… third last… some bad reflections cast for which I humbly beg pardon and acknowledge my fault for it was the heat of my passions. W.M. Esq. I remain sir your most obedient and humble Servt

Fort Misery in good earnest B. Chapman

Sunday Evening going to bed

8th Dear Sir
We seldom see more pleasant days in April than the day past we shall hope for this fine weather in March and April I will that the

lake would freeze over that we might fish &c time passes slowly away &c no news

W.[illiam] M.[orrison] + W. A[itken][27] Your most Obdt BC

Misery
Monday Eve 12 of the clock, Febry 9th

My Dear Sir

I am the only one that is [awake] sleep is a stranger to at this house in this place so I have seated myself to write you another small epistle. The day past has been fine but the wind changed from East to North this evening and is now blowing a gale + is cold the weather has appearance of snow. I have spent the day in reading walking eating singing etc as for trade, I never write for there is none, my provisions are lower every day and yet I have my hogs to feed. The old Roan [Boucher ?] is getting quite unruly and makes his threats very publically although he receives his Rations daily in Fish but this is not good enough for him. He must have flour, butter, tea + sugar _____ and all other necessaries for high living which I have not had wherefore he threatens to brake the canoes burn the houses &c and if he gets mad he is going to kill us all but I have cautioned him against madness or again speaking as he did this morning for he must not flatter himself that we came here to be scared or to be governed by him. He says that it is you that sent him to his father's family friend and made many promises to them which you have not fulfilled and that his father will not be pleased with my conduct toward him for all of which I have told him that I know no promises you have made and I cared not for his father's whither for him or any one of the family &c _____ disputes

W.M. I remain yours most affectionately BC

Friday afternoon, Feby 13th 1824

My Dear friend...
Since I last wrote you we have had cold weather. The small lake or big Toby [?] as you may call it froze over the night of the 9th last yesterday morn there was much ice afloat in the lake last night the wind was off the lake & blew the ice ashore the morning our men speared 2 trout. the ice is so thin and weak that they returned immediately the [wind] is now blowing from the North East and has blown the ice off in the lake again. No news rather sickly among the Indians Ob I remain Sire your most Obvt servt...

Tuesday eve, Febry 17th 1824

My Dear Sir
We have had a variety of weather since my last epistle of the 13th last but nevertheless the Ice continues to stand good and we have had our meal of fresh fish every day since this has been a stormy blustering day but a good day for fishing. The men have speared eight trout. I have set my line this morning with five hooks which is all I have left whether I shall take any fish or not is very uncertain we all enjoy good health but we have a lodge of sick to maintain and there is no probability of their recovery. Disturbing times indeed wish you and all of yours good health I bid your good night very affectionately yours B Chapman

Saturday eve Febry 21st 1824

Mr. Morrison, Esq, Fond du Lac

My Friend Sir
I have taken my pen in hand to write you a few lines. It is late but

sleep is a stranger to my eyes. I have been reading until I am tired. Therefore have I undertaken this short epistle. Navigation is early in this quarter the ice broke up here Thursday last but there is a large bay about 2 leagues[28] from this where our men spear a few fish every day sufficient for our living. when I last wrote you I wrote I had set my line. I have taken nothing. I had also the precaution to take it up before the ice broke up. My sick family of Indians are still living and are hard on me for provisions but here I write you again they will most probability be in peace for there is not hopes of recovery. No news of Indians etc,

Most Obdt Servt. BC

Sunday eve Febry 29th 1824

For M _____

Dear Sir
There has nothing of consequence taken place since my last epistle we are all in good health excepting the sick woman of whom I have before spoken of she is yet alive + seems to be in some small degree recovering. But I have but little hopes of her recovery. On the 26 there fell about a foot of snow the greatest depth that has fallen at any one time as yet. 27th, first snow on the lake shore + in land about ten miles since first this [of February]. I think is not true but we get but few fish in those days there is much floating ice in the lake etc—

wishing a good night rest, Yours BC
Mssrs W. M. + W. A.

Sunday eve March 7th 1824

My Dear Sir

I have seen hard times since my last epistle, we have had a very refreshing shower of rain from the north east which lasted three days beginning on the 3rd last and ending on the 5th every thing has been wet through + through but as bad luck will have it I have no Peltry to get wet My buildings are worse than any hog pens, I am entirely cast down to see my returns, we are now arrived at spring and nothing done, to say we live would be false only stay and hardly that since March began we have taken no fish until this day the boys have speared a dozen small trout, times are dubious, I have still my hogs on hand and if I can find a market for them I assure you I shall not be difficult about price ; the sick [person][29] which I have heretofore made mention of is recovering &c the Lake is full of Ice at this place but all afloat with every wind which makes fishing very precarious &c there is not a day passes over my head but that I think of you all and pray that you may make good returns to cover some of my losses if possible for I bewail my own deplorable situation with tears in my eyes to more effect had I wherewith and were on my own account. I should not let the horrors come near me but as I am situated I find it utterly impossible but hope for the best and prepare for the worst as the saying. I shall do my utmost to get hold of some of the spring hunts if life and health attend me Ob-

I remain dear Sir very respectfully
Mr. Morrison Esq. Your Obdt & Humble Servt
B Chapman

Monday March 15th 1824

Dear Friend

I have got another touch of the H— on me. I would that I had the wings of a Turtle Dove that I might fly away out of this world of sorrow + be at Rest, I pass my time in hunting and making traps to no effect and in the night in reading for I cannot sleep. I have also make another bill of expense for you. I have equipped and sent off the Indian that has been here all winter to try and make something of him if possible. His family I have on my hand sick. We have no fishing. Ice is afloat. No news what so ever Good Bie Yours Ob. BC

M. W. W. A. A.

Thursday March 18th 1824

Sir

I have this morning signed and sent off two Indians to the spring hunt &c We have News from Fort William and the Indians in that quarter. There is a clerk and two men at White Fish Lake to take care of the Indians in that place. They have put down the prices far below par ottors for **3** skins martins **2** for a skin as they come mink also fishers are a skin. Foxes, lynx and wolverines[30] also beaver are **2** skins as they come Rats **6** for a skin bears **2** skins &c this is to encourage the Indians to pay their credits as they had made their credits before we arrived here however the Indians are not well pleased and with them for all their low prices and fair promises they say high time now they have an opposition &c Yesterday I sent my men with am[munition] and some good[s] to a lodge about **5** leagues from this. They brought me one Rain Deer[31] and the rest of the am[munition]. They gave on credit and most of the goods to the amt of **18** skins &c I have noted in some of my last epistle the bad conduct of Boucher when I sent him to White Fish Lake and they found no Indians when they arrived on the lake. They found an old encampment and 1 larger road and there returned. Had they proceeded on to the other end of the Lake they would have found the Indians with Peltries. The Indians say three pack but I judge from their own account to be about **2** pack I intend to pay the Hon. Hudson Bay's clerk a visit as soon as the Lake is free &c no further news

W. M. Esq. Most Resp Yours Ob B. Chapman

Sunday eve March 28th

Sir

Since my last epistle we had had very fine warm weather until this evening which is very blustery and stormy. The Indians in this quarter are making no hunts.[32] There is no martens. What they will do when the spring breaks up is uncertain. It is to be hoped that they will kill some thing. At any rate I intend to pass the spring at the Portage. My canot[33] is much damaged but as soon as the weather will admit of repairing I shall embark. We are nigh the end of our provision and there is no fishing here. I am told early in the spring by all appearance there will be a great str_____ [stress ?] for the spring hunts. The Indians drink rum as free as water. There is in every lodge a small keg whether they get in on credit or have it given them I cannot say. They say it is given them and that the great Englishman is more free with his rum than the traders have been heretofore. I have also been tolerable lavish with mine and too much so. But there is not probability of making anything more with it than to draw the trade of the Indians. We have almost daily news from some quarter and all to the same amount that is no trapping of small animals. All in tolerable health & Respects to all &c Good night, Yours Ob BC

Sunday eve 11th April 1824

Dear Sir

I have once more taken upon me to trouble you with another small epistle of my nonsense. The band of Brutes that I sent off all came back upon me and would have eaten me up alive had it not been for the lucky arrival of the chief who has had mercy enough on me to take them away with him. The chief has made good hunts he has seen no person all winter. I suppose they have better than ? thirteen ? good packs. They are three in number they have killed **7** bears, **1** moose, **4** Rein Deer, **100** martins and **150** castor.[34] I have some hopes of getting a small part of it but not all they have all large credits from the English. They have also small credits from me about **20** skins in all. The chief says that he cannot trade with me unless he should kill more than his credit but his young man will probably trade the greater part with me. I intend to make a bold push for the whole. We have not been able to get bark for our canot as yet but should the weather continues warmer we shall soon be able to have this &c I have much to say to you of my wintering and men but I refrain putting it on paper &c fare you well, BC

May 5th on road[35]

Dear Sir

Since my last epistle nothing new has occurred. the weather has been so bad that we have not been to mend our canot until yesterday and this day we have embarked and have been driven ashore by the wind.

6th

This has been a fine day we are encamped at the small Islands[36]

7th

This has been windy rainy day but we have anchored at the Old Grand Portage[37] I will write you shortly again

20th May Old Portage

Dear Sir

I have no news to write you. My men are gone in search of the Indians. This is the third time I have sent them off and they have turned back on account of snows. What will be the result this time. I know not there has passed a canot bound for the Red River those men and the family of Mr. Stuart[38] ... no fishing Good bie BC

Grand Portage 4 June

Dear Sir

The chief left this morning for Fort Wm with 2 good packs. I have done all that had in my power to trade it to no effect. I have tried the force of flattery and of + of lying and of Rum and he has swallowed all what he had more than his credit. I have not far from half pack The Indians have not yet arrived. No fish in a state of starvation &c Good Bye Your Resp. BC[39]

◆ ◆ ◆

After the journal text and general inventory, there is an inventory of Indians and their debts and credits stemming from Chapman's time in Grand Marais, Grand Portage, and even trading at White Fish Lake. Scribbled on the edge and sometimes on top of the individual entries is the word "Entered," suggesting both debts and credits were rolled up into a larger accounting at Fond du Lac.

The Big Rogue (Grand Coquin)	Debts		Credits
4th Thread	8	By 1 martin	
2 Beaver Traps	8	By 6 Marts. [martens] M[ale]	3
1 Motton [Molton] Capot	4	By 2 ditto F[emale]	1
2 Fathoms strouds	8	By 1 martin	
1 Blanket 3 pts [points]	4	By 6 Rats [muskrats]	1
1 " 2 ½ "	3	By 1 otter	2
1 Tommehawk	1	By 2 marts M.	1
1 file 1 scalper Mts	1		
Am[munition]	9		
1 deer skin	1		
Am[munition]	14		
Tobacco	2		
1 pr Mitassins [leggings]	2		
1 file & parchment	1		
1 axe	2		
Amt [ammunition] say shot	2		

The Big Rogue Lame son	Dts		Cts
1 capot of moulton	4	By 2 Martins	1
1 Pr Mitassins	2	By 3 Martins	1

The Big Rogue Second son	Dts		Cts
1 Motton Capot	3	By 1 Martin F[emale]	
1 Blanket 2 Pts	3	By 2 Martins F.	1
1 Pr Mitassins & cap	3	By 10 " M[ale]	5
1 Pr. Fish spears	1	By 1 Mink	
1 Tommehawk	1		
1 Scalper Mts 1			
Am.t [ammunitions] 1 at Fon du Lac	8		
1 Pr Mitassins strouds	2		
1 Fathom Ribbon	1		
&c Am.t	4		

Le Fils (son) de La Bete	Dts	Le Jeune	Cts
2 Fathoms Stroud	8		
1 Capot	4		
1 roll gartering	2		
1 Blanket 2 ½ Pts	3		
1 Tommehawk	1		
2 Scalpers	1		
Am.t	10		
2 Beaver Traps	8		

1 File	1
Tobacco	2
Capot 4 Ells	4
Am.t	6

Le Fils de la Bete	Dts	The Eldest	Cts
1 Blanket 3 Pts	4		
2 Fathom Strouds	8		
1 Roll gartering	2		
6 Holland Twine	6		
4 Maitres Rai	2		
Exchange on traps	1		
1 Fathom Moulton	2		
1 half axe	2		
1 Tin Kettle	2 ½		
Am.t	11		
1 File	1		

1824

Espanole Step Son	Dts		Cts
1 Capot	4		
1 Blanket 2 ½ Pts	3		
2 Fathoms Strouds	8		
1 Trap	4		
1 Blanket 1 Pt	1		
1 Roll gartering	2		

2 Skines worstead	2
2 Masses White Bead	1
1 Tommehawk	1
1 Small Tin Kettle	1
1 Large Tin Kettle	4
1 File	1
Am.t	11
To 1 Blanket	4
To Tobacco	2
For small capot 1 ½	1
To 2 Pr small scarlet leggins	3
To ½ Bag Flour	6

Espanole. The Chief	Dts	Cts
1 Capot	4	
1 Blanket 3 Pts	4	
2 Fathom Strouds	6	
2 Beaver Traps	8	
1 Tommehawk	1	
2 Holland twine	3	
4 Maitres Rai	2	
1 Roll gartering	2	
1 Tin Kettle	2	
1 File	1	
Am.t	1	
Am.t by his stepson	3	

1824

The White Fisher Son	Dts	Eldest	Cts
1 Blanket 2 ½ Pts	3		
2 Fathoms Stroud	8		
1 Moulton Capot	4		
1 Roll gartering	2		
1 Tommehawk	1		
1 Beaver Trap	4		
1 File	1		
Am.t	9		

The White Fisher Son	Dts	Youngest	Cts
2 Fathoms Moulton	3		
1 small axe	1		

The Crapeau
1824, Septr 17th

	Dts		Cts
To 1 Fathoms Strouds	4	By 9 Male Martins	4 ½
To Am.t	10	By 5 Fem. Ditto [martens]	
To 1 Blanket 3 Pts	4	By 1 Mink	
To Blanket 2 ½	3		
To 1 Beaver Trap	3		
For Cloth Cap & Gatg	1		
To 1 Pr Mitassins	2		
To Britch Cloth, gtg	1		
To 1 Tobacco	1		
To Tommehawk	1		

1 Looking glass [mirror]	1
To Cloth Cap	1
To 1 Pr Mitassins	2
To 1 Fathom Ribbon	1
To Knife	___ 2
To ½ a skin	2
To 1 Ivory comb	1
Am.t	6
Tobacco	1

The Brechee's Son	Dts		Cts
For Blanket 3 pts	4	By 1 Beaver	1
For Capot 4 Ells	4	By 6 Male Marts	3
For " 1 "	1	By 9 Female "	3
To 1 Tommehawk	1		
To 1 Blanket 2 ½ Pts	3		
For Pair Blankets 1 Pts	2		
To 1 Fathom Stroud	4		
" 1 Britch cloth	1		
" 1 Blanket 2 Pts	2		
2 Beaver Traps	6		
Tom am.t	4		

La Chuit the above	Dts	Son	Cts
For Capot 3 ½ ells	3	By 8 rats	
1 Cloth Cape & gartering	1	" 2 Minks	1

1 Tommehawk	1	" 4 Martins M.	2
1 Pr Fish Spears	1	" 6 Females"	2
Am.t	2		

1824 Nov. 10th

Le View, Peau Chat
Eldest Son

½ pr. Blankets 2 ½ Pts	9
2 Fathoms Strouds	8
To Am.t	10
To 1 Capot 3 ½ Ells	4
To Cloth Cap	1
To Tobacco	1
To 1 Beaver Trap	3

Notes

"1 Motton [Molton] Capot": tightly woven but coarse thick woolen cloth made into a coat, frequently closed with a sash. The flannel may have been heavily felted. Blankets and also molton fabric were often made into capots.

"2 Fathoms strouds": twelve feet of a woolen cloth woven and dyed, often red, made in Stroud, England. Florence M. Montgomery, *Textiles in America, 1650–1870* (New York: Norton, 2007), 352.

"1 Blanket 3 pts [points]": Points on a blanket once demarked the value of the blanket in fur trade currency, called "made beaver." Made beaver was essentially a value assigned to fur trade goods. Points later came to denote the size and weight of the wool blanket, with higher points meaning a larger blanket. A three-point blanket was often 54 inches by 70½ inches. Charles Hanson Jr., "The Point Blanket," *The Museum of the Fur Trade* 12, no. 1 (1976): 5.

"1 Tommehawk": Despite the association of a tomahawk with peril and terror, those traded here were primarily tools, a small ax or hatchet with a wooden handle.

"1 scalper": A "scalping knife" was a common fur trade item of the AFC and the HBC. It is a style of knife with a straight-backed blade with one knife edge and with a wooden handle primarily used to flesh hides, cut meat, and so on. It was a utilitarian knife, or what we might call a butcher knife, not a weapon, despite its disturbing name. Charles E. Hanson Jr., "The Scalping Knife," *The Museum of the Fur Trade* 23, no. 1 (Spring 1987): 8–12.

"1 file & parchment": "Parchment" here likely meant a soft animal skin rather than parchment paper, since there is no mention of the prerequisite ink or quill to write. Parchment was most commonly the skin of goat, sheep, or cow that had been limed and scraped under tension.

"1 capot of moulton": Usually spelled *molton,* but Chapman spells it multiple ways. It is a hooded coat made of a thick flannel with a heavy nap on both sides. It was mostly commonly white but occasionally blue or green. Cory Carole Silverstein, "Clothed Encounters: The Power of Dress in Relations between Anishinaabe and British Peoples in the Great Lakes Region, 1760–2000" (Ph.D. diss., McMaster University, 2000), 425.

"1 Pr. Fish spears": A fish spear was made of an iron shaft with two or three sharp barbs. It was often attached to a wooden shaft to extend its length.

"Le Fils de la Bete": La Bete, a renowned hunter, was not listed here, although his two sons were ("Le Fils de la Bete"). He would bring Isle Royale caribou meat to the HBC clerk at Fort William. *La bête* is French for "animal" or "beast." Fort William post, August 9, 1830, July 28, 1834, and August 2, 1836, B231/a/11, 14, and 16, HBCA.

"1 roll gartering": Gartering was made of a combination of wool and silk; it was used to hold up long stockings just below the knee.

"6 Holland Twine": Holland twine was cotton line used for making nets for fish. Most commonly here, it was "knitted" into gill nets to catch lake trout.

"4 Maitres Rai": Maître, heavier than Holland twine, was a fishing line used as a main line to the gill net or to the top and bottom of the gill net to make the net sturdier to attach net floats (on top) and sinkers (on bottom).

"Espanole Step Son": Written on the side of the entry for "Espanole Step Son" is "For small capot ½ Etc 1."

"2 Skines worstead": a length of loosely coiled wool made of long fibers that have been combed, making it finer wool than most traded. Montgomery, *Textiles in America,* 357.

"2 Masses White Bead": These are likely glass "seed" beads, or some of the smallest beads used in embroidery. They were a very common trade bead.

"The Crapeau 1824, Septr 17th": Something is amiss with this date and those that follow under "1824." Chapman would not have been on the North Shore in September 1824; George Johnston had just arrived in Grand Marais by this time, but the ledger is clearly written in Chapman's handwriting. It is possible that Chapman was at another location, possibly Rainy Lake, although the last ledger entry is for Peau de Chat's oldest son, who was clearly a North Shore Anishinaabe. *Crapaud* means "toad" in French.

"For Capot 4 Ells": *Ell* was a unit of measurement, usually defined as 45 inches long. George Quimby, *Indian Culture and European Trade Goods* (Madison: University of Wisconsin Press, 1966), 65.

"1824 Nov. 10th": There was no corresponding journal account for this day, suggesting that Chapman's journal entries did not cover all significant interactions with area Anishinaabeg. The date may suggest that Le View took these debts in one interaction.

The Journal of George Johnston

August 3rd 1824[1]

Dear Friend,

I have heretofore changed my wintering position twice, & this will be the third time. I have taken my License for Pembina on Red River.[2] This is to be a new established post, as I like to see new country and new places it will precisely suit my roving dispositions.

I embarked this morning from the upper end of the Sault de Ste. Marie, in company with Mr. William A. Aitken, and we are to proceed to the American Fur Company head post at Fon du Lac. We this day got as far as Point au Pins,[3] we were here obliged to camp, owing to a severe head wind, we employed ourselves the Remaining part of the day in fixing our Bales & Boxes, regulating and putting them in good order for the voyage.[4] I shall strive to write you twice between this and my departure from the Fon du Lac, and then twice a month.[5] A copy of my Journal to my employers. We arrived without any accident occurring on the 14th Inst. At the Petit Peche near Nontonagan River.[6] The weather being fine, and the Lake quite calm, we landed at the above place. There being Indians camped, & who informed us that a Chippeway war party had this Summer killed four Americans by mistake near the Mississippi.[7] The wind sprang up and became favourable, we hoisted sail and reached Iron River after Sun set.

I Remain
Your Sincere Friend
Geo. Johnston

15th August 1824

Dear Friend,

We started very early this morning although the wind blowing very strong ahead, we however managed to reach about two leagues beyond Black River, and encamped early as our men broke three of their oars.[8] At night we were obliged to unload our Boats owing to the wind blowing from the westward which caused a heavy swell. We remained camped part of the ensuing day. Mr. Lyman Warren overtook us this afternoon, we effected to load our Boats & reached Montreal River.[9] I embarked with Mr. Warren in order to get to La Point before our Boats could arrive there. It began to blow tremendously from the North East creating a very heavy swell we were obliged to put ashore a little beyond, Mauvais River.[10] Mr. Warren and I started on foot and Reached the eastern end of Cha-gaw-wa-mick-ong, we Kindled a large fire, which was seen by the people of the Island and Mr. Cadotte an old resident of the Island sent his sons in a large canoe & landed us safe.[11] His Britannic Majesty's Schooner the New *Recovery* lay at anchor in the Strait, having the naval surveyors on board, Lieutenants Bayfield & Collins.[12] Mr. Warren & I called on board but did not see the gentlemen as they were gone surveying the adjacent Islands. The schooner appears more like a Brig, and is a very strong well built vessel, & well calculated to navigated Lake Superiour, in the afternoon Captain McCargo and Doctor McLean came on shore and on the 19th inst. Mr. Warren & I dined on board.[13] Mr. Aitkin at last arrived having wet his goods at the time when Mr. W. & I were obliged to put ashore, this afternoon it came on to blow accompanied with a Thunder-storm & Rain, after the Rain ceased we got away & camped two leagues beyond La Point,[14] on the 20th we embarked early & did not proceed far when the wind rose ahead, or rather from the N. West, we were compelled to put Back in a deep Sandy Bay & creek, we saw the surveyors tents pitched on an Island opposite to our camp. We again embarked the ensuing day but were obliged to put into a River as It blew too strong for us. I shall write you again once more before I leave Fon du Lac or as soon as we can Reach that place.

I Remain
Your Sincere Friend
Geo Johnston

Fon du Lac Post: 4th Septr. 1824

My Dear Friend,
We arrived here on the 24th August and I found the situation well adapted for carrying on the Indian Trade. Mr. Morrison having got two new stores and a dwelling house built this summer during his absence to Michilimackinac which sets off this place consid-erably, as the greater part of the old buildings look very shabby. There is also a considerable farm under cultivation principally in wheat, Indian corn, squashes & potatoes the latter being the main stay of the Post, and are cultivated for that purpose as also for the quantity consumed, by the men as well as the Indians, the wheat was sown on trial, which has the finest appearance imaginable it being nearly fit for the Sickle and the Indian corn was nearly ripe, the squashes grow to an immense size.

I have been employed since my arrival in outfitting the men, writing Triplicate receipts, or say Rather Invoices for the differ-ent posts of the Interior. All the Clerks and men are gone & I am the last on the list, as Mssrs. Morrison & Aitken have made other arrangements where I am to winter and they resolved on Grand Marais near Grand Portage being employed by the Company to perform my duty I did not for a moment hesitate from their request, however should the Indian agent at the Sault find it derogatory, to his high station, I trust the fault will not lay on my back, as not being licensed for Grand Marais.[15] I shall in the mean time strive to do my utmost endeavors for my employers that I would have done had I gone to the Post I was licensed. A war party of the Fon du Lac Indians had collected themselves this summer, and they started five days ago, without the least appearance to denote them warriors. Lieutenants Bayfield & Collins arrived here in two long boats on the 31st of August, they spent the night with us, as I am to start tomorrow I shall bid you adieu and

Remain
Your Sincere Friend
Geo Johnston

Grand Marais Septr. 11th 1824

My Dear Friend,
Once more will I trouble you with my nonsense, I arrived here this morning a lonely and dismal place it is, by the very first appearance. The Bay is semicircular, and by observing it from the lake, resembles very much a horse shoe, the beach is gravelly, the main shore is perpendicular rocks. It would be a good harbor for two or three vessels at a time on utmost emergencies, and the only one between Fond du Lac & Grand Portage, distance from the former place by computation forty five leagues & from the latter fifteen, about three miles from this passes a high range of mountains, which I am told go beyond Fort William.[16] It is in some

places perpendicular and at others sloping from top to the margin of the lake. The growth of Timber is vis Spruce a few stunted pines, poplar, white birch, cedars, and at some distance into the interior, here and there, a cluster of maple. The appearance of the country in general, is sterile in fact I cannot but lament my situation considering that I have nearly ten months to remain in this I may safely say Siberian exile, no one to converse with but Ignorant Canadians, and the Natives, the latter are chiefly, murderers, Robbers & thieves. I must now desist troubling you any further on such lame subjects, as I must according to promises write a copy of my Journal, a diable boiteaux[17] it will be to you, once more adieu

I Remain
Your Sincere Friend
Geo. Johnston

Elba, 22nd Septr. 1824[18]

Messrs. Morrison & Aitken

Dear Sirs,
I shall attempt to give you a cursory view of our proceedings in this post during our exile in it, intending to reserve something to discuss upon, should the Almighty enable us to meet again. We arrived here on the sixth after leaving Fon du Lac, without unloading or any accident happening [to] our boat. We found all the houses burnt which makes this place look dismal enough. The appearances are that we shall be obliged to get wood from a considerable distance both for building and for fuel. We however got an handler and fixed our Grind Stone ready to commence operations tomorrow and you will not of course be surprised to find our Boat load secured under lock & key the third day in our store.[19]

The fishermen have been particularly successful in catching from twenty to thirty trout daily since our arrival. I intend leaving for this Grand Portage tomorrow, and L'Equier in charge as he is lame, I found Eight Indians at the portage that were waiting for our arrival, I gave as is customary Liquor & Tobacco, &c. And there set the men cutting hay for our buildings at (Elba) and succeeded getting one hundred Bundles, afterwards I sent George & Tasack in search of Indians, expected daily with furs, from White Fish Lake.[20] The guide after having gone up a considerable distance would not proceed any further, with them and they were obliged to relinguish their jaunt. We arrived here today and found the Grand Coquin & Maangozid camped

I Beg leave to Remain
Your Obliged Servant
Geo. Johnston

23rd Sept. 1824

Dear Sirs,
The weather being mild & clear, we began building my house which I intend to be twenty feet by sixteen, and we got the square up on the 24th, we covered it, and the ensuing day began the chimney and finished the mason work, when six Indian Canoes arrived the whole band from Grand Portage. The Grand Coquin having previously sent his two sons to meet them & hurry them on. They all came to my tent headed by the aforesaid Big Rogue, and after a long palaver & smoking of the pipe, I was under the necessity of giving them Half a Keg Liquor with Tobacco &c. They remarked in their speech that they intended leaving this in three or four days for their different wintering grounds. They however managed to be drunk for three or four days. Finished our

chimney, & covered the house with hay & on the 27th began our flooring & cellar. The Indians have remained very quiet these three days

I Beg Leave to Remain Respectfully
Your Obliged Servant
Geo Johnston

October 1st 1824

Dear Sir

I have at last got clear of all the Indians not without infringing on your restricted rules, that of not giving them much credits. But I assure you it could not be easily avoided. I need not mention the Indian Character for you know them much better than I could possible describe them to you. The Big Rogue by the bye being their orator on the occasion and may the Big Rogue the Devil take him. (second) I got into my house this day, & the men began theirs. Maangozid & son took their credits, and started on the 4th Inst. for the Interiour leaving his family here. The fishermen are moderately successful, we get from thirty to forty trout per day. On the 7th It blew a complete storm & consequently we were not able to set our nets. George has been very unwell and I have been doctoring him for these two days, and is now getting much better. I set out the nets, and was uncommonly successful having caught sixty five trout. (fourteenth) Maangozid & son arrived from the interior without bringing one single Rat.[21] They report that, all the small Lakes are frozen, & that there is about a foot of snow on the mountains, this is a good beginning for my Hunters, as Maangozid fell in with two of them moving double quick towards the Lake, & complaining of starving. If they thus begin what must be the result in the course of the winter, they know best, but were I to give my opinion, they will no doubt eat one another as they have hitherto done. I forgot to mention that I began salting on the first inst.[22]

I beg leave to Remain Respectfully
Your Obliged Servant
Geo. Johnston

October 15th 1824

Dear Sirs

Blowing very strong from the westward, I was obliged to send three men in a large canoe to set the nets, which they with difficulty accomplished. We experienced a severe frost last night & caught forty fish this morning. (seventeenth) I had the satisfaction this day of seeing Maangozid's son arrive with a large Beaver, and late this evening the Chiefs step sons arrived from near Roche de Bout & bringing with them a long list or rather enumerating a great number of articles they require, Liquor, Tobacco, & Ammunition &c.[23] Was their first demand, having drank here one night and part of the next day, I managed to get my two noblemen off. Late in the evening, having first fulfilled their orders & and on their departure were obliged to give them four Quarts more. The men made two different attempts to go out to the nets. They first came back with their canoe half full of water, and they laterly succeeded & brought forty four trout. I afterwards went out to the lines with George, and on our return nearly upset our canoe having half filled, the waves running mountains high on a shoal, we however got a shore with great difficulty. (twenty second) I send Tasack and L'Equire to the Indians near Grand Portage they returned on the 24th Inst. And brought fourteen Martins & six Rats, The Indian there, not having as yet gone up to the interior,

I got the store and house covered with about four Inches of earth requiring for that purpose upwards of One Hundred Bags full, which the men were obliged to bring in on their backs from a distance of upwards of a quarter of a mile, it made Jean Bat. swear a little I assure you. (Thirty first) The weather mild and misty with rain.

I Beg leave to Remain Respectfully
Your obliged Servant
Geo. Johnston

November 1st 1824

Dear Sirs,
This is a cold unpleasant day with snow on the 2nd Inst. I send Tasack & Macie near Grand Portage for the purpose of taking Am.[munition] to the Indians. We had a spell of mild weather, for these several days, and on the seventh Tasack & Marcie arrived from their journey & they brought two small Beaver skins, four otters & Thirty Martins. At night the Grand Coquin arrived with his whole race altho he told the men he would not come out of the interior til he had worked ten Beaver lodges which it appears he found, and at the same time requesting that I should send him provisions, here he pops in with his roguish band all on sudden like an apparition. When I asked him why he came so soon, replied that he came for the purpose of making snow shoes. This has been another drink bout for the old villain, he had no sooner got sober, when three Indians, & a woman arrived with five castors.[24] Then the old villain begins again, may he never recover to drink another drop. The Indian who brought the beaver skins is a new source from White Fish Lake. [eleventh], The Indians started not without a small Keg. I prepared George & Tasack for

White Fish Lake and they started on the 13th we had a severe frost last night caught only 29 Fish this morning.

I Beg leave to Remain Your
Obliged Servant
Geo. Johnston

November 15th 1824

Dear Sirs

The wind being from the North East & Blowing a complete storm, we were not able to set our nets, and on the 17th I at last started Grand Coquin with all his band, they having destroyed since their arrival, together with what I gave them on starting upwards of one hundred & forty fish, and unfortunately this has been a very stormy month, we could not set our nets out daily far from it not more than half the time during the thirty days. (twenty third) The weather remarkably mild with a heavy fall of snow, & in the evening an Indian arrived, (say the Crapeau) with his wife, so you see as soon as I get rid of the devil, his nymphs appear, they have come from Roche de Bout or there abouts, they are all starving having burnt their nets, & what is worse (an Indian) one of my creditors cut his knee very badly, consequently we cannot expect anything from him.[25] (Twenty fourth) George & Tasack arrived from their voyage & report that the H.B. people had got to White Fish Lake some time before they reached that place, & that they had got twenty three plus.[26] And it is reported by the men that Mr. Haldane is to send out an outfit immediately to that place, they were waiting for the finishing of sleigh only.[27] They however brought here 5 Castors, one link [lynx] & two minks, we still make good fishing, get from twenty to thirty fish every day, (twenty seventh) The wind being from the North east, and the weather mild, I send Tasack & L'Equier towards Roche de Bout to the Indians, who have fourteen plus in Martins etc. (twenty ninth) I got Grand Coquin son off, and I send George & Maangozid in the interior in search of an Indian reported to be opposite this place. 30th George returned not being able to proceed, having rained all night in torrents.

I Beg leave to Remain
Your obliged Servant
Geo. Johnston

Dec. 1st 1824

Dear Sirs,

It still continues to Rain, and towards evening it blew a complete storm from the South. The wind shifted in the course of the night to the North, and on the morning of the second, George & Maangozid started, finding the snow sufficiently frozen. I begin to apprehend some unforeseen accident has happened to Tasack & L'Equier, this being the eighth day since their departure and have not yet arrived. 5th I make preparations to go in search of them but blowing too strong from the North west prevented me from starting. I left this the ensuing day with a severe cold & headwind. I however managed to reach salmon trout river,[28] But could proceed any further owing to our old canoe filling with water (having no gum) as Tasack took the whole of what we had. 7th I returned and with difficulty reached our houses & on my arrival the men told that L'Equier & Tasack had each of them taken two shirts & 2 pr Mitassens, & the latter a bowel and soap, that being sufficient & evident proof of their desertion to Fon du Lac and to which I have made up my mind. 8th George & Maangozid arrived from the interior, not having been able to find the Indian.

9 th Send Macie in Search of Grand Coquin, he returned the next morning on account of having broken his ax handle. 14th This being a tolerable calm day, I started with George in search of Grand Coquin we reach Burnt River & slept there.[29]

I Beg Leave to Remain
Truly Yours
Geo. Johnston

Dec. 15th 1824

Dear Sirs :

We started early this morning & mounted our snow shoes. We walked all day and at last lost the road owing to the severe fall of snow on the mountains.[30] We consequently could not find the Old Villain. Returned the ensuing day and reached the Lake. The waves were running mountains high, we were obliged to leave our canoe & started on foot along shore. I was glad enough to reach this on the 17th I have only to Remark that it's the Devil's own country, as Cats and dogs would be hardly able to extricate themselves out of it. Maangozid & son came and got ammunition on credit intending to start for the interior with all his family. 21st L'homme du Bois Fort arrived from near Roche du Bout, and brought 2 otters & 1 Bear skins, and says that he gave Tasack ten plus in Martins, as also the Little Englishman four in Marts &c.[31] I here was assured by the Indian that Tasack and L'Equier had gone on to Fon du Lac, on a visit & was to return in twenty days. 22 nd I send George and Macie along with the Bois Fort into the woods for some Rein deers meat, they returned the same day, along with old Grand Coquin, the old villains family as usual all starving, he desired me and the Boys to meet them with provisions, which I accordingly did the ensuing day.[32] The men returned in the evening, bringing with them six large & small Beaver skins & fifteen Martins. 25th I gave the men a dram and a hearty breakfast, from this day to the 31st has been remarkable fine weather & L'Homme du Bois Fort started for Burnt River along with his son in law.

I Beg Leave to Remain
Sincerely Yours
Geo Johnston

Siberia 1st Jany 1825

Dear Sirs,

This being New Years day, I wish you both many happy returns of it. May we all be able to see many of them, in health & happiness is my sincere wish, as also good returns from every quarter, to cover the losses of this place, for I can see no prospect of making any thing here whatever. Never was I more lonesome in any place, or had a more earnest wish of doing something to the benefit of those by whom I am employed. I'll leave all into the hands of him who is all wise, good, & merciful, he only can extricate me from my state of mind, and from my difficulties ----- I had an early visit from the Grand Coquin and all his band, no danger of his leaving this when the others started. I must not make any further remarks whatever of the poor old villain, as we must this day show good will towards all men. 3rd The weather being fine & clear I send George & Macie to White Fish Lake, and at the same time send off Grand Coquin. Since I sent off the men it had been constantly blowing we had an extraordinary appearance in the moon, 8th The weather mild, Maangozid paid me a visit, and is customary in this quarter, all starving is the complaint. 12th we had a tremendous wind from the North East Maangozid arrived with his whole family & camped. **14**th George arrived, but could not find the Indians at White Fish Lake as they had all started for Fort William by appearances all the English people are gone also as they saw a very large path of tranes, and the tracks of men women & children that way inclined.[33] I am of opinion that they are all starving, or they must have heard news of an extraordinary nature, which has induced Mr. Haldane to recall his men at this season of the year, this is how ever mere conjecture of mine. Maangozid set two nets & our men one.

I Beg leave to Remain
Sincerely Yours
Geo. Johnston

15th Jany 1825

Dear Sirs

The wind is from the North East and the waves running so high that Maangozid and our men could not go to their nets. **16**th this is a mild day & calm, we had a fall of about six inches snow our men went out to their net & brought in two trout, and the above Indian five. **20**th we have had very severe cold & boisterous weather since the sixteenth, Grand Coquin & l'Homme du bois fort arrived & as usual starving. The former brought two links & two Marts and the latter two Martins also. This is a poor specimen of good hunting without the least exception. **21**st a fine clear cold day the wind being fair. I got old Big Rogue off once more, not without furnishing him & the other Indian with provisions, which makes our stock run low. **22**nd Wind South with snow & quite mild. I prepared George & Maangozid for a voyage towards Roche du Bout. (Twenty third) the weather still mild started George in search of the Espagnol & his band. (Twenty fourth)

Late this evening an Indian & his wife arrived from White Fish Lake. Both of them starving, having been ten days on their way across the country. They report that there are no French wintering at White Fish Lake, it appears that all the Indians in that quarter are starving. The weather fine & mild reminding one of a March day. (Twenty sixth) This evening an Indian, the Little Englishman arrived having left his wife and all his family in the interior starving, I expect.[34] The Indians will shortly eat us out of house & home. 27th I prepared my Indian Englishman he is to start tomorrow. 28th The weather cold, got the Little Indian Englishman started merry be his heart. I this evening prepared the Indian from White Fish Lake. 29th The weather extremely cold our bay of Elba froze over. Started the Indian & his wife, No sooner had I got them away, the Little Englishman's wife & daughter arrived, saying that George & Maangozid had reached their Lodge, and that they gave all their furs to them. 30th The woman and her daughter are still here waiting for our men, who fortunately arrived this afternoon with thirty eight martins & one otter. They unfortunately could not find the Espagnol nor his band. 31st I have at last got clear of the Englishman, his wife & his daughter

I Beg leave to Remain
Truly Yours
Geo Johnston

February 1st 1825

Dear Sirs,
For the commencement of this month the weather is very mild on the second I got Maangozid & all his family started for the interior, we fished in the bay and caught six salmon trout, and

the ensuing morning we again got three, and unfortunately the Ice cleared out of the bay as well as along the Lake Shore. 5th The weather fine mild & clear, and about last midnight arrived Grand Coquin's two sons starving. The most deplorable objeᵈts I ever beheld not at all having the appearance of human beings, & they say that the younger part of their family are not able to rise. It appears they eat a parched Rein deer skin the day before yesterday. (Seventh) weather clear & cold. The Lake is Frozen once more, how long it will last God alone Knows. I got George & Macie started with provisions, and the next day returned, and in the meantime sent off my two starving Indians. They are to go to Grand Portage, as their father is waiting for them (Eighth) Still cold I was in hopes that the Ice would have held, but it is constantly moving to & fro. We however ventured on the Bay but were not successful in catching trout. There comes Grand Coquin & his Rascally band, (Great God what shall I do to extricate from such a scene of distress) permit me here to say may those who put you up to again establish this post, suffer all the bitter pangs of the distressed in mind. Two months ago the Ice was firmly frozen at Pigeon River, where we might in our present situation get daily subsistence, as also the Rascally band, who are constantly hovering about us like birds of prey. Were I to vent out all my feelings on this as on former occasions, respeᵈting the above band of Indians, I might without the least doubt fill whole pages, resolved must I be to let them starve and go to the devil their own way, or else abandon this post (which is out of the question). The Ninth & tenth, the men ventured on the Lake, and were out spearing all day but were not successful. I have again started the Big Rogue and all his band. (Eleventh) Got George & Macie started to fish at Grand Portage and at the same time to go to White Fish Lake in search of Indians. Rassette was out the whole day fishing with a hook and Line, but did not kill anything (Twelfth) Mild weather and every appearance of the Ice going.

The Little Englishman & his nephew arrived bringing with them twenty eight martins, and as usual starving. (Thirteenth) started the two Indians, & as they met their families they returned and camped here. (fourteenth) Still mild & fine weather with snow, wishing you both all manner of success.

I beg Leave to Remain
Truly Yours,
George Johnston

15th February 1825

Dear Sirs,
This is a mild day with a little fall of snow. Maangozid's son arrived and left this the ensuing day. 17th The wind blowing from the North a complete storm the Ice cleared all out. Eighteenth, The Little Englishman and all his family started out for the Interiour. (Nineteenth) Weather cold with the wind from the North East I sent the Little Englishman's nephew & his wife into the interiour, and I have not the least doubt on my mind but that they return in four or five days, at furthest. Rassette caught a small carp this day, great production of this bay. We have had eight days of the mildest weather imaginable & no sign of our people I sent to White Fish Lake, having read all my books long ago, I spend my time lonely and dismal enough I assure you.

I Beg Leave to Remain
Truly Yours
Geo. Johnston

March 1st 1825

Dear Sirs,

We have had three nights of fine, mild & pleasant [weather]. The little Englishman's nephew & wife arrived, they brought one beaver skin, & one martin. (Fourth) the weather still mild, the Indian and his wife started, & no sign of our men as yet. I do not know what to conjecture, (fifth) the weather continues mild, with wind from the North East. This wind prevailed the part of Last fall and of this winter, I have this day began to make new masts, & grand perches for our boat, and sprits for the sails, by this you will perceive that I am anxious to leave this place, circumstances admitting.[35] I assure you we are getting very low in provisions, as the Indians have been constantly on us during the winter & what is worse have not made any hunts whatever. On the seventh Maangozid and his band arrived starving. You may rest assured he however brought nineteen martins. Eighth, We began squaring our oars, the Indian and his son went out spearing in a bay beyond this, & close in shore, they killed two small trout, unfortunately, the Ice cleared all out the ensuing day, and in the evening they set two nets, and at the same time were out flambeauing, but were not successful in either cases.[36] (tenth) The Indians were out again but to no purpose, the Ice still makes its [lingering ?] appearance a considerable distance in the offing. 11th The wind North East and blowing a complete storm, I am in hopes it will drive the ice entirely from this. 13th I got Maangozid and his family once more started, they are to camp close from this, for the purpose of making sugar I have not the least doubt on my mind, they will be here daily, wishing you both all manner of success.

I Beg Leave to Remain
Truly Yours,
Geo. Johnston

◆ ◆ ◆

The last journal entry is dated March 13, 1825, although Johnston likely stayed in the area a few weeks longer. Perhaps he stopped writing in this journal because he was *en derouine,* traveling to trade with Indian camps. He resumes writing in this journal on August 4, 1825, when he is in Sault Ste. Marie.

Excerpt from the Fort William Hudson's Bay Company Records

This entry from the Fort William Hudson's Bay Company records shows the scale and breadth of "gifts" a leader such as Espagnol would have received at this time. The title says 1833 and 1834, but the records continue into 1835. The book mentions almost twenty Anishinaabe men who received gifts from the Hudson's Bay Company. From "Fort William Indian Gratuity Book 1833/34," microfilm M19, Minnesota Historical Society, St. Paul, Minnesota.

	Spaniard	Gratis
1833 Sept	3 bushel Hulled Corn	
	1 bushel Rough Corn	
	½ barrel Flour	
	1 Lbs Grease	
	4 Lbs butter	
	10 loaf bread + Biscuit	
	1 Brass inlaid knife + 1 yew handle	
	1 ___ Roach a 4 fhs color thread	
	2 Awls, 1 gun worm + gimblet	
	4 lbs Power + 16 lbs shot 20 balls	

	15 gun flints, 10 cod hooks	
	6 # tobacco, 1 pr combs	
	½ lbs tea, ½ lb chocolate	
	¼ _____ ½ keg reduced rum	
	½ bush H. corn	in course of the summer at difft. periods
	6 lbs maple sugar	
	7 lbs flour	
1834 Mar	3 M [measure] Powder	for Ross
	3 M. shot	for Ross
	5 flints & 1 # tobacco	for Ross
May	1 large keg Rum	
	1 lbs tobacco	
	5 lbs Biscuit + 2 lbs Butter	
1834	1 fine camwood knife	
	2 knots maitres (fishing twine)	
	1 knot twine nobs	
June	3 ft. net thread given to the Spaniard	
	Gratis from order of the [HBC] Governor	
	And one large keg reduced Rum	
	3 ft. twine & 4 lbs tobacco	
	2 measure powder & shot	
	10 plug tobacco	
	6 cod hooks & 4 flints	
	1 pr sleaves, 10 balls	

	4 flints, 1 needle + 1 fine knife	
	Needle + 2 fhs [fathoms?] Thread	
1835, Mar	6 At Ammunition	for Michel [Collin]
	1 # tobacco	for Michel
	2 Qts Rum	for Michel
	4 flints	
	1½ bushel Hulled Corn	
	1½ rough hulled corn	
	96 Lbs corn + flour	

Notes

"Roach": Roach refers here to a type of knife, shorter than a "scalper" but also with a straight back and with a somewhat rounded cut blade.

"1 gun worm + gimblet": A gun gimblet was used to extract a ball from a fur trade gun.

"Gratis from order of the [HBC] Governor": Important HBC leaders, such as Governor George Simpson, often took inspection tours. Simpson would instruct HBC men to provide gifts, such as alcohol, to important ogimaa. These visits at Fort William usually occurred in June, thus drawing many North Shore Anishinaabeg to the post.

"for Michel": Michel Collin was a Métis man living in Fort William and married to an Anishinaabe woman from Grand Portage. He was an expert canoe maker.

Acknowledgments

Writing a book may appear to be a solitary act. You do go and write it alone, accompanied perhaps by a mug of coffee or a bored, sleeping dog. But really it is constructed through countless direct and also glancing communications with friends, colleagues, and family. When finished with the writing, you have a contrary feeling of knowing how much you have borrowed and learned from others. You wrote it but not alone.

Many people contributed to this endeavor, some of them long ago. Fellow National Park Service ethnohistorian Tom Theissen first provided me a copy of Bela Chapman's journal. Tom also did much of the yeoman's work in transcribing the Hudson's Bay Company Lac La Pluie journals and district reports and some of David Thompson's journals. I would still be laboring to transcribe these without Tom's generosity. Another Park Service employee, Jeff Richner, was generous with hard-to-find historical records, such as trading licenses. Dr. Theresa Schenck alerted me to the existence of George Johnston's journals; relocating them in the Schoolcraft Papers at the Library of Congress was then relatively easy. She also graciously wrote about other matters besides Johnston, thus preserving the novelty of this manuscript. Dr. Bruce White's professionalism and summary analysis of the Bela Chapman logbook has inspired me to keep thinking and writing. The late Jean Morrison of Thunder Bay offered thoughtful comments on my early ideas about this project.

I'm afraid I have effectively tortured a number of librarians at the Grand Marais Public Library by giving them challenging interlibrary loan requests. Thank you to Anne Prinson Pollock, Patsy

Ingebrigtsen, Linda Chappell, Steve Harsin, and others who were game to track down my requests. Librarian Susan James at the Bayliss Public Library in Sault Ste. Marie was wonderfully helpful to me when I read through the George Johnston papers. Patricia Maus at the Northeast Minnesota Historical Center in Duluth was ever ready to answer my historical queries and requests. A number of Bentley History Library staff at the University of Michigan and reference librarians at the Minnesota Historical Society have been delightful to work with through time. Although we never met, Marianne Stiem graciously translated Father Francis Pierz's rare account of his time in "Grand Portage" from German to English. Similarly, Lenora McKeen sent me further English translations of Father Pierz's letter from the Bishop Baraga Association in Marquette, Michigan. Dr. Mattie Marie Harper trustingly shared her dissertation on the Bonga family while she worked to turn it into a manuscript. Howard Sivertson gave me the occasional boost to keep at it, advised me to render the writing more understandable, and is capable of laughing about the dire times of the AFC in Grand Marais. The Hudson's Bay Company Archives' far-reaching records—and generous access to those via interlibrary loan—form a backbone to this work.

Thank you to those Grand Portage and Grand Marais friends who were subjected to half-articulated parts of this story. Thanks to the good counsel of Shelley McIntire, the late Doug Birk, Dave Cooper, Bill Clayton, and Norman Deschampe, I have solved historical questions often before I knew I had them. Billy Blackwell encouraged me to understand the prominent place of the North Shore Anishinaabeg in history. Thanks to a number of Grand Portage elders, especially Ellen Bah-gwatch-nee-nee Olson, who continue to cheerfully teach me despite my abilities to misspeak virtually every Anishinaabemowin word (*Anishinaabemowin* is the Native term for the Ojibwe, or Anishinaabeg, language). John D. Nichols at the University of Minnesota cheerfully answered my vexing Anishinaabemowin quandaries. Tory Tronrud at the Thunder Bay Historical

Museum Society answered my questions about historical gems in his caretaking.

The meticulous work of editor Mary Keirstead made this text more readable, consistent, and easier to follow. The comments of two anonymous reviewers greatly improved the organization of this manuscript to make it more accessible to a wider audience. Erik Anderson and Kristian Tvedten at the University of Minnesota Press have been supportive from the beginning, all the while making a number of sound suggestions to improve the manuscript.

Working at Grand Portage National Monument provided me access to a great little library, replete with many of the gems that appear in these pages. My former day job as a park manager serendipitously meant business trips to the locations of important primary sources, such as the Library of Congress. I hope my inattention to bureaucratic matters was not too evident while on Washington, D.C., trips, as I was really eager to sneak away to the Library of Congress and National Archives. Grand Portage enthusiasts and devotees Curt Roy, Alan Woolworth, and the large Grand Portage Rendezvous reenactor community spurred me on with their captivation by the fur trade. A final, and perhaps most advantageous, part of my job at Grand Portage National Monument was rubbing elbows with Stephen Veit and Karl Koster—encyclopedias of fur trade knowledge. Karl correctly calls himself a "fur trade geek," and he is very good. For example, a few weeks after pondering about which plant fibers were available locally and thus could be made into rope, Karl presented me with braided twine, made of basswood tree fibers, with the gentle reminder that even though basswood trees are not found in our county, individuals could, and did, trade for it. For these guys, it is not enough to talk about a gun gimblet; they need to find a picture, make it, or otherwise extol its virtue or lament its shortcomings. And to Steve, Karl, and Carrie Johnson, head of the Cook County Historical Society, who read and commented on the manuscript and saved me from a number of blunders, thank you.

Notes

Introduction

1. Chapman's journey was slowed by six windbound days where he and his crew made no progress. Others who made a similar trip completed it days faster than Chapman, though he may not have known this at the time. Francois Victor Malhoit and crew made the longer distance from Fort William to Fond du Lac in nine days, Jean Baptiste Perrault made it in six days from Grand Portage to Fond du Lac, and George Nelson made the same trip in six and a half days. Francois Victor Malhoit "A Wisconsin Fur Trader's Journal, 1804–05," *Wisconsin Historical Collections* 19 (1910): 172; Jean Baptiste Perrault, "Narrative of the Travels and Adventures of a Merchant Voyageur in the Savage Territories of Northern America Leaving Montreal the 20th of May 1783 (to 1820)," *Michigan Pioneer and Historical Collections* 37 (1910): 569; George Nelson, *My First Years in the Fur Trade: The Journals of 1802–1804,* ed. Laura Peers and Theresa Schenck (St. Paul: Minnesota Historical Society Press, 2002), 95, 98.

2. *Anishinaabeg* is the indigenous people's own term for themselves, called by many Ojibwe, Ojibwa, or Chippewa. I am using *Anishinaabeg* as the plural form of the people, while *Anishinaabe* means "an Indian," or person, or human. John D. Nichols and Earl Nyholm, *A Concise Dictionary of Minnesota Ojibwe* (Minneapolis: University of Minnesota Press, 1995), 10.

3. This is conjecture about what the grounds might have looked like. There is little documentary evidence, so I constructed this scenario from reports of similar places and times. Major Joseph Delafield, *An Unfortified Boundary* (New York, privately printed, 1943), 390. For other information on old encampments, I have drawn on Isle Royale's surveyor William Ives's field notes, Public Land Office, May 23, 1847, copy held at Isle Royale National Park, Houghton, Mich.; Bela Hubbard, *Lake Superior Journal: Bela Hubbard's Account of the 1840 Houghton Expedition,* ed. Bernard C. Peters (Marquette: Northern Michigan University Press, 1983), 18–19; and Stephen H. Long, *The Northern Expeditions of Stephen H. Long,* ed. Lucile M. Kane, June D. Holmquist, and Carolyn Gilman (St. Paul: Minnesota Historical Society Press, 1978), 228.

4. John Fritzen, "History of North Shore Lumbering," Fritzen Papers, Northeast Minnesota Historical Center, Duluth. Willis H. Raff cites Fritzen in his *Pioneers in the Wilderness* (Grand Marais, Minn.: Cook County Historical Society, 1999), 3.

5. George Johnston, *The Journal of George Johnston,* Henry Rowe Schoolcraft Papers, Library of Congress, Washington, D.C., September 23, 1824.

6. Carolyn Gilman, *The Grand Portage Story* (St. Paul: Minnesota Historical Society, 1992), 104.

7. W. Stewart Wallace, ed., *Documents Relating to the North West Company* (Toronto: The Champlain Society, 1934), 2.

8. Bela Chapman, *The Log of Bela Chapman,* Henry H. Sibley Papers, Minnesota Historical Society, St. Paul, October 5, 1823. That Espagnol thought this was a good fishing ground is affirmed by his efforts to fish there the winter of 1831–32. Hudson's Bay Company Archives (HBCA) (Winnipeg, Manitoba), Fort William, B.231/a/11, September 12, 1831.

9. Mary Jane Hendrickson in *Grand Portage Chippewa: Stories and Experiences of Grand Portage Band Members,* ed. Donald J. Auger and Paul Driben (Grand Portage, Minn.: privately printed, 2000), 19; Ellen Olson, personal communication with author, April 26, 2006, Grand Portage, Minn.; Carolyn Podruchny, *Making the Voyageur World: Travelers and Traders in the North American Fur Trade* (Lincoln: University of Nebraska Press, 2006), 175; Henry R. Schoolcraft, *Personal Memoirs of a Residence of Thirty Years with the Indian Tribes on the American Frontiers: With Brief Notes of Passing Events, Facts, and Opinions, A.D. 1812 to A.D. 1842* (Philadelphia: Lippincott, Grambo and Co., 1851), 204.

10. A number of external forces separated this group: the international border treaty of 1842 (Webster-Ashburton Treaty), the Lake Superior Robinson Treaty of 1851 for the Canadian North Shore, the 1854 treaty for the Arrowhead region of Minnesota, and the presence of missionaries that heightened divisions between traditionalists and Catholics (and a few Methodists). Government officials dispensing treaty annuities then demanded that Anishinaabeg be either Americans or British Canadians to receive any treaty payments—this also effectively tore the group into two. I have asked a number of Anishinaabeg elders in Grand Portage about what this historic group name might have been, and there is not a widely agreed upon name that is remembered today.

11. William W. Warren, *History of the Ojibway People* (St. Paul: Minnesota Historical Society Press, 1984), 38.

12. "History of the of Town Cornish, Sullivan County, New Hampshire, 1763–1910," posted on Ancestry.com; "Observations—Ex-Mackinac Islander Held Many Earlier Positions," *Cheboygan Daily Tribune,* February 3, 1987, 1, 3.

13. Malhoit, "A Wisconsin Fur-Trader's Journal," 170.

14. Nelson, *My First Years in the Fur Trade*, 18, 205–6.

15. Years later, Reuben Chapman would eventually build one of the nicest hotels, Lake View Hotel, on Mackinac Island, and it would be run by family members for almost one hundred years.

16. Stanley Newton, *The Story of Sault Ste. Marie and Chippewa County* (Sault Ste. Marie, Mich.: Sault News Printing Company, 1923), 137. Chapman was a charter member of the first Presbyterian Church of Sault Ste. Marie.

17. Charles J. Kappler, comp., "Treaty with the Chippewa, 1826," in *Indian Affairs: Laws and Treaties* (Washington, D.C.: Government Printing Office, 1904), 2:272.

18. Grace Lee Nute, *Calendar of the American Fur Company's Papers*, parts 2 and 3 (Washington, D.C.: Government Printing Office, 1945), 5–6, 7, 8, 9, 57, 77, 154, 155, 1579, 1581.

19. "1836 Mixed-Blood Census Register," National Archives, microfilm series M574, Special Files of the Office of Indian Affairs 1807–1904, Washington, D.C.; Nute, *Calendar of the American Fur Company's Papers*, 574.

20. Clarence Edwin Carter, comp. and ed., *The Territorial Papers of the United States*, vol. 12, *Michigan Territory 1829–1837* (Washington, D.C., Government Printing Office, 1945), 55–57, 247–48, 316–17, 344–48, 395–97, 397–99, 920.

21. Dwight H. Kelton, *The Annals of Fort Mackinac* (Mackinac Island, Mich.: John W. Davis and Son, 1887), 48; Eric Freedman, "Schoolcraft Boys No Match for Chapman," *Detroit News*, February 2, 1987.

22. Anon., *The Traverse Region, Historical and Descriptive, with Illustrations of Scenery and Portraits and Biographical Sketches of Some of Its Prominent Men and Pioneers* (Chicago: Page and Co., 1884), 97; General Land Office Records, Mackinac County, February 10, 1852; Bela Chapman and his wife, Mary, received eighty acres of Indian allotment lands outside of Little Traverse; GLO Records, January 13, 1872. Original land patents are available online at *www.glorecords.blm.gov.*

23. Bela Chapman, death record, September 10, 1873, Mackinac County Clerk Records, Mackinac, Mich.

24. Mrs. Thomas Gilbert, "Memories of the 'Soo,'" *Michigan Pioneer and Historical Collections* 30 (1903): 631. The 1826 treaty had land grant provisions for "Susan" and her children: "to Oshauguscodaywagqua, wife of John Johnston, Esq. to each of her children, and to each of her grandchildren, one section." Kappler, "Treaty with the Chippewa, 1826," 193.

25. Henry R. Schoolcraft, *Information Respecting the History, Condition and Prospects of the Indian Tribes of the United States* (Philadelphia: Lippincott, Grambo, 1852), 2:526.

26. Henry R. Schoolcraft, *The Indian in His Wigwam* (Buffalo, N.Y.: Derby and Hewson, 1848), 142, 144.

27. Warren, *History of the Ojibway People*, 219–20; C. H. Chapman, "The Historic Johnston Family of the 'Soo,'" *Michigan Pioneer and Historical Society Historical Collections* 32 (1903): 311.

28. Schoolcraft, *The Indian in His Wigwam*, 134. Schoolcraft added that Ma-Mongositea "was present with his warriors, under Gen. Montcalm, at the loss of Quebec, in 1759."

29. Johnston Family Papers, John McDougall Johnston, "Miscellaneous Notes and Fragments," Bentley Historical Library, Ann Arbor, Mich. One measure of being a distinguished chief was hunting or wartime prowess. Even if this account was an exaggeration, it demonstrates the family pride in their Anishinaabeg forefathers.

30. Alice B. Clapp, "George Johnston, Indian Interpreter," *Michigan History Magazine* 23 (Autumn 1939): 350.

31. Chapman, "The Historic Johnston Family of the 'Soo,'" 306.

32. Ibid., 307.

33. Gilbert, "Memories of the 'Soo,'" 631.

34. Ibid.

35. American Fur Company Papers, 1832 Account Book, "George Johnston," 81, Bayliss Public Library, Sault Ste. Marie, Mich.

36. Clapp, "George Johnston," 354; Chapman, "The Historic Johnston Family of the 'Soo,'" 307; Margaret Curtiss Weaver, "George Johnston (1796–1861)," in *The John Johnston Family of Sault Ste. Marie*, ed. Elizabeth Hambleton and Elizabeth Warren Stoutamire (Washington, D.C.: John Johnston Family Association, 1992), 33.

37. Robert Dale Parker, ed., *The Sound the Stars Make Rushing through the Sky: The Writings of Jane Johnston Schoolcraft* (Philadelphia: University of Pennsylvania Press, 2007), 13.

38. George Johnston Papers, Memorandum book 2, Bayliss Public Library, Sault Ste. Marie, Mich.

39. George Johnston, "Reminiscences by Geo. Johnston, of Sault Ste. Marys, Reminiscence No. 3, 1820," *Michigan Pioneer and Historical Society Historical Collections* 12 (1887): 608–11.

40. Charles C. Trowbridge, "Gen. Cass at St. Marie 1820," *Wisconsin Historical Collections* 5 (1907): 410–13. Trowbridge was also an eyewitness to this event and places more credit on Mrs. Johnston than her son, George, with foiling the plot to kill the Americans. Janet E. Chute, *The Legacy of Shingwaukonse: A Century of Native Leadership* (Toronto: University of Toronto Press, 1998), 31–36; Henry Schoolcraft, *Narrative Journals of Travels, through the Northwestern Regions of the United States Extending*

from Detroit through the Great Chain of American Lakes, to the Sources of the Mississippi River (Albany, N.Y.: E. and E. Hosford, 1821), 135–40.

41. Carter, *The Territorial Papers of the United States*, vol. 11: 308, 578.
42. Lewis Cass, letter to George Johnston, August 28, 1826, George Johnston Papers.
43. Carter, *The Territorial Papers of the United States*, vol. 11: 987–88.
44. Schoolcraft, *Personal Memoirs*, 87.
45. Parker, *The Sound the Stars Make Rushing through the Sky*, 24.
46. Weaver, "George Johnston," 35.
47. Ibid., 36.
48. Alexander Morris, *The Treaties of Canada with the Indians of Manitoba and the North-West Territories* (Toronto: Coles, 1979), 304.
49. George Johnston, letter to Henry Schoolcraft, July 13, 1825, Henry R. Schoolcraft Papers, Library of Congress, Washington, D.C.
50. Alan Knight and Janet E. Chute, "In the Shadow of the Thumping Drum: The Sault Metis—The People In-Between," in *Lines Drawn upon the Water: First Nations and the Great Lakes Borders and Borderlands*, ed. Karl S. Hele (Waterloo, Ont.: Wilfrid Laurier University Press, 2008), 76, 266.
51. Ibid., 99.
52. Lewis Cass, letter to George Johnston, October 22, 1834, George Johnston Papers.
53. Marjorie Cahn Brazer, *Harps upon the Willows: The Johnston Family of the Old Northwest* (Ann Arbor: Historical Society of Michigan, 1993), 176, 186.
54. Kappler, "Treaty with the Chippewa, 1826," 272.
55. Weaver, "George Johnston," 35.
56. Ibid., 37.
57. Ibid., 36.
58. Clapp, "George Johnston," 365; Robert E. Bieder, "The Unmaking of a Gentleman: George Johnston and a Mixed-blood Dilemma," *Hungarian Journal of English and American Studies* 16: 1/2 (Fall-Spring 2010): 133.

1. In Grand Marais

1. Johnston, *Journal*, September 11, 1824. Johnston's superior attitude toward "Indians" was peculiar given the fact that he was a Métis, or mixed blood, and his mother was a notable Anishinaabe.
2. Ibid., September 22, 1824.
3. The type of boat is not named in these journals, but a reference by the Fort William clerk identifies one vessel as a bateau. This type of boat is twenty

to thirty feet long and could be rowed or sailed. It is "double-ended": a sharp bow and stern and flat bottom. The larger bateaux could carry up to two tons of cargo. Chapman, *Log,* October 5, 1823.

4. Ibid., September 23, 1823.

5. Johnston, *Journal,* August 3, 1824.

6. Schoolcraft, *Personal Memoirs,* 112–14.

7. David Thompson, July 21, 1822, as quoted in Grace Lee Nute, *Lake Superior* (Indianapolis: Bobbs-Merrill, 1944), 60.

8. George M. Cannon, "A Narrative of One Year in the Wilderness" (Ann Arbor, Mich.: privately printed, 1982), 30, Bentley Historical Library, Ann Arbor. Cannon was writing of his prospecting time on the North Shore in 1843.

9. Ibid., 25, 27.

10. Ibid., 32.

11. James Ferguson, letter to Daniel Webster, July 25, 1842, *Congressional Globe,* December 9, 1842, 12.

12. James Ferguson, letter to General Peter Porter, July 2, 1822, Peter B. Porter Collection, Buffalo and Erie County Historical Society, Buffalo, N.Y. A few years later, prospector Cannon called this area a "country of rocks," meaning there was an absence of productive soil. Cannon, "A Narrative," 27.

13. James Ferguson, letter to General Peter Porter, August 1, 1822, Porter Collection.

14. David Thompson, Treaty of Ghent Journal, August 9 and 16, 1822, at "Lake Kaseegnagah" or Saganaga, Archives of Ontario, Toronto.

15. John Haldane, "Report on the State of the Country & Indians in Lake Superior Department 1824," B.231/e/1, HBCA.

16. J. D. Cameron, "Rainy Lake Report, 1825–26," B.105/e/6, HBCA.

17. The NWC appears to have run a small, satellite post at Grand Portage occasionally up until their merger. But records of a smaller post at Grand Portage after the NWC left until the 1821 merger of the Hudson's Bay Company and NWC are scant. We do know that in 1816 there was a small HBC post at Grand Portage during the Selkirk incursion to Fort William (Selkirk Papers, National Archives of Canada, 9:2842, 2852). HBC men were at Grand Portage off and on from 1816 to 1817, when Lord Selkirk sent "Mr. Lacrois with a party of men to the Old Grand Portage abt. 40 miles from Ft. Wm. With several months provns with instructions to make hay on the land clear of wood in the neighbourhood of the old Fort, and also at various place along the portage on the road to Lac La Pluie." Selkirk was anticipating the needs of cattle and sheep he had purchased from the NWC, which were to be used by Scottish immigrants

who were bound for the Red River. John Allan, Surgeon, Royal Navy, in Selkirk Papers, microfilm reel C-5, 4626, Library and Archives of Canada, Ottawa, Ontario.

One of the de Meuron soldiers, Lieutenant Friedrich von Graffenried visited the Grand Portage post in fall 1816. He describes the small post: "There we found a rather well preserved house, measuring 12 feet by 12 feet, which would offer sufficient shelter for the winter once it was properly plastered with mud." Friedrich von Graffenried, "Six Years in Canada, 1813–1819," translated by Ingrid Keller, Fort William Historical Park, Thunder Bay, Ontario.

18. Henry Schoolcraft, "Mr. Schoolcraft's Report in Relation to the Fur Trade," October 24, 1831, 22nd Cong., 1 sess. (1832), Senate Document 90, Serial 213, 46.

19. "Report of Fort William Trade and Indians 1830–31," B.231/e/7, HBCA.

20. Journal, HBC, Fort William post, December 15, 1823, B 4/2/1, Thunder Bay Historical Museum Society (TBHMS), Thunder Bay, Ontario.

21. Malhoit, "A Wisconsin Fur Trader's Journal," 172.

22. Schoolcraft, "Mr. Schoolcraft's Report in Relation to the Fur Trade," 43.

23. Malhoit, "A Wisconsin Fur Trader's Journal," 172. Fishing at Grand Marais did not disappoint Malhoit; his men caught "four fine trout, three large ciscaouettes [siscowet, or fat trout, which were considered highly desirable at that time], and a white fish."

24. Grace Lee Nute, "Posts in the Minnesota Fur Trading Area, 1660–1855," *Minnesota History* 4 (December 1930): 353–54.

25. John L. Bigsby, *The Shoe and Canoe: or Pictures of Travel in the Canadas* (London: Chapman and Hall, 1850), 231.

26. Journal, HBC, Fort William post, 1824, B 4/2/1, TBHMS.

27. Reverend Edmund F. Ely Papers, May 4, 1834, transcribed by Veronica House, St. Louis County Historical Society, Duluth, Minn.

28. Much of the NWC's post on the Snake River was built like a row house with apartments connected by interior doors. This construction technique has an advantage of less exposure to winds and cold weather and thus has the potential to be warmer. Doug Birk, *The Messrs. Build Commodiously* (Brainerd, Minn.: Evergreen Press, 2004), 28–33.

29. Chapman, *Log*, October 7, 10, 23, 28, and 31, 1823, and March 7, 1824.

30. Johnston, *Journal*, September 22, 23, and 27, and October 15 and 24, 1824.

31. James Duane Doty, "Northern Wisconsin in 1820," in *Collections of the State Historical Society of Wisconsin*, vol. 7, ed. Lyman Copeland Draper (Madison: Wisconsin Historical Society, 1908), 196.

32. Johnston, *Journal*, October 1, 1824.

33. Chapman, *Log*, November 20, 1823.

34. Johnston, *Journal,* September 4, 1824.

35. Port Mackinac Records, July 19, 1824–August 19, 1825, and Port Mackinac Records, June 15, 1825, in George Johnston Papers, Bayliss Library, Sault Ste. Marie, Mich.

36. Reverend Edmund F. Ely, Journal, 1834, St. Louis County Historical Society, Duluth, Minn.

37. Chapman, *Log,* October 7, 1823.

38. HBC, Fort William post, October 24 and November 11, 1823, TBHMS.

39. "Minnesota (Fort Snelling area) Weather for the Year 1823," http://www.climatestations.com/minneapolis/historical-writeups/minnesota-weather-for-1823.

40. Lieutenant Henry Bayfield, "Abstract of the Meteorological Journal Kept on Lake Superior in 1824, by the surveying party under the command of Lieut. (now Captain) Bayfield, R.[oyal].N [avy]" in Frederick Henry Baddeley, "Geological Sketch of the Most South-Eastern Portion of Lower Canada," *Literary and Historical Society of Quebec* 3 (1837): 282.

41. Schoolcraft, *Personal Memoirs,* 148, 176.

42. Ibid., May 4, 1824.

43. Ibid., 176; HBC, Fort William post, May 10, 1824, TBHMS.

44. David Thompson, letter, June 2, 1824, Thomas Barclay Collection, Maine Historical Society, Portland, Maine; Bayfield, "Abstract of Meteorological Journal," for May through September 1824.

45. Miron Heinselman, *The Boundary Waters Wilderness Ecosystem* (Minneapolis: University of Minnesota Press, 1996), 50, 54, 57.

46. Thompson, letter, September 8, 1824, Thomas Barclay Collection.

47. Ibid.

48. Bayfield, "Abstract of Meteorological Journal," 282.

49. John Franklin, *Narrative of a Second Expedition to the Shores of the Polar Sea in the Years 1825, 1826, and 1827* (Philadelphia: Carey, Lea and Carey, 1828), xvi; Edward De Krafft, comp., *Meteorological Register for the Years 1822, 1823, 1824 & 1825: from Observations Made by the Surgeons of the Army, at Military Posts of the United States* (Washington, 1826), 33–55. The weather records used here are drawn from Fort Brady, outside of Sault Ste. Marie.

50. Lac La Pluie, April 23, 1825, B.105/a /10, HBCA.

51. John Johnston, "An Account of Lake Superior," in *Les Bourgeois de la Compagnie,* ed. L. R. Masson (New York: Antiquarian Press, 1960), 170. The elder Johnston used "Tenerife" as a metaphor for a particularly steep, rugged mountain. Tenerife is one of the Canary Islands known for its steep volcanic rock faces that plunge into the Atlantic Ocean. Johnston would also have known that the NWC partners consumed vast quantities of wines from Tenerife.

52. Chapman, *Log*, November 13, 1823.
53. Johnston, *Journal*, February 1, 1825. Fishing was possible when the bay was either free of ice or completely frozen enough to travel on it and set nets or lines. If the ice was not solid enough, it became dangerous to go out to deeper water and sometimes difficult to "lift" or retrieve a net. Or the net or hooks might be carried off by an ice flow separating from the shore and thus lost. Anishinaabeg fishers, in the depth of winter on Thunder Bay ice, would both spear and set lines for trout. Sometimes the HBC men would catch suckers in gill nets to provide bait to Anishinaabeg to use on their hooks when fishing off the ice. Fort William, January 24 and 24, 1831; January 11, 15, 25, and 31, 1832; and January 20 and 28 and February 2 and 14, 1833, B.231/a/10–12, HBCA.
54. Chapman, *Log*, December 24, 1823; January 19, 1824. Chapman's note saying they experienced earthquakes could not substantiated in the Fort William journal at the time, or at two university websites that note historic earthquakes. The major series earthquakes at New Madrid, Missouri, occurred in late 1811 and early 1812, or more than ten years earlier. "Tectonic Earthquakes Felt or Occurring in Michigan," https://www .msu.edu/~fujita/earthquake/mieqlist.html; http://www.intute.ac.uk/ sciences/hazards/Earthquakes-database.html; Val W. Chandler, geophysicist, Minnesota Geological Survey, personal communication with author, January 19, 2011.

   What phenomenon did Chapman experience? Could some of the rocky headlands above the harbor have splintered off and shaken their buildings? Perhaps the most plausible explanation is that they heard an "ice quake," or cryoseism, made by a sudden cracking in the soil or rock that is saturated with water or ice. It often makes a booming noise, but the sound is highly localized. It is also possible he misinterpreted three "thundersnow" events; however, it seems likely he or his men would have known about these, as they lived much of their lives outdoors. It is also curious that Chapman had a folk belief that earthquake tremors come in three waves, much like the belief about the "three sisters" of menacing waves on Lake Superior.
55. HBC, Fort William post, November 29, 1823, TBHMS; Fort William post, September 1, 1829, B.231/a/11, HBCA.
56. Chapman, *Log*, February 7 and March 7, 1824; Leslie Ritchie, "'Expectations of Grease & Provisions': The Circulation and Regulation of Fur Trade Foodstuffs," *Eighteenth Century Life* 23, 2 (1999): 124–42.
57. Billy Blackwell, personal communication with author, March 4, 2010, Grand Portage, Minn.

58. Ellworth T. Carlestedt, "When Fond du Lac Was British," *Minnesota History* 20 (1939): 13.

59. Perrault, "Narrative of the Travels," 179. Fond du Lac operated from 1793 to 1811, and its successor operated farther upstream on the St. Louis River from 1811 to 1817. Nelson, *My First Years in the Fur Trade,* 98. It is not entirely clear what location Nelson called "Vieu Déser."

60. Michel Curot, "A Wisconsin Fur-Trader's Journal, 1803–1804," *Wisconsin Historical Collections* 20 (1911): 471.

61. John Fritzen, *Historic Sites and Place Names of Minnesota's North Shore* (Duluth, Minn: St. Louis County Historical Society, 1974), 21; and Blackwell, personal communication.

62. Gilfillan, "Minnesota Geographical Names," 454; Chrysostom Verwyst, "A Glossary of Chippewa Indian Names of Rivers, Lake and Villages," *Acta et Dicta* 4, 2 (July 1916): 259. There are examples of North Shore Anishinaabemowin place-names that did not translate into English, such as Beaver Bay.

63. Gilfillan, "Minnesota Geographical Names," 453–54; Verwyst, "A Glossary of Chippewa Indian Names," 265.

64. David Thompson, as quoted in Nute, *Lake Superior,* 60.

65. Léandre Bergeron, *Dictonnaire de Langue Québécoise* (Montreal: VLB, 1980), 310; Louis-Alexandre Bélisle, *Dictionnaire Bélisle de la Langue Française au Canada* (Quebec: Belisle, 1971), 748.

    Alain Nabarra, professor of French at Lakehead University in Thunder Bay, who is interested in historic French contributions to this region, wrote: "I found an interesting piece of information: in New France, and even in some part of Québec today, the word 'MARÉE' was (and is) used with the meaning of 'MARE': an expanse of water. So it is very probable that when using the word: 'Grand-Marée' the voyageurs meant 'an expanse of still, calm (by contrast with the waves, winds, dangers of the lake) and shallow (thus near the coastline) water,' with the connotations a resting place, a cove, a place to harbor. 'Grand-Marée' was and is part of oral dialect. If it has been written 'Grand Marais,' it is probably because of phonetic confusion due to dialectal pronunciation. And the transfer of meaning in the mind of the writer (or an educated person or a cartographer) 'marée' has only the meaning of tide." Alain Nabarra, personal communication with author, August 23, 2011, Thunder Bay, Ontario.

66. Roger J. Steiner, ed., *The New College French and English Dictionary,* 2nd ed. (New York: Amsco School Publications, 1988), 203; Bernard C. Peters, "The Origin and Meaning of the Term 'Marais' as Used on the Lake Superior Shoreline of Michigan," *Michigan Academician* 13, 1 (Summer 1980): 7–16.

67. None of the early explorers (David Thompson, Lieutenant Henry Bay-field, or George Cannon) who came to Grand Marais mentioned a swamp. Geologist David Dale Owen's 1852 geologic survey and diagram of North Shore places (documenting mostly Anishinaabeg place-names) noted the "great sheltered nature of the [Bitobigunk] Bay" and "grooves and scratches" on the rocks on the point, but no marsh-like feature. This is in contrast to noting swamps in a number of inland places. David Dale Owen, *Report of a Geological Survey of Wisconsin, Iowa, and Minnesota* (Philadelphia: Lippincott, Grambo and Co., 1852), 388–89, 395. Nor did the first American surveyor for the area of the town note a swamp. Elias C. Martin, Deputy Surveyor, October 7, 1859, Cook County Recorder's Office, Grand Marais, Minn.

There is a contemporary view that asserts that Grand Marais means "great swamp," the primary evidence being a small pond trapped behind the cobblestone beachline, which was used as a swimming hole in the first half of the twentieth century. It is filled in now. The place-name explanation appears to be apocryphal. Swimming in the pond was fondly remembered, and the accompanying wetland being the source of the name made sense to latter-day residents. This does not explain why the name with its meaning of "great swamp" was bestowed on this place, and this meaning would not have had much relevance to early paddlers on the lake. More than fifty years before Grand Marais was "settled," voyageurs and fur trade clerks had anchored the name to the place. The meaning of Gichi Bitobig, or twin sheltered waters, is not far from the meaning of the Quebecois Grand Marée but quite distant from Great Swamp.

68. Lieutenant Henry W. Bayfield, Lake Superior, sheet III, printed in 1828 by the British Admiralty, Library and Archives Canada, Ottawa.

69. "North America, Sheet IV, Lake Superior, Reduced from the Admiralty Survey," Society for the Diffusion of Useful Knowledge, London, 1832. Copy of the map owned by the author.

70. Harbor Friends, "Grand Marais Harbor Reshaping, 1870 to 2000," 12–13: "6 acres of land at the Northeast corner of . . . the harbor" were excavated and removed.

2. American Fur Company and the Trade

1. Elizabeth Louisa Gebhard, *The Life and Ventures of the Original John Jacob Astor* (Hudson, N.Y.: Bryan, 1915), 101–16; John Upton Terrell, *Furs by Astor* (New York: Morrow, 1963), 61–75.

2. I am using birth year estimates that Mattie Marie Harper devised in her

dissertation. Matti Marie Harper, "French Africans in Ojibwe Country: Negotiating Marriage, Identity, and Race, 1780–1890" (Ph.D. diss.: University of California, Berkeley, 2012), 50.

3. Charles Flandrau, "Charles Flandrau's Reminiscences," read before the Minnesota Historical Society, April 25, 1898. The lack of blacks in this region at this time also led the 1857 Minnesota Territorial Census to list George Bonga's race as "white." September 21, 1857, Minnesota Archives, Minnesota Historical Society, St. Paul.

4. Pierre Bonga was the son of Jean Bonga, a slave servant of the British commandant at Michilimackinac. Apparently, Jean Bonga's family was also at Michilimackinac—one brother and two sisters. When Captain Robertson drowned in 1787, Jean was manumitted, or freed, to marry Jeanne Bonga, "a free Negro woman." Jean and Jeanne Bonga were formally married at Michilimackinac on June 25, 1794; however, they had children prior to formalizing their vows. Six months later, Jean Bonga was dead. Their son, Pierre, married an unnamed Anishinaabe woman, and she gave birth to a daughter on March 12, 1801. The Bonga family were part of the Catholic society at Mackinac. Harper, "French Africans in Ojibwe Country," 24; Reuben Gold Thwaites, ed., "The Mackinac Register of Marriages, 1725–1760," *Collections of the State Historical Society of Wisconsin* 18: 497; and Reuben Gold Thwaites, ed., "The Mackinac Register of Baptisms and Interments, 1695–1821," *Collections of the Historical Society of Wisconsin* 19: 83, 157; George Bonga, "The Letters of George Bonga," *Journal of Negro History* 12 (1927): 54; Paul H. Gaboriault, "Who Was Stephen Bongo?," *Evening Telegram* [Superior, Wis.], August 2, 1982; Peg Meier, "Black Frontiersman," *Minneapolis Star Tribune*, February 6, 1995.

5. Kenneth W. Porter, "Negroes and the Fur Trade," *Minnesota History* 15 (1934): 424–25.

6. Clement A. Lounsberry, *Early History of North Dakota* (Washington, D.C.: Liberty Press, 1919), 42.

7. Jean Morrison, "Pierre Bonga—the Black Engagé," June 16, 1984, Old Fort William, Thunder Bay, Ontario; Jean Morrison, *Superior Rendezvous-Place: Fort William in the Canadian Fur Trade* (Toronto: Natural Heritage, 2001), 97.

8. Lac La Pluie, July 8, 1819, B.105/a/7, HBCA.

9. Doty, "Northern Wisconsin in 1820," 201. Fur traders used the offensive term *squaw* here to mean a female Anishinaabeg woman. Most traders viewed Anishinaabeg women as a lesser form of a human for being both female and Indian. Some traders saw them merely as convenient beasts

of burden or drudges, while a few recognized their fundamental contributions to Anishinaabeg life and society.

10. The NWC and later the HBC must have had high regards for Pierre Bonga. For example, four years after his death, the HBC trader sought out his heirs—then working for their competitor, the AFC—to pay wages yet owed to Pierre Bonga. Nute, *Calendar of the American Fur Company's Papers*, parts 2 and 3, 445, 447.

11. Earl Spangler, "The Negro in Minnesota, 1800–1865," *Manitoba Historical Society Transactions* 3 (1963–64): 2–3.

12. Alfred Brunson, *A Western Pioneer: or, Incidents in the Life and Times of Rev. Alfred Brunson* (Cincinnati: Hitchcock and Walden, 1879), 2:83–84.

13. Meier, "Black Frontiersman"; Gaboriault, "Who Was Stephen Bungo?"; U.S. Federal Census for Minnesota, 1860.

14. "List of Persons Employed by the American Fur Company at Fond du Lac & dependencies 1834," "Register of Men Employed by the American Fur Company's Northern Outfit, 30th May 1841," American Fur Company Papers, New York Historical Society, New York; U.S. Territorial Census for Minnesota, 1849; U.S. Federal Census for Minnesota, 1860; Kappler, "Treaty with the Chippewa, 1842," in *Indian Affairs*, 545.

15. "Stephen Bungo: Voyageur," *Evening Telegram* [Superior, Wis.], August 24, 1983.

16. Ronald N. Satz, "Chippewa Treat Rights," *Wisconsin Academy of Sciences, Arts, and Letters* 79: 1 (1991): 58.

17. Schoolcraft, *Personal Memoirs*, 478; Jean Morrison, *Superior Rendezvous-Place*, 109. The Bongas clearly were fluent Anishinaabeg speakers. However, the Bongas may have given a remarkable gift back to the Anishinaabeg, according to ethnomusicologist Frances Densmore. She stated that the old "Chippewa love songs" of two tribes are strikingly similar to the "nasal, drawling tone that also characterizes the singing of Negroes." Densmore then wonders aloud if the songs she recorded are the product of the Bongas adding a unique tone to Anishinaabeg love songs. Frances Densmore, "Brief Communications," *American Anthropologist* 47, 4 (October-December, 1945): 638–39.

18. Kappler, "Treaty with the Chippewa, 1837," in *Indian Affairs,* 493; Alfred Brunson, *A Western Pioneer,* 2:83.

19. Kappler, "Treaty with the Chippewa of the Mississippi and Lake Superior, 1847," in *Indian Affairs,* 570.

20. Ely Papers, April 26, 1834.

21. Patricia Condon Johnston, *Eastman Johnson's Lake Superior Indians* (Afton, Minn.: Johnston Publishing, 1983), 15. Many of Eastman Johnson's

paintings are held by the St. Louis County Historical Society, Duluth, Minn.

22. Manuscript in Henry M. Rice Papers, perhaps written by Paul Beaulieu, Minnesota Historical Society, St. Paul.

23. George Bonga, letter to Reverend W. T. Boutwell, April 1, 1838, Henry H. Sibley Papers, Minnesota Historical Society, St. Paul. *Aitkin* is a widely used alternative spelling for *Aitken*.

24. Harper, "French Africans in Ojibwe Country," 21.

25. It is likely that George or Stephen had paddled the border route from Fort William to Rainy Lake in the summer of 1819. The HBC Rainy Lake clerk wrote, noting that a NWC canoe brigade went through: "they had apparently lost their Bourguois [sic] and substituted a negroe [sic] in his place." Rainy Lake, July 8, 1819, B.105/a/7, HBCA.

26. George Johnston, letter to General Lewis Cass, December 30, 1845, Grand Traverse Bay, Bentley Historical Library, Ann Arbor, Mich.

27. Theresa M. Schenck, *William W. Warren: The Life, Letters, and Times of an Ojibwe Leader* (Lincoln: University of Nebraska Press, 2007), viii.

28. John Johnston, "Means of Amelioration, Letter Means of Amelioration," Letter 1, St. Mary's Falls, January 24, 1822," in Schoolcraft, *Information Respecting the History*, 2:524.

29. Chapman, *Log*, February 3, 1824. Chapman was likely referring to a fellow clerk Pierre Cotte. Cotte, assumed by some to be "half-breed," was a French man from Montreal. His wife, Margaret, was metis or "half breed." The Cottes were long associated with the AFC Fond du Lac establishment, from which Chapman had just left. He and his wife became renowned for their efforts in providing Roman Catholic instructions to Métis and Anishinaabeg. Anna Mary Keenan, "Pierre Cotte," *Acta et Dicta* 6, 1 (October 1933): 86–96; and Theresa M. Schenck, *All Our Relations: Chippewa Mixed-Bloods and the Treaty of 1837* (Amik Press and The Centre for Rupert's Land Studies at the University of Winnipeg, Madison, Wisconsin, 2010), 52.

There is an irony to Chapman's disparaging comments about Cotte and "half-breeds," since Chapman himself was married to a woman of mixed ancestry, and thus his children would be considered by many as "half-breeds." *Half-breed* became a more common term as British and American pseudoscientific race theory came into play. Once called Bois Brule or simply Canadians, in the first decades of the nineteenth century terms like *half-breed*, or *mixed-blood*, and *Métis* were used commonly for persons of mixed ancestry. A person of mixed ancestry was frequently of French Anishinaabeg descent (Cotte), or British Anishinaabeg descent

(George Johnston), or American Anishinaabeg descent (such as Bela Chapman's children).

During this same period, whites begrudgingly recognized the coalescing Red River Métis settlement and culture as being neither Indian nor white. It would take years and much bloodshed before Métis were formally recognized in Canada. Jacqueline Peterson, "Red River Redux: Métis Ethnogenesis and the Great Lakes Region," in *Contours of a People: Metis Family, Mobility, and History*, ed. Nicole St-Onge, Carolyn Podruchny, and Brenda Macdougall (Norman: University of Oklahoma Press, 2012), 26–29; Mary Lethert Wingerd, *North Country: The Making of Minnesota* (Minneapolis: University of Minnesota Press, 2010), 126.

30. Fur trade scholars Jennifer Brown and Theresa Schenck believe the term *halfbreed* was first used in HBC records in 1814. Jennifer Brown and Theresa Schenck, "Métis, Mestizo, and Mixed-Blood," in *A Companion to American Indian History*, ed. Philip J. Deloria and Neal Salisbury (Malden, Mass.: Wiley-Blackwell, 2004), 326.

31. Carter, *The Territorial Papers of the United States*, vol. 11: 730–31, 738, and 742; Robert Bieder, *Science Encounters the Indian 1820–1880: The Early Years of American Ethnology* (Norman: University of Oklahoma Press, 1986), 66.

32. Frank Straus, "Ambrose R. Davenport," Ambrose Davenport file, Mackinac Island State Park, Michigan Department of Natural Resources; Edwin O. Wood, *Historic Mackinac: The Historical, Picturesque, and Legendary Features of the Mackinac Country* (New York: Macmillan, 1918), 526–27; John R. Bailey, *Mackinac: Formerly Michilimackinac* (Grand Rapids, Mich.: Tradesman Co., 1909), 170.

33. Kappler, "Treaty with the Chippewa, 1826," in *Indian Affairs*, 272. In 1826, "Susan Davenport, granddaughter of Misquabunoqua, and wife of Ambrose Davenport, and to each of her children, one section."

34. S. R., *Friends Intelligencer* 39 (August 1, 1882): 444.

35. Schoolcraft, *Information Respecting the Indian Tribes*, 605. Davenport was the licensed trader at Grand Portage for 1831–32.

36. "List of Persons Employed by the American Fur Company," 1834, American Fur Company Papers, New York Historical Society.

37. Papers of Edmund F. Ely, Journal #2, October 22, 1833, Minnesota Historical Society, St. Paul.

38. 1850 Federal Census for Michigan; Timothy Harrison, "The Davenport Lighthouse Legacy," *Lighthouse Digest*, August 2008.

39. Ambrose Davenport, death record, November 4, 1879, Mackinac County Clerk Records, Mackinac, Mich.

40. Ely, Journal, November 5, 1833, and May 23, 1834; Podruchny, *Making the Voyageur World*, 179.

41. Ely, Journal, 1834.

42. Chapman, *Log*, November 13, 1823. Stephen and Jack Bonga's names appear only on the front page of Chapman's *Log* and not in his written text.

43. Johnston, *Journal*, December 1, 1824.

44. Kerry A. Trask, *Black Hawk: The Battle for the Heart of America* (New York: Holt, 2006), 25–26.

45. William Watts Folwell, *A History of Minnesota* (St. Paul: Minnesota Historical Society Press, 1956), 1:145.

46. Wingerd, *North Country*, 82, 90.

47. Daniel Walker Howe, *What Hath God Wrought: The Transformation of America, 1815–1848* (Oxford: Oxford University Press, 2007), 34.

48. Folwell, *A History of Minnesota*, 1:140; Wingerd, *North Country*, 101.

49. Howe, *What Hath God Wrought*, 207–8.

50. Susan Sleeper-Smith, "'[A]n Unpleasant Transaction on this Frontier': Challenging Female Autonomy and Authority at Michilimackinac," *Journal of the Early Republic* 25 (Fall 2005): 423.

51. Morrison, *Superior Rendezvous-Place*, 73.

52. Howe, *What Hath God Wrought*, 75.

53. Sleeper-Smith, "'[A]n Unpleasant Transaction,'" 424.

54. Michael Chenoweth, "Ships' Logbooks and 'The Year without a Summer,'" *Bulletin of the American Meteorological Society* 77: 9 (September 1996): 2084; and Lee Foster, "1816—The Year without Summer," http://erh.noaa.gov/car/Newsletter/htm_format_articles/climate_corner?yearwithouts.

55. The first year the American surveyors overwintered at Fort William (unlike their counterparts, who returned to eastern Canada), which allowed them to survey Isle Royale in the fall of 1822. Most years, however, the surveyors from both countries were in the field only during the summer months. In a show of good cheer and appreciation for their HBC hosts, lead American surveyor James Ferguson (and the U.S. government) paid for the traditional New Year's regale to Fort William HBC "servants" and Anishinaabeg. James Ferguson, letter to General Peter Porter, January 20, 1823, Porter Collection.

56. David Thompson, letter, March 16, 1822, Thomas Barclay Collection. Thompson's letters were largely written to the British border commissioner, Anthony Barclay, and were not available to the Americans at that time.

57. Thompson, letters, March 17, 1823, and August 22, 1823, Thomas Barclay Collection. Ironically, Thompson's geographical masterpiece once hung

at the Great Hall of Fort William. In this map, Thompson charts much of the Canadian northwest from Lake Superior and Hudson Bay on the east to the Pacific Ocean.

58. Johnston, *Journal,* August 15, 1824.

59. Thompson, letter, September 8, 1824, Thomas Barclay Collection.

60. John D. Haeger, "Business Strategy and Practice in the Early Republic: John Jacob Astor and the American Fur Trade," *Western Historical Quarterly* 19, 2 (May 1988): 184.

61. Terrell, *Furs by Astor,* 297–98.

62. Wingerd, *North Country,* 92.

63. Peter Stark, *Astoria: John Jacob Astor and Thomas Jefferson's Lost Pacific Empire* (New York: HarperCollins, 2014), 287.

64. Encyclopedia of Chicago, Chicago Historical Society, www.enclyclopedia .chicagohistory.org/pages/10958.html.

65. Marjorie Cahn Brazer, *Harps upon the Willows: The Johnston Family of the Old Northwest* (Ann Arbor: Historical Society of Michigan, 1993), 142; Folwell, *A History of Minnesota,* 1:168–69.

66. W. Sheridan Warrick, "The American Indian Policy in the Upper Old Northwest following the War of 1812," *Ethnohistory* 3, 3 (Spring 1956): 110; Kenneth Wiggins Porter, *John Jacob Astor, Business Man* (Cambridge: Harvard University Press, 1931), 710–14.

67. Thomas Jefferson, letter to John Jacob Astor, April 13, 1808, in *The Writings of Thomas Jefferson,* vol. 12, ed. Albert Ellery Bergh (Washington, D.C.: Thomas Jefferson Memorial Association, 1907), 28; "Fur and the Fur Trade, II," *Saturday Magazine* 21, 674 (December 1842): 262.

68. Astor loaned the U.S. government two million dollars during the War of 1812. John H. Humins, "Furs, Astor, and Indians: The American Fur Company in the Old Northwest Territory," *Michigan History* 69 (March/April 1985): 25; Porter, *John Jacob Astor,* 726–27.

69. Terrell, *Furs by Astor,* 249.

70. Ramsay Crooks, letter to John Jacob Astor, March or April 1817, Mackinaw American Fur Company Letterbook, quoted in Rollo C. Keithahn, "The American Fur Company in the Upper Mississippi Valley" (master's thesis, University of Minnesota, 1929), 57.

71. Axel Madsen, *John Jacob Astor: America's First Multimillionaire* (New York: John Wiley, 2002), 173; Terrell, *Furs by Astor,* 173.

72. Porter, *John Jacob Astor,* 725n54; and Humins, "Furs, Astor, and Indians," 27.

73. Morrison, *Superior Rendezvous-Place,* 81–90.

74. John Jacob Astor, letter to Secretary of State James Monroe, December 30, 1816, copy in Thomas Selkirk Papers, Minnesota Historical Society, St. Paul. The South West Fur Company was a hybrid company owned by

both Astor and principals of the NWC. Selkirk's main aim was to bring to justice those who had purposefully harmed HBC settlers at Red River and the ability of HBC to conduct business in the region. Later, Lord Selkirk privately reimbursed the AFC for the high wines and goods taken from Fond du Lac during the conflict. Ramsay Crooks, letter to John Jacob Astor, May 2, 1818, American Fur Company Papers, New York Historical Society; William McGillivray, letter to John Jacob Astor, November 23, 1816, Selkirk Papers.

75. Selkirk Papers, 8588; Kenneth MacKenzie, letter to Duncan Cameron, August 27, 1815, National Archives of Canada, Ottawa, Ontario.

76. Gilman, *The Grand Portage Story*, 124, 104; Ramsay Crooks, letter to John Jacob Astor, November 30, 1821, American Fur Company Papers, New York Historical Society: "by getting our traders appointed Officers of the Customs by the Collector at Mackina [sic] we can seize them if they venture into our territory."

77. Terrell, *Furs by Astor*, 273–74.

78. Porter, *John Jacob Astor*, 707.

79. Schoolcraft, "Mr. Schoolcraft's Report," 43.

80. Haeger, "Business Strategy and Practice in the Early Republic," 197.

81. "Lac La Pluie District Report for 1822–1823," B.105/e/2, HBCA.

82. Lac La Pluie Journal, November 8, 1822, and Simon McGillivray, letter to John McLoughlin, October 30, 1822, B.105/a/8, HBCA.

83. "Lac La Pluie District Report for 1822–1823"; John S. Galbraith, "British-American Competition in the Border Fur Trade of the 1820s," *Minnesota History* 36, 7 (September 1959): 242–44.

84. Lac La Pluie Journal, September 7 and 23, 1822, and October 7, 1822.

85. Lac La Pluie Journal, September 11, 1822; "Lac La Pluie District Report for 1822–1823."

86. John McLoughlin, undated letter [from December 1822] to Simon McGillivray [at Basswood Lake], Lac La Pluie Journal, B.105/a/8, HBCA.

87. John L. Bigsby, *The Shoe and Canoe: or Pictures of Travel in the Canadas* (London: Chapman and Hall, 1850), 273. Also during the 1822–23 winter, HBC trader John McLoughlin had detained AFC employee Cotte and another clerk for "trespass" into Canada and made them promise they would not cross into Canada again.

88. Anna Youngman, "The Fortune of John Jacob Astor," *Journal of Political Economy* 16, 6 (June 1908): 363.

89. Terrell, *Furs by Astor*, 296.

90. Thomas L. McKenney, *Sketches of a Tour to the Lakes, of the Character and Customs of the Chippeway Indians, and of Incidents Connected with*

the Treaty of Fond Du Lac (First published 1827; Minneapolis: Ross and Haines, 1959), 396.

91. Keith R. Widder, *Battle for the Soul: Métis Children Encounter Evangelical Protestants at Mackinaw Mission, 1822–1837* (East Lansing: Michigan State University Press, 1999), 49.

92. Ibid.

93. Ibid., 63.

94. Martin Heydenburk, "Incidents in the Life of Robert Stuart," *Michigan Pioneer and Historical Collection* 3 (Lansing: George & Co., 1881), 58; Donald W. Voelker, "Robert Stuart: A Man Who Meant Business," *Michigan History Magazine*, September/October 1990, 17. Stuart followed his wife's conversion, and his behavior changed noticeably in January 1829.

95. Wingerd, *North Country*, 89–90.

96. "Copy of Mr. Trowbridge's Letter," *Michigan Pioneer and Historical Collection* 3 (Lansing: George & Co., 1881), 54; Voelker, "Robert Stuart," 13–16. Stuart led a remarkable life. He led a handful of AFC men across the continent on an overland route, some of which became the Oregon Trail. He also became the U.S. Indian Agent who negotiated the 1842 La Pointe Treaty, or "Miners Treaty," that ceded much of the western Upper Peninsula of Michigan, northern Wisconsin, and Isle Royale to the Americans.

97. Voelker, "Robert Stuart," 16.

98. Warrick, "The American Indian Policy in the Upper Old Northwest," 111.

99. Ibid., 115.

100. Thompson, letter, August 17, 1822, Thomas Barclay Collection. The death of Lord Selkirk in 1820—the majority owner of the HBC—also created great uncertainty at this time.

101. Thompson, letter, July 29, 1822, from Fort William, Thomas Barclay Collection.

102. *Minutes of the Council, Northern Department of Rupert Land, 1821–33,* edited by R. Harvey Fleming (Toronto: The Champlain Society, 1940), 33–35.

103. Lac La Pluie, January 29, 1825, B.105/a/10, HBCA. This rumor would have spread to Fort William through the winter mail.

104. Lac La Pluie, March 15, 1825, B.105/a/10, HBCA.

105. James L. Clayton, "The Growth and Economic Significance of the American Fur Trade, 1790–1890," in *Aspects of the Fur Trade: Selected Papers of the 1965 North American Fur Trade Conference* (St. Paul: Minnesota Historical Society, 1967), 64.

106. Milan Novak, Martyn E. Obbard, James G. Jones, Robert Newman, Annie Booth, Andrew J. Satterthwaite, and Greg Linscombe, "Furbearer

Harvests in North American, 1600–1984," Ontario Ministry of Natural Resources (1987), 116, 180, 245.

107. Ibid., 40 (for beaver), 83 (for foxes), 127 (for mink), 150 (for muskrat).

108. Ibid., 103 (for lynx); Fort William, September 16, 1831, B.231/a/11, HBCA.

109. The HBC were trading various handmade steel traps to Cree from their major posts along Hudson Bay. Only posts with blacksmiths produced traps. There was a different type of metal trap for each animal species sought. James Isham, *Isham's Observations and Notes,* ed. E. E. Rich (London: Hudson's Bay Company Record Society, 1949), 159; Robin F. Wells, "Castoreum and Steel Traps in Eastern North America," *American Anthropologist 74,* 3 (June 1972): 479, 481.

110. J. B. Tyrrell, ed., *David Thompson's Narrative of His Explorations in Western America, 1784–1812* (Toronto: Champlain Society, 1916), 204–5.

111. A. W. Schorger, "A Brief History of the Steel Trap and Its Use in North America," *Transactions of the Wisconsin Academy of Sciences, Arts, and Letters 4,* 2 (1951): 182ff.

112. John Fritzen, *The History of Fond Du Lac and Jay Cooke Park* (Duluth: St Louis County Historical Society, 1978), 14.

113. Ibid., 12, 15.

114. James Duane Doty, "Papers of James Duane Doty, Official Journal 1820, Expedition with Cass and Schoolcraft," in *Collections of the State Historical Society of Wisconsin,* vol. 13, ed. Reuben Gold Thwaites (Madison: Wisconsin Historical Society, 1895), 202. The expedition paddled up the St. Louis River en route to find the source of the Mississippi River.

115. Johnston, *Journal,* September 4, 1824.

116. McKenney, *Sketches of a Tour to the Lakes,* 276–77.

117. Allan Morrison Papers, Minnesota Historical Society, St. Paul.

118. Robert Stuart, letter to John Jacob Astor, July 22, 1818, New York Historical Society.

119. McKenney, *Sketches of a Tour to the Lakes,* 377.

120. Henry R. Schoolcraft, "Posts to be Established for Indian Trade in the Country of Fond du Lac are as follows," July 31, 1824, Reel 49, Container 61, Henry R. Schoolcraft Papers, Library of Congress, Washington, D.C.

121. J. D. Cameron, "Report of the Transactions at Rainy Lake during the Year 1824–25," June 1, 1825, Rainy Lake, B.105/e /6, HBCA.

122. Ramsay Crooks, letter to John Jacob Astor, July 21, 1817, in *Final Report of the International Joint Commission on the Lake of the Woods* (Washington, D.C.: Government Printing Office, 1917), 126.

123. William Morrison, obituary, *New York Times,* August 21, 1866. This obituary notice made the claim that Morrison was the first white man to discover the source of the Mississippi. Perhaps more reliable was the

information that Morrison had deep fur trade roots; he was the grandson of Jean Etienne Waden, a fur trader, who was murdered by the ambitious Peter Pond. Warren, *History of the Ojibway People*, 381. Further, Morrison is often credited with stopping the Minnesota Anishinaabeg participation with the Shawnee Prophet's efforts to rid North America of whites and "colonial" influences, such as alcohol. "The Red River Trail," *Harper's New Monthly Magazine* 19 (June 1859): 52–54.

124. Kappler, "Treaty with the Chippewa, 1826," in *Indian Affairs*, 272.

125. *Final Report of the International Joint Commission on the Lake of the Woods*, 126.

126. Warren, *History of the Ojibway People*, 382.

127. Allan Morrison Papers, Minnesota Historical Society.

128. William Aitken married Charles Oakes Ermatinger's Métis daughter, Marguerite. Knight and Chute, "In the Shadow of the Thumping Drum," 92.

129. David Lavender, *The Fist in the Wilderness* (Garden City, N.Y.: Doubleday, 1964), 328.

130. Ramsay Crooks, letter to Robert Stuart, December 5, 1821, American Fur Company Papers, New York Historical Society.

131. Schoolcraft, "Posts to be Established for Indian Trade"; Henry R. Schoolcraft, letter, August 2, 1824, Office of Indian Agency, Sault Ste. Marie, in Sibley Papers.

132. Kappler, "Treaty with the Chippewa, 1826," in *Indian Affairs*, 273.

133. The text lists the known fur companies and clerks along the North Shore during these years. Indian license to Bela Chapman published in 19th Congress, 1st sess., House doc. 118, 1826, 30; Johnston, *Journal*; license issued to William Aitken, August 2, 1824, Sibley Papers; 20 Cong. 1st sess., Sen. Doc. 96, 1828, 36; Fort William, July 14 and October 5 and 7, 1828, B.231/a/8, HBCA; Fort William, October 3, 1829, B.231/a/9, HBCA; Fort William District Report, 1828–29, B.231/e/6, HBCA; 21st Cong., 2nd sess., House Doc. 42, 1831, 7; Fort William, November 7, 1830, and April 30, 1831, B.231/a/10, HBCA; Indian license, 22nd Cong., 2nd sess., Sen. doc. 90, 50; microfilm 234, roll 770, Sault Ste. Marie Agency, Office of Indian Affairs, National Archives; Fort William, May 24, 1833, B.231/a/13, HBCA; Fort William, June 11, 1834, B.231/a/14, HBCA; Fort William, September 1, 1836, B.231/a/16, HBCA; Nute, *Calendar of the American Fur Company's Papers*, "Northern Outfit, 1836," 1575; letter, June 26, 1837, 309; letter, September 30, 1840, 834; 1839 Inspection Report, Gabriel Franchere Papers, Minnesota Historical Society, St. Paul; Nute, *Calendar of the American Fur Company's Papers*, letters on November 14, 18, 24, 1840, 1345–47.

134. William H. Keating, *Narrative of an Expedition to the Source of St. Peter's*

River, Lake Winnepeek, Lake of the Woods, etc Performed in the Year 1823 (Minneapolis: Ross and Haines, 1959), 170–72; Kane, Holmquist, and Gilman, *The Northern Expeditions of Stephen H. Long,* 229–30.

135. Ramsey Crooks, letter to William W. Matthews, Montreal, September 1, 1821, in *Final Report of the International Joint Commission of the Lake of the Woods,* 125. Crooks is looking "for a couple of good traders for the Rainy Lake Dept."

136. Johnston, *Journal,* February 1, 1825.

137. American Fur Company Contract with William Morrison, November 24, 1821, quoted in *Final Report of the International Joint Commission,* 126.

138. Ramsay Crooks, letter to Robert Stuart, April 8, 1822, in *Final Report of the International Joint Commission,* 127.

139. C. H. Beaulieu manuscript, 1880, in Henry M. Rice Papers, Minnesota Historical Society, St. Paul.

140. Thompson letter, November 11, 1823, Thomas Barclay Collection.

141. There are seven total references to alcohol use in the Chapman and Johnston journals, while the HBC Fort William clerks more frequently noted alcohol use. The AFC was licensed by the United States to take alcohol into "Indian Country," which included the border posts of "Grand Portage, Vermilion Lake, Rainy Lake, and Pembina." Henry Schoolcraft, U.S. Indian Agent, letter to William A. Aitken, August 2, 1824, in Sibley Papers.

    Alcohol consumption by whites at this time was also voluminous. An average American male adult in 1825 consumed seven gallons of alcohol a year, primarily whiskey and hard cider. Howe, *What Hath God Wrought,* 167.

142. Fort William, November 2, 1827, B.231/a/7, HBCA.

143. Bruce White, "Give Us a Little Milk: The Social and Cultural Meanings of Gift Giving in the Lake Superior Fur Trade," *Minnesota History* 48 (Summer 1982): 65.

144. Fort William, July 14, 1828, B.231/a/8, HBCA.

145. John Johnston, August 1, 1826, and an unattributed fragment, Johnston Family Papers, Bentley Historical Library, Ann Arbor, Mich.

146. Johnston, *Journal,* September 23, 1824.

147. Chapman, *Log,* October 3, 1823, and March 28, 1824.

148. Lavender, *The Fist in the Wilderness,* 299.

149. Lewis Cass, letter to Henry R. Schoolcraft, June 10, 1823, in "The Fur Trade in Wisconsin—1812–1825," in *Collections of the State Historical Society of Wisconsin,* vol. 20, ed. Rueben Gold Thwaites (Madison: Wisconsin Historical Society, 1911), 306.

150. *Final Report of the International Joint Commission,* 127.

151. Ibid.

152. Fort William, May 30, 1828, B.231/a/7, HBCA.

153. Humins, "Furs, Astor, and Indians," 29.

154. Fort William, January 4, 1828, B.231/a/7, HBCA.

155. Twenty-one HBC men and settlers, including Governor Semple, were killed by Métis in a confrontation known as the Battle of Seven Oaks. This violent event was part of a larger clash between the NWC and the HBC known as the Pemmican War. Métis were defending their homeland (with NWC assistance), while the HBC was moving settlers to and claiming jurisdiction over the greater Red River area.

156. March 31, 1815, microfilm C-9, vol. 31, 9213–14, Selkirk Papers, National Archives of Canada.

157. Youngman, "The Fortune of John Jacob Astor," 365.

158. John Haldane, "Report Lake Superior District, 1825," B.231/e/3, HBCA.

159. "Minutes of Council Held at York Factory, July 5, 1823," in *Minutes of Council, Northern Department*, 56.

160. Nicole St-Onge, "The Persistence of Travel and Trade: St. Lawrence River Valley French Engagés and the American Fur Company, 1818–1840," *Michigan Historical Review* 34, 2 (Fall 2008): 30.

161. Fort William HBC post, October 25, 1823, TBHMS.

162. John Haldane, Chief, Factor, "Report Lake Superior District 1825," B.231/e/3, HBCA.

163. Fort William HBC post, December 15 and 20, 1823, TBHMS.

164. William Johnston, "Letters on the Fur Trade 1833," *Michigan Pioneer and Historical Collections* 37 (1909–10), 201.

165. Fort William post, December 17 and 22, 1823, January 1, February 23, and April 24, 1824, TBHMS. Mr. Grant then moved to a portage off White Fish Lake and closed the White Fish Lake post. Fort William post, January 20 and 22, 1824, March 6, 10, 16, and 28, 1824, TBHMS. The HBC established a satellite post at Arrow Lake the winter of 1830–31. There was a secondary advantage to establishing an outpost besides intercepting more Indian trade: those men were living off the country and less reliant upon Fort William rations.

166. Joseph Delafield, *The Unfortified Boundary* (New York: privately printed, 1943), 400–402.

167. Also the guests at Fort William illustrated its significance. During the winter of 1823–24, Royal Navy personnel—Lieutenants Bayfield and Collins, and naval surgeon Mr. McLean—resided in Fort William quarters.

168. Threatened with a policy of no alcohol and as a strategy for exercising their control, Leech Lake Anishinaabeg threatened to burn the AFC

post. However, they did not. Tim E. Holzkamm, "Fur Trade Dependency and the Pillager Ojibway of Leech Lake, 1825–1842," *Minnesota Archeologist* 45, 2 (Fall/Winter 1986): 10.

169. David Thompson, letter, from Kingston (on Lake Ontario), November 12, 1822, Thomas Barclay Collection. These maps, once thought to have been lost, are part of the Thomas Barclay Collection at the Maine Historical Society.

170. Thompson letter, August 17, 1823, from Saganaga Lake, Thomas Barclay Collection. Eventually his son, Samuel Thompson, would assemble this knowledge and do the fieldwork on this portion of the border route. Though derived, in part, from "Indian information," it is a formal survey map. For example, it has notations about tributaries and their watersheds entering the border route that were apparently not examined by survey crews. Further it states that the border lakes were "the usual route of the canoe." Map F51, Collection 26, Barclay Collection.

171. Thompson, letters, March 3, 1823, and April 5, 1823, Thomas Barclay Collection.

172. James Ferguson, letter, July 2, 1822, Porter Collection.

173. Doty, "Northern Wisconsin in 1820," 205.

174. Schoolcraft, "Mr. Schoolcraft's Report," 44. There is no evidence that Chapman brought guns of any manufacture to Grand Marais for trade.

175. John Tanner, *A Narrative of the Captivity and Adventures of John Tanner* (New York: Penguin, 1994), 51.

176. Journal 3, April 26, 1834, Ely Journal, St. Louis County Historical Society.

3. Espagnol's Dilemma and the Anishinaabeg

1. Fort William, July 26, 1828, and August 21, 1830, B.231/a/8 and 10, HBCA.

2. David Thompson, letter, November 12, 1822, Thomas Barclay Collection; George Simpson, *Narrative of a Journey round the World* (London: Henry Colburn, 1847), 245–46.

3. Grand Portage elder Billy Blackwell mentioned that one of his teachers, the late Theresa Thibeault, also of Grand Portage, confirmed this name. Blackwell and other elders believe that traders misheard the Anishinaabemowin name "Aysh-pay-ahng" and rendered it "Espagnol" instead—a name they were more comfortable saying. Billy Blackwell, personal communication with author, May 6, 2014, Grand Portage. I have located only one historical reference reaffirming this Anishinaabeg name, although it is spelled very differently. Reverend Hurlburt, letter to James Evans, December 17, 1838, in John Mclean, *James Evans, Inventor*

of the Syllabic System of the Cree Language (Toronto: Methodist Mission Rooms, 1890), 135.

4. Fort William HBC post, July 8, 1824, B 4/2/1, TBHMS; October 5, 1828, July 13, 1830, May 25, 1832, and August 22, 1837, B.231/a/8, 10, 11, and 17, HBCA.

5. Father Francis Xavier Pierz, letter, October 1, 1838, *Berichte* 13: 49.

6. Ibid.; "Correspondence Book," Michipicoten, B.129/b/4, HBCA. Fur trader George Keith further described Espagnol in 1830 as "the most eminent living character at present . . . and who I am informed is a very brave, and well informed comparatively and sagacious character."

7. "Baptismal and Marriage Register," Father Francis Xavier Pierz Papers, Minnesota Historical Society, St. Paul.

8. Janet E. Chute, *The Legacy of Shingwaukonse: A Century of Native Leadership* (Toronto: University of Toronto Press, 1998), 10, 21. Little Pine, or Shingwaukonse, was the son of a British officer and an Anishinaabe woman. Chute explained that while he was "biologically of metis ancestry, Little Pine hailed from an exclusively Anishinaabeg cultural background." Shingwaukonse obtained great power through vision quests and was then included in the Plover dodem, or clan.

9. Fort William post, July 1, 1824, TBHMS; Fort William, March 18 and 29, 1827, B.321/a/7, HBCA.

10. Fort William, June 11 and 14, 1826, and August 21, 1830, B.231/a/6 and 10, HBCA; Fort William post fragment, January 10 and February 7, 1844, microfilm # M19, Minnesota Historical Society, St. Paul.

11. Ellen Olson, interview by Carolyn Gilman, November 1, 1989, Grand Portage. A copy of the interview is held at Grand Portage National Monument.

12. We know that a "delegation from old Grand Portage" went to the 1826 treaty but did not sign it. However, one leader, Little Caribou, or Attikonse, received a medal from the Americans. Henry Schoolcraft, "Treaty of Fond du Lac," *National Journal* [Washington, D.C.], October 7, 1826; and Henry Schoolcraft, *Narrative of an Expedition through the Upper Mississippi to Itasca Lake* (New York: Harper, 1834), 234.

13. Not all ogimaag attending the 1826 treaty were sketched. Attikonse, or Little Caribou, was sketched, and later his portrait was completed by James Otto Lewis.

14. Grace Lee Nute, "Journey for Frances," *The Beaver* (March 1954): 15.

15. Simpson, *Narrative of a Journey*, 245–46.

16. Fort William, September 1, 1829, B.231/a/9, HBCA.

17. Fort William, February 21, 1830, September 12, 1831, and September 9, 1832, B.231/a/9, 10, and 11, HBCA.

18. Fort William, May 18, 1834, B.231.a/13, HBCA; Fort William, "Report for Fort William District 1828–29," B.231/e/6, HBCA.

19. Chapman, *Log*, April 11, 1824. Espagnol was renowned for being a good price negotiator, and thus he might have had other relatives' furs in this lot. Espagnol's winter "hunting lands" were west of White Fish Lake, likely even west of Arrow and Rose Lakes. Fort William HBC post, February 10, 1824, TBHMS.

20. Other contemporary Anishinaabeg ogimaag also scrutinized Christianity. Maangozid had also been "taught by the Catholics when he was a boy" and then temporarily converted to Methodist faith. Shingwaukonse, or Little Pine of Garden River, near Sault Ste. Marie, "investigated" various Christian faiths and was eventually baptized as an Anglican. Rebecca Kugel, "Religion Mixed with Politics: The 1836 Conversion of Mang'osid of Fond du Lac," *Ethnohistory* 37, 2 (Spring 1990): 128ff; Chute, *The Legacy of Shingwaukonse*, 47–60.

21. Reverend Hurlburt, letter to James Evans, December 17, 1838, in John McLean, *James Evans*, 135. The author alternates naming the Anishinaabeg leader "Ashueoo" and the Spaniard. The letter states, "This Ashueoo sent for the priest before he went to the Manitoulin, and since his return he has been baptized again by the priest." Father Pierz, "Baptismal and Marriage Register," Minnesota Historical Society. "Francois Espagnol" was baptized on September 30, 1838, at Grand Portage.

22. "Lac La Pluie District Report for 1829–30," B.105/e/9, HBCA; Billy Blackwell, personal communication with author, March 4 and 17, 2010, Grand Portage. Father Pierz stated that Espagnol killed a windigo that had killed twenty-two "human beings." Father Pierz, letter, October 1, 1838, *Berichte* 13: 49, translated by Marianne Stiem.

23. Nectam's Anishinaabemowin name was spelled in a variety of ways including "Nittem." His Anishinaabeg name meant "the first," or what he was often called in English, the Premier. Charles M. Gates, ed., "The Diary of John Macdonell," in *Five Fur Traders of the Northwest* (St. Paul: Minnesota Historical Society, 1965), 103; J. A. Lovisek, "The Political Evolution of the Boundary Waters Ojibwa," in *Papers of the Twenty-Fourth Algonquian Conference*, ed. William Cowan (Ottawa: Carleton University, 1993), 288–89.

24. Alan Woolworth, personal communication with author, March 22, 2000. Woolworth recalled what Paul La Garde of Grand Portage, his foreman on a number of archaeological digs, recollected about the point being locally called "The Premier's Point." Keating, *Narrative of an Expedition*, 156. A few decades later, the North Shore Anishinaabe leader Joseph

Peau du Chat also tried to extend his influence to other bands on the Canadian North Shore during treaty negotiations. Peau du Chat was less successful in this endeavor than Nectam. Lise C. Hanson, "Chiefs and Principal Men: A Question of Leadership in Treaty Negotiations," *Anthropologica* 24 (1987): 47.

25. Billy Blackwell confirmed that Aysh-pay-ahng, or Espagnol, was the overall chief of the North Shore Anishinaabeg. Blackwell further noted that this area ran from just north of Duluth to past Thunder Bay. Billy Blackwell, personal communication with author, March 8, 2007, Grand Marais, and February 17, 2010, Grand Portage.

26. Fort William, "Report on the State of the country, & Indians in Lake Superior Department, 1824," B.231/e/1, HBCA.

27. Father Pierz, letter, October 1, 1838, in *Berichte* 13 (1840): 56.

28. Theresa M. Schenck, *The Voice of the Crane Echoes Afar: The Sociopolitical Organization of the Lake Superior Ojibwa, 1640–1855* (New York: Garland, 1997), 75.

29. John Kinzie, letter to Thomas Forsyth, July 7, 1812, in Carter, *The Territorial Papers of the United States,* vol. 16: 1948. There is also the material evidence of gifts from the British to recognize their allies—a Red Ensign flag and silver peace medals of King George III—that came into the possession of the Grand Portage people at the time Espagnol was a band leader and perhaps principal chief. The flag and medals were recognized as coming from the Maymushkowaush family, or Espagnol's stepson. Since Paul Maymushkowaush was too young to participate in the War of 1812, the medals and flag must have been given to an older family member. And since Espagnol did not have a son to give these to, it was following traditional custom for him to give them to his stepson, Paul Maymushkowaush. Gilman, *The Grand Portage Story,* 48.

30. The written documentation of who wore the medals as significant regalia begins with Paul Maymushkowaush, but the story likely started earlier. For more on these medals see Carolyn Gilman, "Grand Portage Ojibway Indians Give British Medals to Historical Society," *Minnesota History* 47: 1 (Spring 1980): 26–32; and "Notice of Intent to Repatriate Cultural Items from Grand Portage, Minnesota, in the Possession of the Minnesota Historical Society, St. Paul, Minnesota," *Federal Register* 65: 184 (September 21, 2000).

31. Nancy L. Woolworth, "Miss Densmore Meets the Anishinaabe: Frances Densmore's Ethnomusicology Studies among the Grand Portage Anishinaabe in 1905," *Minnesota Archeologist* 38 (August 1979): 110.

32. Fort William, November 26, 1831, B.231/a /11, HBCA.

33. Fort William, September 12, 1831, B.231/a/11, HBCA.

34. Fort William, May 8, 1832, and September 9, 1832, B.231/a/11 and 12, HBCA.

35. Fort William HBC post, February 21, 1824, TBHMS; Johnston, *Journal*, January 15, 1825; Fort William, December 7 and 8, 1831, B.231/a/11, HBCA.

36. Lac La Pluie, John McLoughlin, letter to John Haldane, March 18, 1824, B.105/a/9, HBCA.

37. Chapman, Log, undated, list of Anishinaabeg with whom he traded and or extended credits.

38. Fort William, December 27, 1830, July 23, 1835, August 22, 1837, B.231/10, 15, and 17, HBCA; Fort William post, April 11, 1824, TBHMS.

39. Ibid.

40. Fort William, September 1, 1829, B.231/a/9, HBCA.

41. For example, over six thousand whitefish were caught in the seine nets placed in the Kaministiquia River in 1825. John Haldane, "Report Lake Superior District 1825," B.231/e/3, HBCA; Fort William, December 18, 1836, B.231/a/16, HBCA.

42. Fort William, February 11, 1836, B.231/a/15, HBCA.

43. Cannon, "A Narrative," 24.

44. Ellen Olson, personal communication with author, February 17, 2006, Grand Portage.

45. Fort William, September 12, 1831, B.231/a/11, HBCA.

46. "Lac La Pluie Report, 1825–26," B.105/e/6, HBCA.

47. Fort William, "Report of Fort William Trade and Indians, 1833–34," B.231/e/9, HBCA.

48. Fort William, October 5, 1829, B.231/a/9, HBCA.

49. Lac La Pluie, August 23, 1824, B.105/a/10, HBCA; "Lac La Pluie Report, 1824–25," B.105/e/4–5, HBCA. High water from summer months into September flooded wild rice beds.

50. Lac La Pluie, September 9, 10, 13, 24, 25, 1823, B.105/a/9, HBCA. These records illustrate how Rainy Lake Anishinaabeg regularly paid their debts with bags of rice.

51. Donald McIntosh, Chief Factor, "Report of Fort William Trade and Indians 1830–31," B.231/e/7, HBCA.

52. "Lac La Pluie Report, 1825–26," B.105/e/6, HBCA.

53. Laura Peers and Jennifer S. H. Brown, "'There is no end to relationship among the indians': Ojibwa Families and Kinship in Historical Perspective," *History of the Family* 4, 4 (2000): 538.

54. Duncan Cameron, "The Nipigon Country, 1804," in *Les Bourgeois de la Compagnie,* ed. L. R. Masson (New York: Antiquarian Press, 1960), 258, 255.

55. There are too many HBC records of these activities to list here. One good example is Fort William, June 28, 1832, B.231/a/12, HBCA.

56. Fort William, August 2, 1827, B.231/a/7, HBCA. "[Anishinaabeg mothers of two Metis HBC employees] . . . and other old women went off to make berries, at the Grand Encampment."

57. Fort William, November 11 and 19, 1832, B.231/a/12, HBCA.

58. The specific quotations in this hypothetical seasonal round are drawn from the "Thermometrical Journal Kept at the Hudson's Bay Company Trading Establishment Fort William in the Lake Superior District for 1839," B.231/a/19, HBCA.

59. Some of the HBC clerks were more attentive to those who traveled mid-winter to trade some furs and receive some necessary supplies. Quite often the traveler was the spouse of a hunter/trapper. Fort William, February 5, 1831, January 4 and 13, and February 12, 1833, and March 10, 1834, B.231/a/10, 12, and 13, HBCA.

60. Barry M. Gough, ed., *The Journal of Alexander Henry the Younger, 1799–1814* (Toronto: The Champlain Society, 1988), 1:188.

61. "List of the Total Number of Indians at Grand Portage and Its Vicinity in the Spring, 1825," in Henry R. Schoolcraft Papers, container 61, Library of Congress, Washington, D.C. It was highly likely that George Johnston took this census for his brother-in-law while in Grand Portage in the spring of 1825. Johnston thus wrote down the following men: "Espagnoul chief, Mah mash caw wash, Pat tick eous Kay, May bau a ca mig isk kay, Omis sah tay scance, Gitchy gaw me soiu way, the above sons, Osuack Kackince, Osk Kan dah gance, Shaw gaw ashence, Ace e ban c wayan, May mash caw wash, Way gee caugence, Mah nah ekechick. And old men."

62. Leo G. Waisberg and Tim E. Holzkamm, "'Their Country Is Tolerably Rich in Furs': The Ojibwa Fur Trade in the Boundary Waters Region 1821–71," in *Actes du 25e Congres des Algonquinistes,* ed. William Cowan (Ottawa: Carleton University, 1994), 178.

63. Father Pierz, letter, November 5, 1838, Grand Portage, in *Berichte* 13 (1840): 51.

64. James Duane Doty, "Northern Wisconsin in 1820," 201.

65. Lac La Pluie, John McLoughlin, letter to Simon McGillivray Esqr., March 31, 1824, B.105/a/9, HBCA.

66. Fort William post, March 16, 1824, TBHMS; Fort William, February 21, 1830, B.231/a/9, HBCA.

67. Fort William, April 28, 1833, B.231/a/12, HBCA.

68. Cameron, "The Nipigon County," 256.

69. Anishinaabeg women most often harvested and traded the split spruce

root, or watap, in late June or early July. Fort William, June 19, 1829, and July 10, 1833, B.231/a/8 and 13, HBCA; Fort William post, July 6 and 8, 1825, TBHMS. Canoe "gum" was traded at approximately the same time of year. Fort William, July 17, 1829, July 6, 1832, and July 10, 1833, B.231/a/9, 12, and 13, HBCA.

70. Sylvia Van Kirk, *"Many Tender Ties": Women in Fur Trade Society in Western Canada, 1670–1830* (Winnipeg: Watson and Dwyer, 1980), 58; Cameron, "The Nipigon Country," 257.

71. Cannon, "A Narrative," 25.

72. Van Kirk, *"Many Tender Ties,"* 54; Van Kirk, "The Role of Native Women in the Fur Trade Society of Western Canada," *Frontiers: A Journal of Women Studies* 7, 3 (1984): 10.

73. Van Kirk, *"Many Tender Ties,"* 58. Local barrels were made out of white pine staves and large spruce root wrapped around the staves, much like iron hoops. Straight-grained and thus good barrel wood was much sought after in this area.

74. Van Kirk, "The Role of Native Women," 10; Van Kirk, *"Many Tender Ties,"* 57.

75. Fort William, July 17, 1829, and October 4, 1833, B.231/a/9 and 13, HBCA (40 lbs. gum).

76. Fort William, July 11, 1833, B.231/a/13, HBCA.

77. The Fort William clerk occasionally noted hunting "territories" of Anishinaabeg. See Fort William post, February 10, 1824, TBHMS; Fort William, December 28, 1831, July 27 and October 14, 1832, B.231.a/11 and 12, HBCA. I am unaware of the Anishinaabemowin names for Le View and La Bete, names used by both the HBC and AFC traders alike. Le View was the son of Peau de Chat the elder, and the nephew of Grand Coquin. La Bete was a particularly good hunter, who would occasionally resort to Minong (Isle Royale). The HBC clerks noted he hunted at Isle Royale during the summers of 1830, 1834, and 1836. Fort William, August 9, 1830, July 28, 1834, and August 2, 1836, B.231/a/10, 14, and 16, HBCA.

78. Lac La Pluie, January 4, 1833, B.105/a/17, HBCA.

79. There is a small possibility there were two Grand Coquins. My primary evidence for suggesting there was just one is that in the thirty-nine references that name him in the region, there is no conflict in dates and places. He is either in the Rainy Lake country or for a shorter period on the North Shore.

80. Lac La Pluie, April 15, 1826, B.105/a /11, HBCA.

81. Bigsby, *The Shoe and Canoe,* 265.

82. "The Lac La Pluie District Report for 1829–1830," B.105/e/9, HBCA.

83. Lac La Pluie, January 20 and 31, 1820, B.105/a/7, HBCA.

84. "Chiefs and Old Men of the chipeway and kichicamngue Indians at Grand Portage," July 30, 1798, MG 10, Indian Affairs, vol. 266, 163, 028–163, 378, National Archives of Canada, Ottawa. Peau de Chat, "the elder," or Essebaneoyiane in Anishinaabemowin, is of the Fish clan. The difference in clan membership (Lynx versus Fish) is reported in the same district report. Peau de Chat, or Misk-we-co-ne-a, is identified as a Catfish "totem" or Fish clan. "Lac La Pluie District Report 1829–30," B.105/e/9, HBCA.

85. Fort William post, February 10 and March 17, 1825, TBHMS; Lac La Pluie, January 30 and 31, 1820, B.105/a/7, HBCA.

86. Lac La Pluie, January 30, 1820, B.105/a /7, HBCA.

87. After April 1, 1825, there are sporadic references to a Grand Coquin at the Rainy Lake HBC post through 1833. Lac La Pluie, April 1, 1825, B.105/a/10, HBCA.

88. Lac La Pluie, January 31, 1820, April 23, 1825, September 17, 1825, October 15, 1825, B.105/a/7, 10, and 11; "Lac La Pluie District Report, 1829–30," B.105/e/9, HBCA.

89. Lac La Pluie, September 17, 1825, and January 4, 1833, B.105/a/11 and 17, HBCA.

90. Lac La Pluie, September 23, 1822, B.105/a/8, HBCA.

91. Lac La Pluie, May 7, 1833, B.105/a/17, HBCA.

92. Lac La Pluie, December 5, 1825, B.105/a/11, HBCA.

93. Lac La Pluie, January 25, 1826, B.105/a/11, HBCA.

94. Chapman, *Log,* November 15, 1824; Johnston, *Journal,* January 1, 1825.

95. Chapman and Johnston record nine instances of Anishinaabeg "starving." Interestingly, Johnston records eight times, and Chapman only one. Chapman, *Log,* November 11, 1823; Johnston, *Journal,* October 1, November 15, and December 15, 1824, and January 1, 14, and 15, February 1, and March 1, 1825.

96. David Thompson, letter, November 12, 1822, Thomas Barclay Collection.

97. Mary Black-Rogers, "Varieties of 'Starving': Semantics and Survival in the Subarctic Fur Trade, 1750–1850," *Ethnohistory* 33, 4 (Autumn 1986): 354.

98. Our current American custom is the reverse; namely, when arriving at our hosts' house, we deny we are hungry, even if we haven't eaten in quite some time.

99. "Lac La Pluie Report, 1825–1826," B.105/e/6, HBCA.

100. Schoolcraft, *Personal Memoirs,* 295, entry for July 19, 1828.

101. Theresa M. Schenck, ed., *The Ojibwe Journals of Edmund F. Ely, 1833–1849* (Lincoln: University of Nebraska Press, 2012), 245. Ely estimated Maangozid's age at fifty years old in 1837, making him thirty-seven at the time he was in Grand Marais.

102. Cary Miller, *Ogimaag: Anishinaabeg Leadership, 1760–1845* (Lincoln: University of Nebraska Press, 2010), 71–72.
103. William Warren, "Tribal Organization," in Schoolcraft, *Information Respecting the History*, 159–60; Knight and Chute, "In the Shadow of the Thumping Drum," 261n47.
104. Kappler, "Treaty with the Sioux and Chippewa, Sacs and Fox, Menominie, Ioway, Sioux, Winnebago, and a portion of the Ottawa, Chippewa, and Potawattomie, Tribes, 1825," and "Treaties with the Chippewa of 1826, 1837, 1842 and 1854," *Indian Affairs*, 2:254, 271, 493, 544, 651.
105. W. Brian Stewart, *The Ermatingers: A 19th-Century Ojibwa-Canadian Family* (Vancouver: University of British Columbia Press, 2007), 28.
106. Kugel, "Religion Mixed with Politics," 131.
107. Ibid; Schoolcraft, *Personal Memoirs*, 295; Johann George Kohl, *Kitchi-Gami: Life among the Lake Superior Ojibway*, trans. Lascelles Wraxall (1860; reprint, St. Paul: Minnesota Historical Society Press, 1985), 152–54.
108. Loon's Foot's and his father's clan membership are identified in Schoolcraft, *Information Respecting the History*, 2, 160–61; Warren, *History of the Ojibway People*, 88, 89; Schenck, *The Ojibwe Journals of Edmund F. Ely*, 247.
109. Kugel, "Religion Mixed with Politics," 128, 145.
110. Johnston, *Journal*, October 14 and 17, 1824, and March 1, 1825.
111. Ibid., December 1, 1824, and January 15, 1825.
112. Olson, interview by Gilman.
113. These three clans are the only ones documented in the 1798 treaty. "Chiefs and Old men of the chipeway and kichicamngue Indians at Grand Portage," July 30, 1798, National Archives of Canada; R. G. Thwaites, ed., *The Jesuit Relations and Allied Documents: Travels and Explorations of the Jesuit Missionaries in New France, 1610–1791* (Cleveland: Burrows Brothers, 1899) 56:203; Billy Blackwell et al., *A History of Kitchi Onigaming: Grand Portage and Its People* (Cass Lake, Minn.: Minnesota Chippewa Tribe, 1983), 8.
114. Norman Deschampe, personal communication with author, June 20, 2002, Grand Portage, Minn.
115. Timothy Cochrane, *Minong—The Good Place: Ojibwe and Isle Royale* (East Lansing: Michigan State University Press, 2009), 94–95.
116. Cameron, "The Nipigon County," 247.
117. Olson, interview by Gilman.
118. Maymushkowaush was of the Crane clan. "Notice of Intent to Repatriate Cultural Items," 65: 184, 57209.
119. Cochrane, *Minong*, 14–15. Another example of Anishinaabeg experimenting in new areas was when Michipicoten Anishinaabeg came to the

Grand Portage area during the winter of 1832–33. Fort William, October 20, 1832, B.231/a/12, HBCA.

4. "Fort Misery"

1. Johnston, *Journal*, December 15, 1824.
2. Ibid., January 1, 1825. It was a widely held fur trade custom to celebrate the New Year by giving the "servants" the day off, and the company provided extra quantity of foods. The company also gave its employees a "regale" on New Year's, which typically meant free or freer access to drink. The New Year's gift of alcohol was often extended to Anishinaabeg visiting the post at the time.
3. Chapman, *Log*, March 7, 1824.
4. Ibid., January 29, 1824.
5. Johnston, letter to Schoolcraft, July 13, 1825, Schoolcraft Papers.
6. Fort William, "Report for Fort William District 1828–29," B.231/e/6, HBCA.
7. For example, by 1822, there was no chief factor at Fort William, and it was absorbed as part of the Rainy Lake district. It became a footnote in the official notes of the HBC managers. *Minutes of the Council, Northern Department*, 15–16, 23, 24, 39–41, 71.
8. Ramsay Crooks, letter to John Jacob Astor, June 23, 1817, in *Final Report of the International Joint Commission*, 125–26; Morrison, *Superior Rendezvous-Place*, 87, 109; Straus, "Ambrose R. Davenport," Ambrose Davenport file.
9. *Minutes of the Council, Northern Department*, 5.
10. William Aitken, letter to Ramsay Crooks, December 25, 1834, and George Simpson, letter to William Aitken, July 10, 1837, American Fur Company Papers, New York Historical Society.
11. Chapman, *Log*, January 1, 1824.
12. Among James Schoolcraft's complaints about his election loss to Bela Chapman was his ironic claim that "some full blood Indians, or at best ¾ breeds were allowed to vote." James L. Schoolcraft, letter to Henry R. Schoolcraft, Saut [sic] Ste Marie, March 14, 1835, and James L. Schoolcraft, letter to Henry R. Schoolcraft, Saut [sic] Ste Marie, May 15, 1835, in Carter, *The Territorial Papers of the United States*, vol. 12: 878–79, 920.
13. Andrew Jackson Chapman is named in the 1850 Federal Census for Michigan as a son of Bela Chapman, and Andrew Jackson Davenport is named in the 1860 Federal Census for Michigan as the son of Ambrose Davenport Jr.

Susan DeCarreaux was the granddaughter of Misquobonoquay, the wife of Waubojeeg. Kappler, "Treaty with the Chippewa, 1826," *Indian Affairs,* 272; Henry Blatchford (brother of Susan DeCarreaux Davenport), obituary in *Ashland* [Wisconsin] *Daily Press,* February 16, 1901; Woodrow W. Morris, introduction to Henry W. Longfellow, *The Song of Hiawatha* (Gutenberg Ebook, 2007), 3.

14. Doty, "Northern Wisconsin in 1820," 205.

15. William A. Aitken, letter, December 25, 1834, American Fur Company Papers, New York Historical Society.

16. Ellen Olson, personal communication with author, September 13, 2001, August 23, 2002, and April 25, 2006, Grand Portage; Billy Blackwell, personal communication with author, February 17, 2010, Grand Portage.

17. Fort William, "Report on the State of the Country, 1824," B.231/e/1, HBCA.

18. Lord Selkirk, "M.S. by Lord Selkirk Related to Red River," microfilm reel C-12, 12661, Selkirk Papers. This is undated but written as part of Lord Selkirk's testimony about his role during the Red River "troubles" of 1815 and 1816. Nonetheless Selkirk gives a good sense of contemporary knowledge of area Indians.

19. William Lonc, S. J., trans., *Fort William Jesuit Mission House Diary 1848–1852* (privately printed, 2010), 4ff.

20. Fort William, "Report on the State of the Country, 1824," B.231/e /1, HBCA; May 18, 1834, and June 3, 1835, B.231/a /13 and 14, HBCA.

21. J. P. Suppantschiltz [Joseph Peau du Chat], letter from Grand Portage to Ramsay Crooks, New York, April 30, 1840, American Fur Company Papers, New York Historical Society.

22. Tyrrell, *David Thompson's Narrative,* 297–98. Thompson made this estimate for the year 1798. Charles E. Cleland, "From Ethnohistory to Archaeology: Ottawa and Ojibwa Band Territories of the Northern Great Lakes," in *Text-Aided Archeology,* ed. Barbara J. Little (Boca Raton, Fla.: CRC Press, 1992), 99.

23. *Minutes of the Council, Northern Department,* 126, 170.

24. Lac La Pluie, "Rainy Lake District Report for Years 1825/1826," B.105/e/6, HBCA.

25. Ibid.

26. Report of the Agent on behalf of His Britannic Majesty, October 5 and 6, 1826, RG 76, International Boundary, Northern Boundary, National Archives at College Park, Md.

27. The American commissioner and later American statesman Daniel Webster asked about the relative value of the Arrowhead country before the Webster-Ashburton Treaty was concluded in 1842. The head of the

American survey party, Lieutenant Delafield, responded that the country was worthless for agricultural purposes but somewhat valuable for furs and fish. Delafield also observed that the fur traders thought of it as of "national importance." Joseph Delafield, letter to Mr. Fraser, July 20, 1842, in *The Congressional Globe* 12 (1842): 21.

28. August 7, 1840, Douglas Houghton Papers, Clarke Historical Library, Mount Pleasant, Mich. Houghton, the first Michigan state geologist, was primarily inspecting Isle Royale, but they sailed also to Grand Portage. He noted one exception to the barren quality of the land, namely, that the AFC clerk at Grand Portage, Pierre Cotte, "has cultivated a fine field of potatoes & they are in a flourishing condition."

29. Cannon, "A Narrative," 30.

30. There was a least one AFC building standing at Grand Marais in 1839, because they proposed to repurpose it as a warehouse for salted fish in barrels. AFC manager Gabriel Franchere wrote: "At Grand Marais, however, there is a building of sufficient capacity to store all the fish which could not be brought away [by AFC schooner]." In the late 1830s Grand Marais became a fishing station for the AFC. Gabriel Franchere, "G. Franchere's Journal of His Voyage in the 'Brewster' with Mr. Scott to Grand Portage, Ile Royale & the Ance in August 1839," Minnesota Historical Society, St. Paul.

The Journals

1. "Sketches of the Upper Peninsula," No. 5, Schoolcraft Papers, Library of Congress 63, Washington, D.C.

2. Rhoda R. Gilman, *Henry Hastings Sibley: Divided Heart* (St. Paul: Minnesota Historical Society Press, 2004), 67–68, 84; Henry H. Sibley Papers, Minnesota Historical Society, St. Paul.

3. Rhoda R. Gilman, "Apprentice Trader: Henry H. Sibley and the American Fur at Mackinac," in *The Fur Trade Revisited: Selected Papers of the Sixth North American Fur Trade Conference* (East Lansing: Michigan State University Press, 1994), 325. In an earlier article, Gilman further declared, "The elaborate charade of Indian treaties and land purchase was only the political and diplomatic window dressing necessary to disguise a subsidy to the fur companies." Rhoda R. Gilman, "Last Days of the Upper Mississippi Fur Trade," in *People and Pelts: Selected Papers of the Second North American Fur Trade Conference*, ed. Malvina Bolus (Winnipeg: Peguis, 1972), 104–5.

4. Kappler, "Treaty with the Chippewa, 1854," in *Indian Affairs*, 2:649.

5. Schoolcraft, *Personal Memoirs,* 245. Interestingly, the Grand Portage delegation, while apparently awarded peace medals, were not signatories to the treaty.

6. George Johnston, "List of the Total Number of Indians at Grand Portage and Its Vicinity in the Spring 1825"; George Johnston, letter to Henry Schoolcraft, July 13, 1825, Container 61, Schoolcraft Papers.

7. Dr. Tory Tronrud, personal communication with author, February 1, 2017, Thunder Bay Historical Museum Society, Thunder Bay. See also Judy Petch, "Fort William Post Journals of the 1820s and 1830s: Some Extracts," in *Lake Superior to Rainy Lake: Three Centuries of Fur Trade History,* ed. Jean Morrison (Thunder Bay: Thunder Bay Historical Museum Society, 2003), 139–51.

8. There are no references to Alexander Stewart in the post journal, only a note when his family left. According to Governor Simpson, "Sandy Stewart" was "an easy, mild tempered, well-disposed little man . . . speaks Cree well, and acquires influence over Indians by his kind treatment and patient attention to them; but his diminutive size and retiring diffident manner, unfit him very much for the 'rough & tumble' of the business." George Simpson, "The 'Character Book' of Governor George Simpson," in *Hudson's Bay Miscellany 1670–1870,* ed. Glyndwr Williams (Winnipeg: Hudson's Bay Record Society, 1975), 170.

9. Ibid., 186. Simpson wrote of Roderick McKenzie Sr.: "A very honest well-meaning warm hearted correct man altho' irritable and short tempered to such a degree that it is unpleasant to do business with him."

10. Elizabeth Arthur, "Haldane, John," in *Dictionary of Canadian Biography,* vol. 8, University of Toronto/Université Laval, 2003, accessed February 7, 2017, http://www.biographi.ca/en/bio/haldane_john_8E.html.

The Log of Bela Chapman

The Log of Bela Chapman is archived in Henry H. Sibley Papers, Minnesota Historical Society, St. Paul.

1. "Portage" was likely the portage over the sandbar that makes up Minnesota Point, or in Anishinaabemowin, *Onigamiinsing,* "at the little portage." The "old portage" was roughly located where the ship canal and High Bridge are today in Duluth. It was 24 miles upriver from Onigamiinsing to the AFC post on the St. Louis River. Robert B. McLean, "Reminiscences of Early Days of the Head of the Lakes," in J. Wesley White, "Historical Sketches of the Quetico-Superior," vol. 2 (unpublished

manuscript, copy at Grand Portage National Monument), 1; McKenney, *Sketches of a Tour to the Lakes,* 271.

2. The "portage" to Knife Island is a distance of 19 nautical miles. "Knife River" is an English translation of the Anishinaabe place-name: *Mokomanizibi.* Gilfillan, "Minnesota Geographical Names," 454.

3. Knife Island to Encampment Island is a distance of 16 miles along an increasingly exposed and thus unprotected shore. In Anishinaabemowin it would be simply *Miniss,* or "island." Gilfillan, "Minnesota Geographical Names," 454.

4. Despite the use of the term *rowed,* which could indicate some men were in a bateaux, others were traveling in canoes (as mentioned later on February 9). *Rowing* as used here is synonymous with *paddling.* In addition, fur trade canoes were opportunistically sailed. However, they were transporting a great deal of trade goods, food, and even animals (dogs and hogs) by canoes and perhaps bateaux. Two leagues northeast of Baptism River is slightly south of the present-day Little Marais, using a British league measurement. This last leg would have been an approximate distance of 30 miles.

5. I am assuming that Chapman meant Two Island River, and he inadvertently left the "Island" out of his document. There is a well-known Two Island River, which is located off Taconite Harbor, whereas a "Two River" is not known in this area.

6. Impatient with being windbound, that is, not able to safely paddle in rough seas, Chapman's party apparently began to "march," or carry their goods northeastward along the shore. I do not know what Chapman means by "Entm." It cannot be an abbreviation for Encampment River as they have long since passed it. He was likely in the Cross or Temperance River area.

    A contemporary described a *road* as "merely two Pieces of Timber placed together [over wet locations . . . and is] cut through the Woods." Francis N. A. Garry, *Diary of Nicholas Garry, Deputy Governor of the Hudson's Bay Company, 1822–1835* (Royal Society of Canada, 1990), 119.

7. This was likely the Poplar River, near where Lutsen is now located. Balm of Gilead, a type of poplar, is an uncommon tree in this region. It has very pungent smelling buds. The species grows best on moist, rich, low-lying ground such as at river mouths. The historic Old World balm of Gilead is a small evergreen used for healing in some countries.

8. He was also known by the name the Big Rogue and in Anishinaabemowin as Wau waish e Kaow, translated by a trader as "Handsome Figure." Fort William post, February 10, 1824, TBHMS; La Pluie post, April 14, 1826, B.105/a/11, HBCA; Lac La Pluie District Report for 1829/30,

B.105/e/9, HBCA. The "chief" was known as L'Espagnol in French, the Spaniard in English, and Aysh-pay-ahng in Anishinaabemowin.

9. It was most likely that Chapman and men gave the liquor as a means of demonstrating their interest in trading with them as well as to curry favor with Espagnol and others, including their family members.

10. Chapman was speaking of his child, Reuben, born in Grand Marais.

11. "Making nets" was a term of art for knitting the twine into a usable gill net. Cotton twine was provided early on as a trade item but was also used by company men to manufacture nets used by the company or free men. Made nets were expensive, which meant they were rarely a trade item with Anishinaabe women, who would more likely knit their own nets. Cotton nets were more durable and effective than nettle or basswood or cedar fiber nets.

12. Plastering likely meant filling the gaps between logs with clay. Sometimes, if the gap was large enough, a sapling would be placed in the gap, then clay packed around it.

13. Chapman does not provide any information about how his leaky roof might have been constructed or with what materials. HBC employees covered a barn and maple sugar boiling huts with cedar bark strips, as may have been done here. HBC Fort William post, July 6, 1825, TBHMS; Fort William, March 14, 1832, B.231/a/11, HBCA.

14. "Boucher" appears to be a son or relative of Francois Boucher, a long-time interpreter at Fond du Lac, who had worked for the NWC there at least through 1816 and became a "freeman" thereafter. Douglas Birk, *John Sayer's Snake River Journal, 1804–05* (Minneapolis: Institute of Minnesota Archaeology, 1989), 31.

   Losing two gill nets was a costly loss as they were the most efficient fishing technique available and were time-consuming "to knit," or make. Stormy seas with water surges and debris in the water could break lines to anchors or floats, and thus gill nets could be lost or torn up. Ice, too, could snap lines, and nets could be lost.

15. In the wintertime, North Shore Anishinaabeg traveled in extended family groups, sometimes called "bands." The group might be as large as ten to fifteen individuals. Grand Coquin and his two sons likely had spouses and children.

16. Unlike the Fort William clerk, Chapman did not report much about the weather. The HBC clerk reported that the Kaministiquia River was "nearly frozen over" on November 11, and by December 8 it had been 26 degrees below zero. Fort William post, November 11 and December 8, 1823, TBHMS.

17. Chapman was describing the paradox of the situation; that is, he did

not have the provisions to win over the Anishinaabeg to come to and trade with him. Supplying food was a common way to encourage Anishinaabeg to focus more on trapping than subsistence pursuits.

18. Chapman meant he sent his men to White Fish Lake with a hundred skins worth of merchandise to trade. "Skins" is used here as a unit of measure of his trading goods. He was trying to intercept Anishinaabeg who were trading at Fort William.

19. The HBC clerk reported a "continued heavy falls of snow for this day" and a month later on February 24. Fort William post, January 13 and February 24, 1824, TBHMS.

20. This was likely what today is known as the Brule River, roughly halfway between Grand Marais and Grand Portage. *Brule* is French for "burnt." In Anishinaabemowin the name is *Wissakode zibi*, or Half-Burnt Wood River. Gilfillan, "Minnesota Geographical Names," 453.

21. This was perhaps the most optimistic of Chapman's entries. His men traded successfully for two packs of furs and for the most valuable of fur, beaver. Further, they appear to have created a relationship with some Indians that made him hopeful about future prospects.

22. Chapman did not mention it directly, but he had sent his men back to the White Fish Lake vicinity. And his reference to the wind suggests they may have canoed some of the way, or the wind must have been very strong to prevent a snowshoe trip. If they canoed, they likely paddled to the Grand Portage and then snowshoed up the traditional trail (usually used to travel to the wild rice beds) to White Fish Lake.

23. Chapman's ability to trap marten in the vicinity and not other animals tells us something about the forest conditions. The marten, a member of the weasel family, prefers thick forest cover, be it conifers or even some deciduous trees. They avoid burned-over areas. About the size of a cat, they opportunistically eat mice, voles, red squirrels, snowshoe hare, and some birds. A. W. F. Banfield, *The Mammals of Canada* (Toronto: National Museum of Natural Sciences, 1974), 315–18.

24. *River Tourt* is French for Pigeon River, or Omimi-zibi in Anishinaabemowin, named for the flocks of passenger pigeons that used to pass through the area. Gilfillan, "Minnesota Geographical Names," 453.

25. It is unclear what Chapman meant by "small lake." It was likely his provisional name for the west harbor. Even without the latter-day breakwaters, the west bay was more sheltered than the bay to the east, eventually called the East Bay. See his entry for February 4, in which he reports that this small lake froze. If it was truly a small pond, separate from Lake Superior, it would have frozen a couple months earlier.

26. Chapman was likely referring to his fellow clerk Pierre Cotte. Cotte, a

French man, came to the North Shore and operated the American Fur Company's fishing operation at Grand Portage in 1837. Keenan, "Pierre Cotte," 86–96.

27. Chapman signed off to William Morrison, as Morrison was a partner in his outfit. He was also the senior American Fur Company official at Fond du Lac, so the journal was addressed to him. It also appears that he addressed William Alexander Aitken, the next most senior partner.

28. This bay, with sufficiently strong shore ice from which men could spear fish through holes in the ice, is difficult to identify. There are two possibilities, both closer than 6 miles away. About 5 miles southwest of Grand Marais is Good Harbor Bay, where Cut Face Creek enters Lake Superior. This is a more sheltered bay than the other option to the northeast of Grand Marais. Six miles away would put the "large bay" roughly northeast of Red Cliff Point, or in the present-day Colville area. There is very little shelter there, and thus it is less likely for steadfast shore ice to accumulate over deep water.

29. As this individual is not named, it likely another mention of the "sick woman." More significantly, Chapman knew if she died, her family's grief and honoring the dead would preclude them from trapping, thus diminishing his returns. Fur trade clerks also gave gifts to grieving families of important persons.

30. Apparently, wolverine, though once rare, were present enough in this area to "have a price" for their pelt. They are extirpated from the area now and live in the circumpolar north, the northern Rocky Mountains, and Alaska. I found reference to two wolverines trapped in the border region, one in 1827 in the Rainy Lake area, and another in 1831 in the Seine River area. Their fur was much sought after because when used in jacket ruffs, it does not ice up easily. Lac La Pluie, May 17, 1831, B.105/a/15, HBCA; Lac La Pluie, February 3, 1827, B.105/a/12, HBCA; Howard S. Hash, "Wolverine," in *Wild Furbearer Management and Conservation in North America*, ed. Milan Novak, James A. Baker, Martyn E. Obbard, and Bruce Malloch, 575–77 (Toronto: Ontario Ministry of Natural Resources, 1987).

31. The "Reindeer" was really a woodland caribou, fairly common in the Arrowhead region at this time. Anishinaabeg regularly hunted caribou and brought them to trade and curry favor with traders. Fort William traders and clerks welcomed the caribou meat, given they were heavily dependent upon a fish diet. Fort William post journal, March 4 and 7, 1824, TBHMS.

32. Chapman was correct that hunting would have tapered off, as this was the season to make maple sugar. Many Anishinaabeg returned to their traditional sugar bush to collect and boil down the sap. For example, many Anishinaabeg left Fort William on March 18 to return to their

traditional sugar bush above Grand Portage, and boiling maple sugar continued there as late as April 16. The Anishinaabe man Pacutchininies brought forty-three pounds of dried sugar to trade at the HBC post. Fort William post journal, March 18, 29, 30, 31, and May 1, 1824.

33. This is the French spelling of *canoe*.

34. "Good hunts" would be more accurately rendered "good trapping." These furs attributed to Espagnol, or the Spaniard, may have been from family members as well. Fort William post journal, February 10, 1824, TBHMS.

35. Chapman only had one journal entry for the month of April, suggesting his situation had not improved—he would have reported successes. April's weather included rain on April 22, followed by heavy snow a few days later, and then warm wind from the southwest. Ice remained on Thunder Bay through April, but it had "nearly cleared away" by May 9, 1824. Fort William post journal, April 22, 23, 27, and May 9, 1824, TBHMS.

36. Judging by the geographic context of being en route to Grand Portage, they are likely camped in one of the islands off Cannonball Bay, on what is now the southeast corner of the Grand Portage Reservation.

37. "Old Grand Portage" is where the Grand Portage National Monument is now located. For the AFC men coming from Fond du Lac, the "Grand Portage" or sometimes "new Grand Portage" was the long, grueling portage around the many rapids of the St. Louis River.

38. Alexander Stewart was chief factor at Fort William.

39. This is the end of Chapman's daily entries while on the North Shore. His log next details a "Fond du Lac Inventory General for Rainy Lake, Sandy Lake, Fond du Lac, June, 1824." I am omitting this inventory, but it is instructive to note that by sometime in June, Chapman and crew are back at Fond du Lac, and he is conducting normal business for a clerk.

The Journal of George Johnston

The Journal of George Johnston is archived in Henry Rowe Schoolcraft Papers, Library of Congress, Washington, D.C.

1. This was the first entry of his three-year journal. However, Johnston was in Grand Marais for only nine months.

2. Pembina was located on the Red River near its junction with Pembina River, just south of the international border between what is now Minnesota and North Dakota. In 1824, it was a log cabin village largely populated by Métis and an Anishinaabe band, and a few Scottish settlers. Pembina was becoming a growing nucleus of Métis people. Rhoda R.

Gilman, Carolyn Gilman, and Deborah M. Stultz, *The Red River Trails: Oxcart Routes between St. Paul and the Selkirk Settlement, 1820–1870* (St. Paul: Minnesota Historical Society, 1979), 1–6.

3. "Point au Pins" was only a few miles from the Sault and was where some observers said Lake Superior truly began. George Johnston's father described Pointe aux Pins as "a sand bank of several miles . . . covered with red and white pine, the best of which have been cut down and used by the North-West Company for building their vessels." John Johnston, "An Account of Lake Superior," 149.

4. "Bales" refers to the ninety-pound packs used in the fur trade. The packs contained trade goods or furs being transported to posts and to depots by voyageurs. They were carefully wrapped in canvas or leather to protect them from water and damage.

5. It is not clear to whom Johnston was writing, as the greeting and signature lines change throughout his journal. It is likely that this copybook contains copies of letters to both his brother-in-law Henry Schoolcraft, whom he addressed as "Dear Friend," and to his employers.

6. *Petit Peche* was a common name denoting a small fishery or good fishing location. The same name was used for locations along the North Shore and on Rainy Lake. In French it literally means "small fishing" or "to fish small." The name has not survived on modern maps. *Nontonagon* is the historic rendition of the Ontonagon River, it being derived from an Anishinaabe place-name that meant "fish trap" or "fish weir" river. An Anishinaabe band used fish traps or weirs to catch a portion of the large run of sturgeon in the Ontonagon River. Malhoit, "A Wisconsin Fur-Trader's Journal," 172; "Geographic Place Names in the MI 1836 Ceded Territory," *Mazina'igan* (Summer 2007): 15.

7. A Chippewa war party from Lac Vieux Desert seeking Sioux victims instead fell upon four "Americans" near the mouth of the Chippewa River, near Lake Pepin. The four Americans killed were a trader named Finley and three Canadian voyageurs. After the murderers were seized by other Indians and held in jail in Mackinaw, they escaped. Schoolcraft, *Personal Memoirs*, 198–200, 209–13; Warren, *History of the Ojibway People*, 390–93.

8. A league was a historic unit of measurement for distance. An English league—thought to be in use here—was three statute miles. Black River reaches Lake Superior just west of the Porcupine Mountains. It appears to be named for its dark, organic, and tannin-laden water. Peters, *Lake Superior Place Names*, 15–16.

9. Mr. Lyman Warren was a senior AFC trader at La Pointe on Madeline Island. Yankee-born, Warren married Marie or Mary Cadotte, daughter of a French Canadian trader who also lived at La Pointe. A few years after

Johnston arrived at La Pointe, the AFC reorganized, and Warren became one of six partners of the Lake Superior Outfit, which eventually shifted interest to include commercial fishing. Schenck, *William W. Warren*, 1–7.

At its Lake Superior mouth, the Montreal River forms the border between Wisconsin and the Upper Peninsula of Michigan. Why it was so named is not exactly known. However, the dominant theory is that it was named by voyageurs in honor of their home city. Peters, *Lake Superior Place Names*, 102.

10. Mauvais River is French for Bad River. It was so called because it was difficult to ascend by canoe, as it was a very broad and shallow stream. J. Johnston, "An Account of Lake Superior," 167. The Anishinaabe place-name is Swamp River. Verwyst, "A Glossary of Chippewa Indian Names," 255.

11. *Cha-gaw-wa-mick-ong* was Johnston's rendition of the Anishinaabe word that has now been rendered as *Chequamegon*. His father, John Johnston, spelled it *Chagowiminan*. The Anishinaabe place-name means a long, sandy point of land projecting into water. J. Johnston, "An Account of Lake Superior," 167; Verwyst, "A Glossary of Chippewa Indian Names," 255.

The Cadotte family had long-standing trading roots on Lake Superior. The first Cadotte is said to have been at Sault Ste. Marie in 1671. Three generations later the Cadotte being spoken about was the longtime independent French Canadian fur trader Michel Cadotte. Cadotte married a daughter of the celebrated Anishinaabe leader Waub-o-jeeg, granfather to George Johnston. Schenck, *William W. Warren*, 4; Schenck, *All Our Relations*, 35; and Warren, *History of the Ojibway People*, 9–11.

12. The "New *Recovery*," or *Recovery II*, was an HBC ship that was charted by the British Royal Navy for the purposes of surveying Lake Superior. It "went off the stocks in good style" under a salute of nine guns from Fort William on October 18, 1823, with the British officers and crew watching. Next April they were still at work "Rigging the new Schooner." And finally, on May 26, 1824, it set sail, and the survey began. At the time of the survey (mostly completed in 1824–25), it was the only sailing vessel on Lake Superior and was one hundred and thirty-three tons burden.

In charge of the British survey of Lake Superior, Bayfield considered his crew to be "lightly manned" for a vessel this large. Lieutenants H. W. Bayfield and Philip Collins based their overall survey work from the *Recovery II* but did much of the measurements from smaller "long boats." Bayfield served a distinguished career in the Royal Navy and eventually became an admiral. He surveyed all five great lakes, Superior being the last. Fort William post, October 18, 1823; April 28, 1824 and May 26, 1824, TBHMS; *Fort William Hinge of a Nation*, vol. 1, part 1, n.p., n.d., National Heritage Limited, Historic Fort William Library, Thunder

Bay; Lieut. Henry Bayfield, letter to Joseph Delafield, 15 July 1824, Falls of St. Mary's, in Joseph Delafield Papers, Princeton University Library, Princeton, N.J.

13. Captain Robert McCargo was formerly a captain of NWC vessels on Lake Superior. His knowledge of Lake Superior would have been a great boon to Bayfield and Collins. Captain McCargo is perhaps best known for secreting the NWC vessel *Recovery* in a deep cove on Isle Royale during the War of 1812, thus avoiding detection by the Americans. The fjord-like cove now bears his name, McCargoe Cove.

    Dr. McLean was the British naval surgeon assigned to the Lake Superior survey under the command of Bayfield. Little is known about Dr. McLean's efforts on Lake Superior. Naval surgeons treated common illnesses, sometimes became scribes, and were often the intellectual companions of captains. The Royal Navy considered a naval surgeon to be a part of a standard complement of men for a Royal Navy vessel.

14. At this time, La Point, or La Pointe, was an important Anishinaabe village. It was a traditional home for a sizable Anishinaabe community for many years. It would eventually become the main depot for the AFC's operations on Lake Superior. It was also the site of important treaties of 1842 and 1854, as well as the site for the Isle Royale Compact in 1844.

15. A license was applied for, and received, for a specific location. Johnston was worried that he was being sent to a location where he did not have permission to go. The Indian agent at the time was Henry Schoolcraft, with whom Johnston wanted to stay in good stead. For Johnston to spurn his brother-in-law's authority would be troubling and must have been a topic of merriment among his employers. Thomas L. McKenney made clear traders were to go where they "took" their license, and if they did not go to that location, they were breaking the law and might have to forfeit their bond. Thomas L. McKenney, Indian Department within the War Department, letter to Lewis Cass, June 5, 1824, in Schoolcraft Papers.

    Later in his diary, Johnston suggested why his superiors were not troubled by the change in posts. On August 10, 1825, Johnston wrote, "I shall here relate Mrs. Ashman's story, relative to a conversation that took place between Mssrs Aitkin & Warren at St. Marie, the former observed that the Indian agents made laws & restricted him, but the moment that he Mr. Aitkin got into the interior would do as he thought proper, and that he did not care a damn for their laws no further than the time being, or whilst at St. Marys."

    Johnston may or may not have been aware that Aitken had indeed a license in the previous year, 1823, for Grand Portage, Vermilion Lake,

Rainy Lake, and Pembina. For Aitken, this lapse was likely unimportant, but for Johnston, it was worrisome, as it could affect his relationship with Schoolcraft, and he could be denied a trader's license in "Indian County" for future years. Henry Schoolcraft, letter, August 2, 1824, in Sibley Papers.

It is unclear if Johnston knew that his family benefactor and Indian agent Schoolcraft and his sister would soon be leaving Sault Ste. Marie for the East Coast. However, it is likely that he knew of Schoolcraft's intentions to go east. This may have further contributed to his sense of isolation. Schoolcraft left for New York in September 1824. Schoolcraft, *Personal Memoirs*, 200.

16. "Mountains" are the Sawtooth Range, sometimes called the Superior Highlands, which parallel Lake Superior and indeed rise abruptly in a number of places. Johnston was describing the geography of Grand Marais for the first time. What little reconnaissance he had of the area may have come from his employers, Aitken or Morrison, or from his father.

17. *Diable boiteaux* translates from French to mean the "Lame Devil." The term was popularized by the 1707 novel by Alain-René Lesage.

18. Elba is a Mediterranean island off the coast of Italy. At this time it was a French possession and is where Napoleon was exiled for three hundred days prior to returning to France and leading French armies at Waterloo. Elba, here, becomes Johnston's expression of exile from what he might consider the cultured world.

19. That a storehouse could be built in three days suggests it was small and was roughly built.

20. Grass might be used for both thatch on the roof and for bedding. This relative lack of grass at Grand Marais suggests infrequent human use, or at least little settlement with accompanying domestic grasses.

White Fish Lake is shallow and sandy and has a slight current; it was great wild rice habitat. There is a legend about how White Fish Lake was sown with wild rice from Nett Lake (and indeed it is reputed to taste like Nett Lake wild rice). Thomas Vennum Jr., *Wild Rice and the Ojibway People* (St. Paul: Minnesota Historical Society Press, 1988), 69.

21. "Rat," or muskrat, was the least valuable of sought-after furs. An AFC trader at Rainy Lake told his competitor of the HBC that he would credit Indians one beaver skin as worth fifteen muskrats, or four martens, or three lynx, or one large bear. Lac La Pluie post, October 2, 1823, B.105/a/9, HBCA.

22. Preserving fish in rough salt increased the length they could be safely kept and then eaten. Most commonly, fish were layered with salt in a watertight or "wet" barrel. If Johnston was salting fish, he must have brought

kegs to use. He may have been salting and then freezing the fish, which would increase its preservation time. Freezing and smoking fish were common Anishinaabe methods of preserving this important food source.

23. It is unclear exactly where Roche de Bout is. *Roche de Bout* is a generic fur trade name, much like Grand Marais, meaning "great, upright rock." There was a Roche de Bout southwest of Grand Marais, likely the one spoken of here. And there was a Roche de Bout northeast of Grand Portage, on the eastern side of the Black Bay peninsula. J. Johnston, "An Account of Lake Superior," 168. Another trader, Malhoit, mentions that Roche de Bout was a full, hard day's paddle southwest of Grand Marais. Malhoit, "A Wisconsin Fur Trader's Journal," 172. On October 3, 1829, an HBC clerk at Fort William recorded information from a local Anishinaabe: "An Indian called Messetinass arrived from the Grand Marrais [sic] along with his mother. He reports the Americans to be building at the Roche de Boute 45 miles beyond Grand Marrais their usual establishment." Fort William post, October 3, 1829, B231/a/9, HBCA. One possibility is that Roche de Bout is Shovel Point or Palisade Head, both of which are forty-some miles by water from Grand Marais.

24. Johnston here was using *castor,* short for *castor gras* in French, as a synonym for beaver skins.

25. *Crapeau* appears to be a misspelling of the French word *crapaud,* meaning "toad." As the *d* is silent in the French pronunciation, Johnston's spelling was not far from how the word is pronounced.

26. By "H.B." Johnston undoubtedly means the Hudson's Bay Company. In fur trade measurements, "twenty three plus" is the value of twenty-three good beaver skins. "Plus" was a fur trade monetary unit worth one good beaver pelt.

27. John Haldane was the chief factor at Fort William.

28. It is unclear what North Shore river Johnston was referring to as "Salmon Trout River." Lake Superior place-name scholar Bernard Peters believes "Salmon Trout" was a translation from Anishinaabemowin for "brook trout." A Salmon Trout River survives as a place-name on the south shore of Lake Superior. Peters, *Lake Superior Place Names,* 92–94. A newspaper article from 1854 reported of "great sport trolling for Salmon Trout in the same Grand Marais Harbor," in "Interesting Letter from Lake Superior, September 11, 1854," *Minnesota Daily Pioneer,* September 26, 1854. If "Salmon Trout River" means a river with brook trout, it could be virtually any river on the North Shore.

29. Burnt River is today called the Brule River. *Wissakode zibi* became *Brule Riviere,* which then became *Brule River.* Gilfillan, "Minnesota Geographical Names," 453.

30. "Road" in fur trade parlance meant an identifiable trail, on good ground, often with blazed trees. If heavily used, windfall trees would be cleared from it. A "road" was also an identifiable trail in the snow made by snowshoes or dog teams. Douglas Birk, *The Hudson Bay Trail: A Study of Nineteenth Century Travel Routes between Grand Portage, Minnesota, and Fort William, Ontario* (Minneapolis: Institute of Minnesota Archaeology, 1998), 12.

31. *Bois Fort, or Bois Forte,* is French for "strong men of the woods." In this specific designation, it likely meant an Anishinaabe from the next band to the west. Warren, *History of the Ojibway People,* 39; Jeffrey J. Richner, "People of the Third Fur Woods: Two Hundred Years of Bois Forte Chippewa Occupation of the Voyageurs National Park Area," Midwest Archeological Center Special Report no. 3, National Park Service, Lincoln, Neb., 2002, 4.

32. By "Rein deer" traders meant woodland caribou. Various clerks at Fort William traded for caribou meat on July 18, 1831, August 12, 1833, March 29, 1833, and September 10, 1834. Fort William post, B.231/a/11, 12, and 13, HBCA; Fort William post, March 4 and 7, 1824, TBHMS.

33. A "trane" was a toboggan with sides, called a *cariole* in French Canada. In this context, a trane was a dogsled with a wood and rawhide frame laden with supplies or goods wrapped in canvas. The presence of a snow trane path meant that a large party and goods had moved to another location, precluding fur trading at White Fish Lake.

    This entry seems to have been borrowed, much interpreted, and inserted into a Senate document by Henry Schoolcraft. In an 1831 Senate document, Schoolcraft wrote:

    > Men, and even clerks, carried off by foreign opposition, I have not the means at present of naming, nor the number of Indians who have been temporarily, either by force or persuasion, carried across the lines, to prevent their furs from being sold to American traders. In the winter of 1824, persons in the service of the Hudson's Bay Company carried off in trains the band of Chippeways, living near old Grand Portage, (Lake Superior), after the arrival of an American trade (Mr. Johnston) on the ground.

    Schoolcraft presumed the Anishinaabeg were forcibly removed from White Fish Lake by the HBC traders and did not mention the HBC had a small outpost there to keep the Anishinaabeg from trading furs with the Americans! He also did not mention the possibility they regularly resorted to Fort William for food and supplies.

    Either Schoolcraft was unaware that White Fish Lake would have been traditionally considered "within the British lines" and thus his statement was an innocent mistake, or he was playing with American lack of knowledge of geography in this region to arouse a patriotic response to the fierce fur trade competition along the border. Johnston, on the other hand, knew he had sent his men repeatedly to White Fish Lake, within British territory. Lac La Pluie, "Report of 1824–25," B.105/e/4-5, HBCA.

It was also unclear if Schoolcraft knew that White Fish Lake was a longtime gathering place for Anishinaabeg and the NWC and HBC traders as well as an important wild ricing location. Schoolcraft, "Mr. Schoolcraft's Report in Relation to the Fur Trade," 43; "Extract from the Journal George Johnston stationed at the trading post of Grand Marais, during the fall & winter of 1824 '25," (two extracts: November 24, 1824, and January 14, 1825), Schoolcraft Papers, Library of Congress.

34. At this point in time, Little Englishman, or Sha-ga-nash-ins, was an Anishinaabe hunter residing along the North Shore, who would eventually become a leader, or ogimaa. He was a Grand Portage Band signatory to the 1844 Isle Royale Compact and the 1847 and 1854 treaties.

35. Johnston, and likely his men, were making new parts for his boat, including the main mast, perches to hold the oars (as part of the oarlocks in case rowing is done), and a sprit rig for sailing. A sprit-rigged sailboat was a relatively simple sailing boat, easy to handle, with only a free-standing mast and a sprit spar and a four-sided sail. Johnston was describing sailing equipment used in a mackinaw boat, a type of vernacular watercraft particular to the upper Great Lakes. For more on mackinaws, see Timothy Cochrane and Hawk Tolson, *A Good Boat Speaks for Itself: Isle Royale Fishermen and Their Boats* (Minneapolis: University of Minnesota Press, 2002), 69–80.

36. "Flambeauing" was the use of a birch-bark lit torch to attract fish to the light, and then they could be speared as they neared the surface. This is an unusual reference in that most torchlight fishing was done during the ice-free months.

Index

Adams, John Quincy, 61
African Anishinaabeg, 4, 53–54
Aitken, William, 81
alcohol, 61, 66, 86, 231n168; ceremonial
use of, 85; destructive effect of, 85,
86; as provision for border trade, 86,
87; scale of use, 85, 87, 230n141
American Fur Company, 6, 32, 33, 48,
88, 127; buildings, 34–35, 78; clerks,
1, 40, 82; commercial fishing effort,
82, 83, 243n30; as customs inspectors,
65, 69; diversity of men at post, 48;
economic strategy, 6, 7, 33, 66, 68, 69,
79, 81, 84, 85; grudge against HBC,
79; lack of geographic knowledge,
39; Northern Department, 65, 69,
72; profits, 6, 65, 71–72, 76, 93, 128;
working on shares, 13, 68, 93
Anishinaabeg: customary sharing, 100,
102, 115, 235n29; Fond du Lac, 30, 112,
133, 137; Fort William, 10, 30; Grand
Portage, 10, 53; Leech Lake, 231n168;
loyalty to British, 9, 62, 74, 235n29;
Pillager, 53; Michipicoten, 240n119;
name, 9, 10; Nipigon, 30, 133, 137;
pressure on, 132, 134–35; Rainy Lake,
79, 81, 101, 115, 129, 137, 236n50. *See
also* women, Anishinaabeg
Anishinaabeg movement, 8, 33, 95, 96,
100, 110–14, 116, 119, 133–34
Anishinaabemowin, 42, 43, 58; dialects, 58
Apostle Islands, 14
Arrowhead region, 48, 74, 139, 242n27;
poverty of the country 29–30, 53,
107–8, 136

Arrow Lake, 104, 231n165
artichokes, 31
Astor, John Jacob, 6, 7, 47, 65, 68, 84,
128, 225n68; influence, 7, 66–67, 69
Astoria, 66, 128
Attikonse (Little Caribou), 98,
233nn12–13
Aysh-pay-ahng. *See* Espagnol

barrel wood, 114, 238n73
Basswood Lake, 70, 101, 135
Batchawana Bay, 22
bateau, 26, 213n3, 245n4
Bayfield, Henry W., 32, 44, 45, 64, 182,
184, 231n167, 251n12, 252n13
Bayliss Public Library, 149
bears, 15, 30, 100, 167, 169
beavers, 30, 72, 76, 77, 97, 100, 108, 135,
138, 159, 189, 193
Berketh, George, 81
berries, 2, 30, 89, 114, 237n56
Big Rogue. *See* Grand Coquin
birch bark, 2, 35, 92, 109, 110, 114,
256n36; canoe bark, 89
blacksmithing, 78, 228n109
Bonga, George, 48–51, 53–54, 59
Bonga, Jack, 48–49, 59
Bonga, Maragatt, 50
Bonga, Pierre, 48–49
Bonga, Stephen, 48–53, 59
border: "customary route," 10, 63, 64,
112; international, 10, 29, 64, 138,
210n10; uncertain, 32, 48, 63, 64
Boucher, 40, 55–56, 58, 59–60, 129, 156,
157, 159, 161, 168, 246n14

British Canada, 6, 63, 81, 139
British military, 4, 56, 58, 103
Brule River, 29, 39, 43, 247n20, 254n29
Brunson, Alfred, 50
burbot, 31, 106
Bureau of Indian Affairs, 61
burning buildings, 2, 26
Burnt Wood River. *See* Brule River

Cadotte, Joseph, 70
Cadotte, Michel, 182, 251n11
Cannon, George, 28–29, 139
canoes, 5, 26, 30, 32, 110, 119, 186, 188,
    191, 249n33; brigade, 6, 17, 47, 50, 68,
    222n25, 245n4; making, 114, 129, 203;
    travel, 38, 42, 46, 64, 112, 122, 182
caribou, 30, 89, 100, 107, 110, 122, 138, 178,
    248n31, 255n32
Cass, Lewis, 17–20, 22, 50, 67, 68, 74, 75,
    87; near skirmish at Sault Ste. Marie,
    17–19, 20
Catholicism, 55, 73, 99, 100, 210n10;
    converts, 101, 134; mission, 75, 222n29
change, 60–62
Chapman, Bela, 3, 11–13, 55–56, 74;
    background, 4, 11, 12; delegate to
    Michigan territorial congress, 14;
    feeling of isolation, 82, 126, 129, 138,
    163; frustrations, 1, 13, 126, 153, 155–57,
    161–62, 166–67; logbook, 7, 141–45;
    struggles, 8, 38, 60
Chapman, Reuben, 12
Chaurette, Mary, 2, 12, 13, 38
Chaurette, Simon, 12
Cheboygan County, Michigan, 14
Chippewa. *See* Anishinaabeg
Chippewa City, 5
Chippewa war party, 27, 181, 250n7
Civil War, 24
clans, 110, 123; Bear, 110; Caribou, 15, 89,
    110, 122, 133; Crane, 110; Eagle, 123;
    Fish, 110; Loon, 121, 123; Lynx, 115,
    122, 123; Marten, 110; Moose, 110
cloth trading, 31, 108, 171–77, 193
Collin, Michel, 99, 103, 203

Collins, Philip E., 45, 64, 182, 184, 203,
    251n12
copper rush, 23
corn, 31, 36, 86
Cotte, Pierre, 56, 83, 222n29, 243n28,
    247n26
Crane Lake, 70
Crapeau, 117, 131, 175, 179, 190, 254n25
Cree, 133
Crooks, Ramsay, 6, 7, 67, 78, 84
Crow Wing, Minnesota, 15, 51
Curot, Michel, 42
customs inspectors, 65, 69, 70, 84,
    226n76

Dakota, 12, 15, 27, 61, 73, 75
Davenport, Ambrose, Jr., 4, 56–58, 59
Davenport, Ambrose, Sr., 4, 56
Davenport, Susan, 57–58
Davenport, William, 57
deer, 15, 29, 107
Delafield, Joseph, 31, 65, 90, 242n27
Des Carreaux, Susan O Ge Ma Quay.
    See Davenport, Susan
desertion, 59–60
Detroit, 56, 62
Dog Lake, 111
dogs, 151, 144; dog teams, 38, 255n30,
    255n33
Duluth, 3, 46, 244n1

earthquakes, 41, 158, 159, 217n54
Ely, Edmund, 53, 94, 121
Erie Canal, 62
Espagnol, 2, 30, 92, 96–98, 102–5, 113,
    123, 127, 135, 174, 201–3; leadership, 3,
    30, 94, 99, 102, 105, 135, 233n7, 235n29;
    religious experimentation, 100, 101,
    121; travels, 5, 95, 100, 135

factory trade system, 66
failure, fear of, 56, 93, 125, 127, 129, 142
Ferguson, James, 29, 65, 93, 224n55
firewood, 35, 37, 46
fish, 31; salt preservation of, 36, 114

fishing, 89, 243n30; gill nets, 2, 36, 40, 100, 106, 111, 114, 178, 217n53, 246n11, 246n14; hook and line, 40, 111, 126, 164, 196, 217n53; spearing, 40, 100, 106, 107, 111, 126, 164–66, 178, 198; by torch light, 106, 256n36
flags, 91; American, 32, 34; British, 18, 19, 103, 235n29
Folle Avoine, 12, 51
Fond du Lac post (Fort St. Louis), 60, 77, 78
food at post, 36
food caches, 2, 29, 37
forest, 25, 29, 61; fires, 39
Fort Misery. *See* Grand Marais
Fort Snelling, 39, 61, 62
Fort William Post, 2–4, 7, 25, 32, 41, 49, 50, 53, 64, 65, 68, 74, 82, 83, 85, 88, 90, 96, 104, 107, 113, 114, 128, 167, 194, 203; country produce, 88, 89; crops harvested at, 88, 129; downsizing, 8, 85, 127, 133; journal, 141–42, 147–49
foxes, 30, 76
Franchere, Gabriel, 243n30
Franklin, John, 82–83
"freemen," 48, 75, 89, 142
French Canadian. *See* Métis
frost, 39, 63, 149, 188, 190
fur companies merger (1821), 8, 33, 75, 83
fur trade: bales, 51, 56, 78, 159, 161, 168–70, 247n21, 250n4; competition between AFC and HBC, 69, 70–71, 81, 83, 84, 88–91, 127–28, 131–32, 136–37; customs, 9; hardware, 108, 171–78, 201–3; history in Grand Marais of, 3, 6; regale, 41, 224n55, 241n2; securing goods and, 26, 157, 182

gap in historical record, 3
Garden River, 97, 133
geese, 37, 110
Gichi Bitobig. *See* Grand Marais
gifts, 75, 132, 201–3
Gilman, Carolyn, 7
Good Boat Harbor. *See* Grand Marais

Good Harbor Bay, 107, 248n28
Grand Coquin, 2, 8, 94, 98, 105, 111, 115–18, 122, 131, 133, 154, 157, 171, 186, 189, 190, 192–94, 196, 238n79
Grand Marais: 1–5, 7, 12, 13, 31–36, 39–41, 48–49, 78, 81–84, 88–91, 99–100, 103, 113, 115, 126–29, 136–39, 184; breakwater, 45, 247n25; as camping ground, 1–2; corporate beginning, 5, 130, 243n30; environment and, 1, 25–28, 46; as fishing grounds, 9, 136, 154, 186, 215n23; geology of, 28; location of post, 45–46; place name, 41–44, 218n65, 219n67; as shelter from Lake Superior, 1, 42, 46
Grand Marée. *See* Grand Marais: place name
Grand Portage, 3, 5–7, 9, 10, 32–35, 45, 47, 53, 57, 62–64, 79, 81, 83, 84, 90, 96–98, 100–102, 111–13, 122, 128, 133, 139, 147, 170, 184, 186, 188, 203, 214n17, 237n61, 249n36, 249n37; census of, 111
Grand Portage National Monument, 7
Grant, James, 68
grease, 41, 201
"great swamp." *See* Grand Marais
guns, 93, 109

Haldane, John, 30, 105, 133, 148, 194
"half breed." *See* Métis
headlands of North Shore, 1, 43, 217n54
Henry, Alexander, 49
historical change, 60–61
hogs, 37, 41, 144, 157, 162, 166, 245n4; confusion about, 144
Houghton, Douglas, 139, 243n28
Hudson Bay Company, 6, 7, 36, 64, 65, 70, 87, 104–6, 117, 214n17, 227n100, 231n165, 253n21; agreement with American Fur Company, 82, 129; archives at Winnipeg, 147; clerks, 32, 41, 75, 108, 148; conservation strategy, 137; documents from, 7; merger with North West Company, 33, 83

ice, 27, 38–40, 90, 106–7, 111, 164–65, 196; unpredictability of, 40, 126, 166, 196
immigrants: Scandinavian, 3, 4; Scottish, 214n17
interpreters, 22, 48–50, 53, 246n14; duties of, 53
iron, 35
Isle Royale, 82, 105, 122, 178, 224n55, 238n77, 252n13
Isle Royale Compact, 98, 252n14, 256n34

Jackson, Andrew, 61
Jay's Treaty, 62
Jefferson, Thomas, 66
Johnson, Eastman, 53
Johnston, Anna Maria, 130
Johnston, George, 2, 11, 14–24, 74; clan roots, 4; conception of self, 54–55, death, 23–24, feeling of isolation, 25, 82, 138, 185, 193, 196; frustration, 23, 84, 189; interpreter, 22; journal, 7, 144; personality, 16, 58, 132; pressed plants, 149; struggles, 23, 60
Johnston, Jane (Mrs. Henry Schoolcraft), 16, 56
Johnston, John, 15–17, 55, 86
Johnston, John McDougal, 16
Johnston, Lewis, 15, 16
Johnston, Louisa Raymond, 22–23
Johnston, Mary Rice, 23
Johnston, William Miengum, 57

Kaministiquia River, 33, 38, 88, 91, 97, 100, 106, 110, 111, 136, 139, 148: route, 10, 112
Kinistenokwe, 12
Kishkemun, 12
Knife Island, 152, 245nn2–3
Knife River (Mokomani-zibi), 43

La Bete, 115, 117, 127, 178, 238n77
Lac de l'Orignal, 43
La Chuit, 176
Lac des Mille Lacs, 70, 107, 111
Lac Superior. See Lake Superior

Lake Huron, Georgian Bay, 7, 81, 100
Lake Michigan, 58
Lake of the Woods, 63, 64, 79, 81, 92
Lake Superior, 10, 27; crossing, 26: purity, 27; vessels, 63, 252n13; waves, 1, 112, 125, 188, 192
lake trout, 2, 40, 106
language, 58, 72; English, 58; French, 58; multilingual, 72, 74; Quebecois, 43–44
La Pointe, 14, 20, 182–83, 250n9, 251n11, 252n14
league (British measurement), 250n8
Leech Lake, 51, 53, 54
L'Equier, 59–60, 186, 191, 192
Le View, 115, 177, 238n77
L'homme du Bois Fort, 131, 192–94
licenses for Indian trade, 67, 68, 81, 181, 184, 229n133, 252n15
Little Englishman, 192, 195, 197, 198, 256n34
Little Pine (Shingwaukonse or Shingwackhouse), 18–19, 97, 233n8, 234n20
Little Rat, 107
Long, Stephen, 65, 82
Long Lake, 63
Loon's Foot. See Maangozid
lynx ("cats" and "links"), 30, 76, 117, 194

Maangozid, 118–21, 123, 133, 186–87, 191–95, 198, 239n101
Mackinaw, 56, 69, 72, 73
Maine Historical Society, 146
Ma-Mongositea (Big Foot), 15
Manitoulin Island, 100, 234n21
maple sugar, 5, 29, 37, 89, 99, 110, 113–14, 132, 136, 149, 202, 248n32
maps, 31, 45, 64, 92, 146, 232n169
marriage, Indian–White, 12, 22, 56, 57, 73, 79, 81, 220n4, 222n29, 250n9, 251n11
martens, 30, 59, 76, 100, 108, 121, 135, 160, 169, 171–72, 175, 247n23
Maymushkowaush family, 98, 103, 133, 235n29; Paul, 98, 123, 133, 240n118
McCargo, Robert, 182, 252n13

McGillivray, William, 68
McKenzie, Daniel, 50
McKenzie, Roderick, Sr., 91, 147–48, 244n9
McLean, John, 182, 252n13
McLoughlin, John, 70, 105
medals, 99, 103, 119, 233n12, 235n29, 235n30, 244n5
Métis, 9, 12, 13, 23, 35, 47, 48, 53–56, 59, 67, 73, 75, 76, 161, 222n29, 250n9, 251n11
Michigan territory, 14, 20, 49, 60, 74; territorial congress of, 4, 130
Michilimackinac, 4, 12–14, 58, 62, 65, 66, 69, 72–74, 183, 220n4. *See also* Mackinaw
Michilimackinac County, Michigan, 74
migration, American westward, 60–61
minks, 76, 172, 175–76, 190
Minnesota Historical Society, 144, 201
Minong. *See* Isle Royale
Misquabunoqua, 57
missionaries, 50, 53, 73, 99, 210n10
Mississippi River, 61, 62, 77; headwaters of, 20, 63, 228n123
mocassins, 31, 108, 114
Monroe, James, 67
Montreal, 6, 15, 16, 50, 58
Montreal River, 15, 182, 250n9
moose, 29, 30, 97, 107, 108, 117, 138
Moose Lake, 43
Morrison, William, 40, 59, 68, 69, 78–81, 84, 92–93, 127–28, 143–44, 183–84
mosquitoes, 28, 29
muskrats, 72, 76, 85, 93, 117, 188

Nabarra, Alain, 218n65
National Archives, 146
Nectam, 101, 102, 134, 234nn23–24
Nelson, George, 42
Nett Lake, 133, 253n20
New Year's customs, 9, 73, 224n55, 241n2
New York, 47, 65
Noka, 15
Northern Light Lake, 110
northern pike, 31, 106, 111

North Shore Anishinaabeg, 5, 11, 22, 74, 91, 95, 101, 105–12, 119, 131–36, 218n62; illness, 97, 133, 164–65, 167; mobility, 109–11, 133; population, 97, 111; resilience, 134–35; territory, 123, 136, 235n25
North West Company, 3, 4, 6, 47, 62, 63, 69, 77, 97, 214n17; competition with Hudson Bay Company, 33, 68, 88; "Indian manifesto" and, 88; merger with HBC, 33, 83
Nute, Grace Lee, 33

Ogibwayquay, 49
Ojibwa. *See* Anishinaabeg
Old Grand Portage. *See* Grand Portage
old Northwest, 5, 60–61, 63
Ontonagon River, 27, 250n6
O Shau-gus-co-day-way-qua, Susan, 14
Otakaki-on, Josette, 97
otters, 30, 76, 117, 135, 189, 192

passenger pigeons, 30, 100, 247n24
Patisckquseng, 98
Peau de Chat, the elder, 96, 98, 114–16, 122, 135, 136, 239n84
Peau de Chat, Joseph (younger), 98, 135, 234n24
Pembina, 49, 51, 181, 249n2
Perrault, Jean Baptiste, 42
Pierz, Francis Xavier, 96, 97, 100, 102, 112, 234n22
Pigeon River, 22, 40, 63, 64, 92, 100, 106, 139, 196, 247n24
place names, 41, 42, 250n6: Anishinaabemowin, 43, 44, 219n67, 251nn10–11; English, 43, 44, 219n67, 254n28; French, 43, 44, 219n67
Poplar River (River of Gilead), 1, 29, 39, 245n7
posts: buildings, 33–35, 37, 44, 72, 78, 91, 97, 126; life, 37; leaky roof, 34, 246n13
potatoes, 8, 31, 36, 78, 88, 117, 183, 243n28
Prairie du Chien, 13, 119
Presbyterianism, 12, 121

rabbits, 30, 37, 108, 111, 114

racial categories, 53–56

Raff, Bill, 3

Rainy Lake, 31, 39, 63, 69–71, 81, 101, 107, 115, 116, 253n21

Rat River, 30

Recovery, 64, 91, 148, 182, 251n12, 252n13

Red River, 47, 49, 75; colony, 75, 222n29; Pemmican War and Battle of Seven Oaks, 68, 76, 88, 225n74

roads, 90, 125, 153, 168, 192, 245n6, 255n30

Robinson-Superior Treaty, 22, 255n30

Roche de Bout, 60, 188, 190–91, 254n23

Roussi, Eustache, 68

Royal Navy, 32, 44, 45, 64, 231n167, 251n12, 252n13

Rupert's Land, 6, 68

Saganaga Lake, 64, 118

Salmon Trout River, 60, 191, 254n28

Sandy Lake, 119; death march, 51

Sault Ste. Marie, 13, 15, 17, 20, 22, 38, 39, 56, 69, 73, 82, 129, 144, 149, 181, 252n15

Sawtooth Mountains, 25, 40, 139, 184; Tenerife, 40, 253n21; "The Thunder," 40

Schoolcraft, Henry, 20, 56, 143, 147; 1831 Senate document, 255n33; Indian agent, 20, 38, 75, 81, 87, 184, 252n15; nepotism charge, 20; papers at Library of Congress, 146

Schoolcraft, James, 14, 23, 130, 241n12

Selkirk, Thomas Douglas, 50, 68, 88, 128, 133, 214n17, 225n74, 227n100, 242n18

Semple, Robert, 231n155

Sessaba, 17–19

Shagoinah Islands, 110

Shaughunomonee, 79

Shingwackhouse. *See* Little Pine

Sibley, Henry, 144

Simpson, Francis, 98

Simpson, George, 6, 70, 87, 96, 98, 148, 203, 244n8, 244n9

Sioux. *See* Dakota

siscowet trout, 106

smallpox, 97, 133

snowshoes, 5, 33, 38, 108, 111, 114, 247n22

South Fowl Lake, 32, 110

South West Company, 62, 67, 68, 77

Spaniard. *See* Espagnol

starving, 117–18, 187, 190, 156–57, 192–98, 239n95; custom of feeding Indian guests, 105, 118, 162; hunger, 28

Stewart, Alexander, 147, 244n8

St. Louis River. *See* Fond du Lac post

Stuart, Robert, 73, 74, 78, 87

suckers, 106, 111, 217n53

sugar bush. *See* maple sugar

sugar maple groves, 2, 29, 113

Superior, Wisconsin, 53

surveyors, 31, 63–65, 82, 139, 146, 224n55. *See also* Delafield, Joseph; Ferguson, James; Whistler, George W.

Tasack, 59, 60, 188–92

technological change, 61, 62

Tecumseh, 62

Thompson, David, 28, 30, 43, 64, 75, 76, 85, 92, 118, 146, 224n57

Thompson, Samuel, 232n170

Thunder Bay area, 3, 4, 33, 38, 62, 89, 106, 111, 149, 249n35

Thunder Bay Historical Museum Society, 147

Thunder Cape, 110

tobacco, 17, 18, 68–69, 86, 96, 102, 110, 132, 135, 171, 186, 188, 202–3

trade credits, 58, 71, 167, 169, 171–72, 175, 187; debts, 33, 60, 66, 71, 88, 91, 111, 114, 116–17, 127, 131, 171–77

trade goods: cloth, 31, 93, 108, 171–77, 193; metal; 108, 171–77, 201–3; protecting, 26, 157, 182

trails, 33, 112, 136, 247n22. *See also* roads

trapping grounds, 33, 108, 110

traps, 76–77

treaties, 53, 92, 98, 132, 144, 145–46, 210n10; 1825 Prairie du Chien, 13, 119; 1826 Fond Du Lac, 13, 22, 135, 147, 233n12; 1837 Treaty of St. Peters,

119; 1842 Treaty of La Pointe, 51, 119, 233n12; 1854 treaty, 3, 119, 146, 256n34; Treaty of Ghent, 62, 63

treaty payment, 13, 145, 146

Upper Midwest. *See* old Northwest

U.S. government, 20, 61, 68

Vermilion Lake, 70, 81

Vieu Déser, 42

voyageurs, 1, 4, 6, 28, 34, 42–44, 47, 59, 67, 250n4, 250n7

warfare, Indian, 12, 14, 61, 63

War of 1812, 4, 56, 62; British allies, 9, 62, 235n29

Warren, Lyman, 182, 250n7

Warren, William, 10, 55

Waubojeeg (White Fisher), 14–15, 130

Webster-Ashburton Treaty, 64, 242n27

Welcome Islands, 111

Whistler, George W., 31, 65

whitefish, 31, 40, 89, 106, 110, 155–56, 236n41

White Fish Lake, 32, 100, 107, 132, 157, 158, 168, 186, 189–90, 193–97, 247n22, 253n20, 255n33; "watch tent" for HBC, 90, 167, 231n165

wild rice, 32, 36, 70, 107, 110, 253n20

windbound, 1, 27, 126, 152–53, 209n1, 245n6

windigo, 101, 135, 234n22

Winnipeg, 147

winter, 31, 38; of 1823–24, 38–39; deep snow, 37, 38, 125, 157, 162, 165, 170, 187, 190, 192, 194

Wissakode zibi. *See* Brule River

women, Anishinaabeg, 8, 37, 73, 89, 92, 109, 111, 113–14, 220n9, 237n69, 246n11

XY Company, 12, 33, 79

Yankees, 5, 6, 56, 105, 116

"year without summer, the," 63

Timothy Cochrane served as superintendent of the Grand Portage National Monument for twenty years. His books include *Minong— The Good Place: Ojibwe and Isle Royale* and *A Good Boat Speaks for Itself: Isle Royale Fishermen and Their Boats* (Minnesota, 2002, with Hawk Tolson). He lives near Grand Marais, Minnesota.